*Lesbian Teachers*

SUNY Series, Feminist Theory in Education
Madeleine Grumet, Editor

SUNY Series, The Psychology of Women
Michele A. Paludi, Editor

# Lesbian Teachers

## *An Invisible Presence*

## Madiha Didi Khayatt

State University of New York Press

Grateful acknowledgment is made to Sharon Dale Stone and to Between the Lines Press for permission to use a version of my article "Lesbian Teachers: Coping at School" from *Lesbians in Canada,* © 1990 by Sharon Dale Stone.

Published by
State University of New York Press, Albany

For information, address State University of New York Press,
State University Plaza, Albany, N.Y., 12246

Production by M. R. Mulholland
Marketing by Bernadette LaManna

**Library of Congress Cataloging-in-Publication Data**

Khayatt, Madiha Didi, 1944–
    Lesbian teachers : an invisible presence / Madiha Didi Khayatt.
        p.    cm. — (SUNY series, feminist theory in education)    (SUNY
    series, the psychology of women)
    Includes bibliographical references and index.
    ISBN 0-7914-1171-0 (CH : acid-free). — ISBN 0-7914-1172-9 (PB :
    acid-free)
        1. Lesbian teachers—Ontario.    2. Lesbian teachers—Ontario—
    Social conditions.    I. Title.    II. Series.    III. Series: SUNY
    series in the psychology of women.
    LB2837.K43 1992
    371.1'008'664—dc20                                              91-30545
                                                                          CIP

10 9 8 7 6 5 4 3 2 1

*To S. M. R.*
*and to both my sisters and my mother,*
*with all my love and my thanks.*

# Contents

# Acknowledgments

There are several key people without whom this work would not have been possible to conceive or to accomplish. I would like to thank Frieda Forman for her guidance in showing me what to read, what to know, and how to think about it. I would also like to thank Kathy Arnup and Gary Kinsman, for their help in locating material; Joan Gilroy, for her gentle but firm direction in raising my feminist consciousness; Ann Manicom, for many of her ideas, the readings she suggested, and the daily "grump" sessions as we were both writing our final chapters; Ruth Roach Pierson, for teaching me to appreciate the role of history in sociological analysis, for helping me enjoy the field, for the unlimited time she spent giving direction to many of my speculations, and for her detailed editing of the various drafts; Mary O'Brien, for all I learned from her classes, for the time she gave, and for the advice she proferred; Jeri Dawn Wine, for letting me sharpen my interviewing skills; Ron Silvers and Vivian Darroch-Lozowski, for advising me to register in sociology and for their interest in my progress, Dorothy E. Smith, my thesis supervisor, without whose patient direction, suggestions, and rigorous scholarship my ideas could not have developed; Susan M. Robertson, for her infinite encouragement and practical advice, and for never letting me down; Judith Millen, for her long-standing intellectual challenges; and Marian McMahon, for her intelligence and her help in refining my thinking. For my friends who had patience with me, who fed me and took me out on walks, I offer thanks with all my heart. All these people have given me friendship, laughter, help in innumerable ways, strength in times of stress, and warmth in moments of need.

In addition, I want to thank my family for their financial help, their unequivocal encouragement, and their transatlantic support. I want to mention specifically my father, whose death in 1986 meant he did not see the completion of my doctorate or of this project and did not know his vital role in their accomplishment.

And, of course, I want to thank all the women who agreed to be interviewed, to acknowledge their courage and support, as well as the time they gave me and the glimpse of their lives they allowed me to share. I also want to convey my appreciation to all those friends who trusted, encouraged, prodded, talked, and argued with me but were always supportive and believed in this work. I want to express gratitude especially to those women who could not or would not be interviewed themselves but who were able to suggest others. And, of course, I wish to express my gratitude to Lois Patton of SUNY Press, whose support was always welcome on those "down" days. And to my feminist colleagues and students Glendon College, to Lorraine Gauthier in particular, thank you for providing me with an almost ideal place to work.

Finally, I want to express my gratitude to Glendon College, York University, for the specific research grant I was given, as well as to the Canadian Research Institute for the Advancement of Women for its contribution to this research.

I would like to acknowledge the significant contributions of the sisterhood of women whose constant vigilance, significant influence, political activism, rigorous erudition, and vital vision made this work possible as part of the ongoing feminist struggle.

# Introduction

"She's a lesbian," said one student to another in that stage whisper that is meant to carry. The class gazed. I froze. They were referring to me, the teacher, the lesbian. It was 1982.

In the summer of that year, I had returned to teach summer school for the Northern Ontario school board that had employed me for almost ten years. It had been two years since I had left that small town where I lived and taught because I had chosen to go to Toronto to obtain my doctorate. I was still on nonpaid leave but was attempting to earn some money to go back to graduate school for a third year. That summer—my last, as it turned out, as a secondary school teacher—was interesting, informative, and intimidating.

I had left my partner, my teaching job, and the small house we had just bought to learn, I thought, about the pedagogical theories behind the teaching and counseling that made up my daily working life for more than ten months out of every year. What I learned was feminist theories, the presence and power of a women's movement, and hints regarding the existence of a lesbian/gay movement. Suddenly, all my previously unexamined assumptions, my relatively indifferent acceptance of the status quo, and my detached understanding of the possibilities of change—of the "revolutionary" notion that what is does not have to be forever but can be transformed, rethought, reworked to achieve more equitable prospects for women and men alike—suddenly my whole life and beliefs were challenged. I thrilled and thrived. I learned and I questioned. But I also survived and developed. I absorbed and appropriated women's perspectives, women's culture, women's theories, women's analyses. Never before had my intellect been so shaken; never again would I be so unequivocally moved.

I went back to teaching that summer of 1982, carrying with me the first flush of my political changes. I was going to show my students the way; I was going to stand firm on my newly acquired understanding of feminist politics. I was bravely going to declare my feminist convictions and live by my new analyses. I did not know what awaited me.

One of my students that summer, a young woman of about nineteen, took it upon herself to "expose" my sexual preference. I knew that her intentions were not malicious but that she was acting out her attraction to me. I thought I could handle the situation with all my newly acquired analyses. However, I did not count on her fury and my terror. The more she goaded me about my sexuality, the more I ignored her and the more she made her accusations publicly. Because my other students liked and respected me, their response was to silence her, to disbelieve and discredit her intimations that I was a lesbian. To them, I was a teacher they liked; therefore I could not be a lesbian. One young man even asked my permission to "beat her mouth shut" if she did not stop. I discouraged him emphatically and vigorously. But it was my own fear of exposure that almost paralyzed me. The anguish of wanting to say to her, "Yes, I am a lesbian" battled with the discomfiture of my fears of that label, a label I willingly adopted privately. That summer was pivotal because I had to face my confusions. On the one hand, I desperately wanted to help the young woman "understand" the emotions and feelings she was undergoing (after all, I was a trained counselor and a lesbian), and, on the other hand, I could not overcome my own terrors surrounding the stigma of being known as "lesbian." Why could I not demonstrate my newfound pride as a feminist and as a lesbian? Why did I resort to all the subterfuge that had characterized my life until then? How could I be proudly active politically, and strangely silent in my teaching job?

I have described in detail the confusing incidents of that summer in a short article published elsewhere, written under the pseudonym of D. D. Taylor because I was not (and never was) out at work.[1] That very short, poignant piece demonstrated some of the questions I was beginning to pose to myself after two years of graduate feminist studies. I was caught between, on the one hand, wanting to be out, needing to claim my lesbian identity, compelled to articulate that hidden part of my experiences, and even thinking—in my innocence—that I could patch up the fragments that were my life then, and, on the other hand, having to face the terror that the label *lesbian* held for me, a teacher. I had the (mistaken) impression that I could combine the thrill of what I was learning with the reality of what I was living. I did not know that it does not, and cannot, happen overnight. Years of hiding my love for women, of silencing that essential part of my life that is my relationship with my partner, and a lifetime of "passing" as heterosexual made it virtually impossible for me not to respond with fear and lies to the accusation by a student that I was a lesbian—which I was, and am.

No, I was never out when I was a secondary teacher. My lover and I lived a quiet life, out to a handful of very close friends. At work we often interspersed our conversation with mention of men friends, men who did exist and who were friends but who were also gay. We pretended for the most part that our lives did not differ from those of our colleagues, that we lived together only as two straight friends sharing living accommodations. Although we taught for the same school board, we worked in different schools, hers nearby, mine over twenty-five miles west of where we lived. It suited me to brave winter driving conditions in northern Ontario just to be able to leave the small community in which my school was located every evening, and to leave with it that public part of me that I exposed to staff, students, and parents.

We did not think we were alone as lesbians. We both had a keen eye for other gay and lesbian teachers who were hiding. We knew on some level, without ever having to test it, that if we ever came out at work, by choice or by accident, we would have a difficult time surviving the experience and continuing to teach. However, it was not that simple. The act of hiding often depends on more than one person playing the game. The one who hides is responsible for producing all the "right" clues and cues. But the ones from whom she is hiding are also responsible to read these "correctly." Where the former creates a safe environment for herself, the latter play along because they do not have to be confronted with uncomfortable information about this person/neighbor/teacher they have learned to like, admire, or respect. However, a good part of the rules demand that the one who hides, the lesbian teacher in this case, does not "flaunt" her sexual orientation, that she pretends that she is "like everybody else."

My lover and I lived quiet lives. We each excelled at what we did, we each made sure that our public and our private lives did not intersect. In my case, I often spoke about "friends" with whom I went camping, or to Toronto, or to the movies. I spoke in the plural to avoid any identifying pronouns. I spoke vaguely of activities over the weekend, and only in response to direct questions. I hardly ever ventured information, and even less talked about my home. I often got asked by students and inquisitive staff why I was not married. My answer, always flippant, never inviting further inquiry, usually postponed the intrusive curiosity of my questioner.

Not politicized (yet), we lived away from any direct confrontation with the women's movement. Feminism may have been present in our small town, but it was certainly outside my ken. I remember

driving one morning to school listening to the radio announcer talking about a group of women who were organizing a rape crisis center. I remember he called them a "vigilante group," and although I
got angry on their behalf, there was no thought in my mind to respond to his dismissive description. But then, I did not even have
the language or the arguments to take him on. Whereas my feminism, at that time, was but an exciting hope, almost a rumor, my
lesbianism was a sexual preference and not an identity. It was
something I called myself only in the presence of those "in the
know," rarely spoken in a normal voice, but as a dip in a whispered
sentence.

     I think I was a very good secondary teacher. I was interested
in what I was doing, gave willingly of my time to students and to
tasks, and generally got along with staff and administration. I was
respected and often encouraged. I never sought promotions, but I
was active in and worked my way up federation (union) hierarchies
to gain a place in the negotiating team for two years. As a classroom
teacher I stood out, not because of my teaching techniques but because I was clearly and sincerely liked by my students. Consequently, when I became a guidance counselor, I was a popular choice
in the department. My sexual orientation combined with my being
the only Egyptian for miles around made me particularly sensitive
to students who felt out of place. This does not mean that I was always able to help them. For instance, no amount of arguing and
pleading with the vice-principal not to suspend a young male student because of chronic lateness made any difference. I knew that
that student was being sexually harassed and sometimes assaulted
by older and bigger boys, but that "excuse" somehow did not wash
with the vice-principal. However, I did have an uncanny ability to
recognize those young women and men I suspected of being lesbian
or gay. Although not out to them, I was often able to guide them
through whatever traumatic "crushes" they were experiencing or
through their daily confrontation of their "differentness." We spoke
to each other always in veiled terms, protecting both our privacies.

     At the time I was teaching, my life did not stand out to me as
being difficult but rather as being hidden. Although I often wished
I did not have to hide or lie about the nature of my relationship with
my partner, it was more because it was often troublesome to relate
my weekend activities and not because I felt compelled to talk about
my private life. When I took the decision, as a graduate student, to
write about lesbian teachers, it was my life, as well, that I wanted
to uncover and discover. There were so many questions that were
beginning to haunt me, questions like "Why did I have to hide?"

"What compels me and those like me to keep silent?" "How did I (and others) choose to be lesbian(s)?" and "How did I come to label myself lesbian when other women who were involved sexually with women preferred other labels—if any?" and so on.

The present work was finished over five years ago, and yet I was not ready to have it published. After I obtained my doctorate in 1987, I was able to teach at the university level. With the changes in politics, the appearance of AIDS, and the recognition of lesbian and gay rights in the Ontario Human Rights Code, it has become easier both to be recognized and to come out. Many of my students, colleagues, and administrators in my college are aware of my sexual orientation. To date it has not been an issue. Thus this book was not possible for me until I had gone through the process that enabled me to believe I was relatively safe in speaking out, through whatever it took for me to be able to break the silence. Lesbian (and gay) teachers do exist in great numbers, and despite our difficulties, we survive, we excel, and we are here to talk for ourselves.

Teachers in general are hired in conformity with an assumed standard. They are expected, to some extent, to reflect a conventionality that corresponds with the state's ideologically sanctioned model of behavior. Not only are teachers often perceived as the "formal" transmitters of a hegemonic ideology in a capitalist system that needs to reproduce a labor force preferably complicit with the status quo, but as unofficial representatives of the state, they are commonly assumed to embody the dominant values of the society that hires them. More specifically, female teachers historically were admitted as educators on the basis of their "natural" propensity to nurture, their proper place as child rearers. They were also cheaper than male teachers. Teaching, as a profession, was seen to embody a practical training for young women, for whom the "real" vocation was believed to be marriage and motherhood. The notion of lesbian teachers therefore inevitably and indubitably contradicts mainstream assumptions of the female teacher, a woman who was traditionally and stereotypically portrayed as either a "mother-teacher" or a "spinster" (a woman who remained "chaste" and allegedly frustrated, hoping for eventual fulfillment of her "true" role of wife and mother). Although either of these images corresponds (even today) with and implicitly conveys traditional female virtues of purity, dedication, and nurturance, of the two, of course, motherhood holds the higher status, given heterosexual hegemony.

The problematic explored in this book is that of the lesbian teacher's disposition not to reveal her sexual orientation. The need not to draw attention to her sexuality, not to provoke questions,

suspicions, or harassment because of her sexual preference, leads
many lesbians in the teaching profession to take precautions against
their private lives becoming public. This study addresses the historical, ideological, political, and social contexts that would make such
reticence a necessity. It is an ethnographic study of lesbian teachers'
everyday life in the classroom; how they deal with the split between
their public and private worlds; what precautions they may adopt to
deflect suspicions; how they answer certain direct enquiries about
their personal lives; how they handle their relationships with their
students, their colleagues, the administration, the parents, and
the community in which they work; and what behavior they adopt
to make their lives "safe" and productive. Also discussed is what
circumstances the teachers anticipate would make their professional life more open, more universally acceptable, and therefore
more secure.

This book is set in the Canadian context in the early to middle
1980s. More specifically, it deals with the institution of the Ontario
tax-supported school system, which includes both the elementary
and the secondary sectors. The teachers interviewed are all women
who identify themselves as lesbian, whether or not they use that
particular term.[2] Each of their stories has been recorded in in-
depth interviews conducted between the years 1982 and 1986. The
details they disclose for the sake of this study are not meant to be
statistical or quantitative data but the unique experiences of each
woman talking about her own life.

Although this study is set in Canada, the theoretical and an-
alytical sections, along with the descriptions of the lived experiences of the women interviewed, can be applied, for the most part,
to lesbian teachers living in other English-speaking, Western capitalist countries. The methodology used is based on Dorothy E.
Smith's analysis, (whose work is discussed in greater detail in a
later chapter) which compels the researcher to begin from women's
experiences while at the same time to understand the social organization that gives meaning to such personal experiences. The work
is grounded in feminist discourse but takes into consideration a
wide variety of other intellectual traditions, discussing, incorporating, or discarding each on the basis of their relative worth from the
point of view of this work.

Medical, psychiatric, and sociological treatises abound on the
subject of homosexuality, its causes and its possible cures.[3] Also in
abundance are historical accounts that review the prevalence and
the universality of that sexual phenomenon.[4] Anthropological re-

ports reveal how culturally and geographically widespread forms of homosexuality appear to be,[5] and recurrent religious condemnations testify to its existence despite the most stringent restrictions and admonitions.[6] However, none of these sources provide more than a background overview or a historical footnote for the work covered in this book. They can be readily discarded, first, because they treat homosexuality as a problem, a type of sexual deviance, an anomaly, a set of behaviors practiced, accepted, and rejected by "primitive" or ancient peoples. Second, they treat homosexuality as a legal, medical, psychiatric, and sexological term. As such, it is defined, described, dissected, dismissed, and/or decreed against. Moreover, homosexuality is discussed as implicitly covering both the male and the female phenomena, yet upon closer examination it is evident that female homosexuality is relegated to a minor paragraph or chapter, viewed as not warranting separate treatment because it is not statistically (or otherwise!) significant, or it is addressed from a male perspective without considering the lived experience of the women involved. Finally, female homosexuality is constructed as a mild, immaterial, inconsequential expression of its more prevalent and/or more serious male counterpart.

Whereas there is no dearth of the above sources, even a preliminary review of the recent feminist and gay literatures reveals a more promising analysis, one that conceives of the lesbian option as intrinsic to, as well as a part of, the continuum of female sexuality,[7] one that explores every facet of that experience using the lives, the words, the perceptions, and the various articulations of the women themselves, and one that situates lesbianism within the framework of women's oppression. Thus it makes visible that, historically, socially, and materially, lesbians are stigmatized more because of their rejection of patriarchal prescriptions (which would keep them and other women under male control) than because of the "deviance" of their sexuality. This is especially apparent when one is reminded that, traditionally, female sexuality has not been taken seriously in and of itself but has been perceived almost exclusively in relation to men, and that passionate friendships between women were not condemned until they threatened the historical domination of and often unconditional access to women's bodies that males had enjoyed.

However, the same preliminary review of the literature quickly demonstrated a paucity of Canadian sources[8] and, of even more immediate and distressing concern, an almost comprehensively gross silence surrounding the topic of lesbian teachers, a silence that renders them invisible, their presence unacknowledged and unappreciated. Fortunately, the silence is slowly being broken, and several books have come out, which are mentioned in the Selected Bibliography.

The term *teacher* is used in this book to refer exclusively to those (in this case) women who instruct in elementary and secondary institutions. The reason postsecondary educators are not considered is that they are not "in charge" of children; they do not stand "*in loco parentis*" while on the job, as do elementary and secondary school teachers. Although the latter, like their college and university counterparts, have some form of tenure (based on seniority, gained and maintained through collective bargaining), they are protected only insofar as they are competent and do not breach set standards of moral turpitude. However, because of Ontario's Human Rights Code, where sexual orientation has been included as a prohibited ground of discrimination in housing, employment, and services, teachers are, in a sense, protected from losing their jobs.[9] I say "in a sense" because, in 1990, I did go back to the same set of teachers I interviewed for this study to ask them if they felt secure in their employment since the passing of Bill 7 (the sexual orientation clause), and their responses, published elsewhere, were not very encouraging.[10] In addition, because they teach (legal) minors and are considered officially to be in positions of trust (according to the Badgley Reports),[11] their overt presence as identified, admitted, and/or politically or publicly active lesbians and as teachers working for a board of education causes several problems: (a) it could possibly be interpreted as implicity condoning homosexuality; (b) given their position as teachers, they could conceivably be viewed as representing a role model (for children), which, in turn, is tacit approval of the option to be or become lesbian; and (c) the "public" often perceives homosexual men and women as "preying on" or "preferring to seduce youngsters," a misconception that is all the more glaring in the face of statistical evidence that sexual assault against minors is most frequently committed by "heterosexual" men.[12]

A final explanatory note is necessary to clarify why it was necessary to deal with two different discourses, in this case, lesbian and gay literature as well as pedagogical analyses. The subject of lesbian teachers as dealt with in this book is historically and culturally specific. This is not to deny that same-sex relationships have occurred in other ages and in different locations; however, the term

*lesbian* is a social construct that could only have surfaced with
its particular meanings as a result of circumstances peculiar to
North America and those cultures that share a similar history
and culture.

Homosexual acts are present and have existed in almost all
cultures at different times around the world.[13] Female homosexuality traditionally has received far less attention than the male
phenomenon. Until very recently, little consideration was given to
female sexuality in general except as it reflected upon the concerns
of men and their possessive interest in procreative sex. The relatively recent discourses, of which this study is an example, are concerned with the problematic only as it is discussed by the women in
question. Lesbians of all types, races, and classes describe their
lives, create their culture, and analyze their own issues. The gay
movement produced the support to become visible. The feminist
perspective provided the women-positive context.

Since the topic is "lesbian teachers," the latter part of the construct is important. Even as female homosexuality is currently informed by recent political and ideological discourses, the treatment
of women in education has a history of its own. Both as teachers and
as students, women had been previously overlooked, especially as
subjects rather than objects of study. The reasons for this oversight
may vary, but at least two explanations are possible: first, male historians and educators were more concerned with male subjects, and
so women featured often peripherally; second, women have only in
recent history been allowed a public education that is, if not equal
to, at least similar to, that granted to men.

In the following chapter I shall present a short historical overview of homosexuality leading to the gay liberation movement in
the Western, English-speaking industrial world. I shall discuss the
development of various discourses on homosexuality with particular emphasis on current conceptions. I shall outline how these differ
from past sexological scientific works, which treated homosexuality
as a perversion and, for that reason if for no other, could not admit
the reality of "lesbian teachers."

The next chapter traces the progression of women in the teaching profession, describes their position hierarchically and currently,
and discusses the pedagogical literature that has made women,
both as teachers and as students, visible in the discourse today.
Only by covering what transpired for women in education historically and by understanding the development of recent notions of gay

and lesbian identities can we achieve a clear picture of how the concept of *lesbian teacher* is constructed and is both historically and culturally specific.

Chapter 3 elaborates on the theoretical discourses and provides much of the background analyses for the book, and Chapter 4 describes the methodology used, explaining why that particular one was chosen, who got to be included in the study and how. Succeeding chapters are based on the data gathered: the words and lives and coping experiences of the lesbian teachers with whom I spoke.

Much of this book is based on my doctoral dissertation work. I have greatly modified and updated it in sections, without erasing its strength. It is only with the distance of five years, the increased visibility of lesbians and gays in general, and my own continual process of coming out that this book has become timely. The words and experiences of these teachers, what they offered of their lives, is the prime reason for this work.

1

# Homosexuality in Perspective:
## The Discourse

Sexual acts between members of the same sex constitute a
phenomenon that has existed and has often been denounced
throughout the ages and in many cultures around the globe. Isolating these acts and labeling them, describing and eventually diag-
nosing them as pathological, is an element of the social organization
of Western capitalist societies,[1] which, in turn, has its historical
roots in Judeo-Christian morality. Sexual acts between members of
the same sex are referred to as "homosexual behavior."

Homosexual behavior has been recorded throughout historical
time. Whether condemned (the Sumerians, the ancient Hebrews,
the Zoroastrians) or accepted (the Greeks in certain contexts; the
Romans, although not officially condoned), this type of behavior was
a social fact that had to be taken into consideration in those cultures that presumably influenced Western capitalist societies.[2]

With regard to the subject of sexuality in general, historians
consider institutionalized religious morality fundamental to any
discussion dealing with the foundations of Western social organization. The ancient Hebrews, as founders of Judaism, designated exact prohibitions and regulated sexual behavior to conform to a set of
rules encoded in the biblical scriptures. Basically, "Judaism placed a
negative value on sexual behavior outside the marital bed and considered the primary purpose of sex to be procreation, best exempli-
fied in the Biblical injunction, 'Be fruitful and multiply.' "[3] Male
homosexual behavior was reproved,[4] as was any action that would
precipitate male seminal emissions (outside of sexual procreative
acts), such as masturbation, bestiality, and anal intercourse. Even
coitus interruptus was forbidden because the procreative potential was wasted.[5] The Judaic admonitions did not include women.
Judith Plaskow explains that, whereas male homosexuality was

condemned as an abomination, Talmudic references to it are few and "indicate no knowledge of homosexual orientation in the modern sense." However, she adds, "Lesbianism, because it involves no intercourse and no 'wasting of seed,' was a less serious offence."[6] Vern Bullough observes that the ancient Hebrews, "with their male-oriented view of sexuality and penetration, . . . assumed that women could do little among themselves."[7] It was not until the New Testament scriptures that women were mentioned. St. Paul's very ambiguous verse in Romans 1:26 decries the heathens' lack of belief in the Creator and says that "for this cause God gave them up unto vile affections: for even their women did change the natural use unto that which is against nature." Given Paul's misogyny, Bullough, for one, speculates that this passage may simply have referred to women assuming the superior position in heterosexual intercourse.[8] There is no doubt that both the Old and the New Testaments condemn male homosexuality, whereas females are neglected except in the above-mentioned statement.

It is mostly true that male homosexuals were regularly singled out for persecution much more than their female counterparts. Writing in 1955, Derrick Sherwin Bailey, author of a standard study in early antihomosexual legislation, is cited by Louis Crompton as asserting that lesbian acts were disregarded by both medieval and modern law.[9] Over two decades later, in 1977, Hanley, Schlesinger, and Steinberg present a viewpoint similar to Bailey's: "Female homosexuality has . . . been met with more acceptance or less condemnation in the past and at the present time."[10] However, a more recent study by Crompton provides a long list of laws and documented cases gathered from across Europe that condemned sexual acts between women. He leaves no doubt in readers' minds that lesbian acts were denounced regularly and publicly (at least since medieval times) and that the perpetrators of such acts were severely punished. Still, it is undeniable that the male homosexual—as homosexual—has been more visible longer in history. Moreover, his persecution has been more conspicuous, his elimination (by death, imprisonment, castration, excommunication, or therapy) has been more concerted, and his condition has been more researched at all times. Some reasons for this may simply be that men are usually more concerned with what other men do, think, or say; that men's sexual lives are often conducted in the public as well as the private spheres (which makes them more obvious and therefore more vulnerable to changes); and that, traditionally, women's homosexuality was seldom acknowledged as sexual. Lesbians were more likely to be accused of being witches, spinsters, or anarchists.[11] Finally, another plausible speculation is that men's interest in women's sexual behavior is frequently limited to regulating it to ensure legitimate heirs, to control their access to women's sexuality and labor, and to maximize their own pleasure. Laws and customs reflect the central position men have reserved for themselves, particularly in sexual matters. "No matter what is going on, or . . . *not* going on, with respect to female arousal or orgasm, or in connection with the vagina, a pair can be said without semantic deviance to have had sex, or not to have had sex; the use of the term turns entirely on what was going on with respect to the penis."[12] Sexual acts between two women were often trivialized by men, if not denied completely,[13] except in those instances where women were seen as having stepped outside their designated sphere in the private realm. In short, it can safely be said that lesbian behavior was condemned but that its denunciation was embedded in different social and historical bases from that of male homosexuality.

Louis Crompton reports the earliest secular laws enforced against lesbian acts (of which he is aware) as dating from 1270. They occurred in France and were an adaptation of or an addendum to a law meant to forbid male homosexuality.[14] The first incident of capital punishment for lesbianism that Crompton cites is the drowning of a girl in Speier in 1477.[15] From then on, records of condemnations of female homosexual acts are available from all over Christian Europe. Many of the women who were executed were caught cross-dressing or assuming the identity of men.[16] Historical records are replete with examples of women who passed as men marrying women who were presumably (but not always) complicit in the deception.[17]

Although the most massive known persecution of women for sexual reasons occurred during the Inquisition in Europe, historical records indicate that women were frequently executed in Protestant Europe for similar "crimes." Mary Daly notes that the majority of those tortured and punished were females who were single or widowed, women who, she maintains, were "outside patriarchal control" because of their independence from men.[18] The charge most frequently brought against them was indulgence in lewd acts with the devil, sexual promiscuity, and taking part in orgiastic rituals. Consequently, the Inquisitors felt righteously justified in burning witches once their "crimes" were established (usually after they were horrifyingly tortured). Good Christian men had to be protected. It was believed that women were more likely to fall prey to

demonically inspired desires because they are "more credulous, . . .
are naturally more impressionable, have slippery tongues, are fee-
bler both in mind and body, are more carnal than men(!) to the extent of having insatiable lust, have weak memories, [and] are liars
by nature."[19]

During the Renaissance in Europe there was an increase in
the number of laws that specifically condemned sexual acts between
women. Crompton mentions Spanish, French, Russian, and Swiss
(Calvinist) cases where women were tried and executed under these
laws.[20] North America was not immune to European influence.
Crompton cites examples from New England early in the seven-
teenth century, where laws denouncing "carnal fellowship of man
with man or woman with women" were considered but were not necessarily adopted.[21] Contrary to the rest of Europe, England never
had laws that specifically referred to female homosexual acts. Likewise, Canadian jurisprudence, which is based on English codes, at
no time proscribed sexual acts between two women.[22] Similarly, co-
lonial Americans condemned nonprocreative sexual acts, sodomy,
and buggery as sinful and therefore punishable, but, according to
John D'Emilio and Estelle Freedman, "the laws almost always applied to men, not women, because they typically referred to the unnatural spilling of seed, the biblical sin of Onan."[23]

Religious and legal treatises were the major serious sources of
discourse on the subject of sexuality until well into the nineteenth
century, when the focus began to shift from "sin" to "crime" to a recognition that certain behavior can be isolated and described, and
thus diagnosed and cured. Historians identify this period as transitional in that homosexual behavior began to be perceived in
medical terms, and hence as a disorder rather than a sin. In 1869,
Dr. Westphal of Berlin was one of the first to publish cases about
what he identified as "contrary sexual feelings."[24] A few years later, American and British doctors referred to "sexual inversion"
and "sexual perversion" as parallel appellations to Wesphal's German phrase.

The explanation of what constituted those terms (*sexual inversion* or *perversion*) can be understood within the context of contemporary beliefs about sexuality in general. Early Victorian ideology
propagated a cult of "true womanhood" and "true manhood" that
ascribed to women and men characteristics from which they were
not permitted to deviate if they "truly" belonged to their respective sex.[25] Katz explains: "The concept of true woman and true man
equated biological femaleness and maleness with those constella-

tions of qualities collectively called 'femininity' and 'masculinity'. . . . Ministers, doctors and other ideologists of gender identified physiological sex with what may now be distinguished as socially determined, historically relative, gender-specific personality traits and temperaments."[26]

This ideology also viewed women as passionless, incapable of sexual feelings, submitting to male aggressive desire only for the purpose of procreation. Chauncey observes that since the expression of women's sexual arousal was perceived as pathological by a number of sexologists of the time, "there was no place for lesbianism as it is currently understood: if women could not even respond with sexual enthusiasm to the advances of men, how could they possibly stimulate sexual excitement between themselves?"[27] Evidently, lesbian behavior contradicted the widely held view of women's passivity and complete lack of interest in sexual matters. Thus, to overcome the inherent contradiction between what was believed and what was observed, the theories of *sexual inversion* (congenital) or *sexual perversion* (acquired) were introduced. "A complete inversion or reversal of a woman's sexual character was required for her to act as a lesbian; she had literally to become man-like in her sexual desire."[28] Both these terms were applied to males as well and, in the same way, point to the Victorian belief in "naturally" determined gender roles. Thus a man described as an "invert" was perceived as effeminate, soft, gentle, and passive—in other words, "unmanly." Expressed in this way, it becomes apparent how fundamental to this theory was the conviction that sex was tied to notions of femininity and masculinity, that the behavior ascribed to each gender was radically different, distinct, and based on "natural" and/or "biological" characteristics. "Anatomy equalled mentality. A woman who did not display alleged mental, moral, and emotional qualities of her sex was a nonwoman."[29] In essence, Victorian polarization of gender roles, which dictated social behavior, provided the paradigm for gender-based sexual expectations. A woman who actively desired another woman ceased to be a woman. She became masculinized, a sexual invert or pervert. Lillian Faderman summarizes Victorian views of women's sexuality thus:

> To the very end of the century . . . , the sexual potential of love between decent, healthy women was still unacknowledged by many seemingly sophisticated authors: sound women were asexual. It was doubtful enough that they would concern themselves with any form of sexual satisfaction, but that they would

seek sexual expression without a male initiator was as incredible as claiming to hear thunder play "God Save the King."[30]

The concept of sexual inversion imbued the literature from the late nineteenth century well into the 1930s. For Kraft-Ebbing and George Beard, as well as for Havelock Ellis and Sigmund Freud, homosexual object choice implied an inversion of sexual character. Beard maintained in 1880 that "men became women and women men in their tastes, conduct, character, feelings and behaviour."[31] Krafft-Ebbing described sexual perversion in terms of people whose behavior, thought, and character corresponded to those of the opposite sex rather than being congruent with the manner appropriate to their physiology and anatomy.[32] Ellis noted in his *Sexual Inversion* that female inverts, from their "straightforwardness and sense of honour" to their "toleration for cigars," from their "incapacity for needlework" to their "brusque energetic movements," were unequivocally masculine in taste and behavior.[33] Finally, as Chauncey contends, "Freud, like Ellis and the whole turn-of-the-century sexology, continued to assert their 'character inversion' was a regular feature of *female* inversion, although no longer maintaining that this was true of male inverts."[34]

The "sexual inversion" explanations were concerned primarily with the masculinized woman and neglected the partner, who seemed to fit those characteristics deemed appropriate to her gender. Jonathan Katz observes, "Quite often in the early medical literature, the 'feminine' member of a female couple was spoken of as if she was not also a 'pervert'; even her sexual activity with a 'pervert' did not affect essentially her own 'normal' status."[35] Apparently, the more aggressive woman posed a much greater threat to the Victorian perception of women's sexual and social role. Her behavior challenged the idea of females as passive, passionless, and powerless. This position is reinforced by historical evidence, which clearly demonstrates that women were persecuted far more for cross-dressing than for romantic involvements with members of their own sex.[36] Vern Bullough mentions St. Hildegund (died 1188), whose father dressed her in boys' clothing at age twelve to disguise her presence with him on his pilgrimage to the Holy Land. When her father later died, she continued to cross-dress even into adulthood to protect herself during her journey home. After a long series of adventures she finally returned to Germany and joined a monastery, where she remained until she died. Only then was she discovered to be a woman. She was later canonized. However, Joan of Arc

(1412–1431) was charged and executed precisely because she adamantly refused to don female clothing in addition to venturing into men's domain by engaging in combat.[37] Bullough concludes, "For a woman to assume a male guise for holy purposes was permitted, but to compete with men on such masculine grounds as warfare was simply not permitted, and a woman who was successful at such efforts must have been a witch."[38] Although his interpretation is questionable, given that the French people saw Joan as a saintly figure and that to play a masculine role is not necessarily to compete with men, it is curious that Bullough, himself a man, would perceive Joan's efforts as in contest with her male contemporaries.

One could argue that the Bible specifically forbade cross-dressing: "The woman shall not wear that which pertaineth unto man . . . for all that do so are an abomination unto the Lord thy God" (Deuteronomy 22:5), but then, why burn one woman as a witch for the same behavior that earned another sainthood? In addition, why were those women documented by Jonathan Katz and Alan Berube[39] put in asylums, jailed, or heavily fined? Their transgressions were not necessarily of a sexual nature; their crime was the adoption of the male prerogative to operate in the public sphere and in gender-reserved occupations. Conversely, Carroll Smith-Rosenberg and Nancy Sahli each cite abundant letters and diaries of women who formed passionate friendships with each other and who overlap in time with the "passing women" mentioned above. Both these authors agree that romantic attachments between women—and it is irrelevant for the argument whether these were sexual or not—fit more readily in the Victorian social organization and did not threaten the social order. Passionate love between women was considered, as Smith-Rosenberg notes, "both socially acceptable and fully compatible with heterosexual marriage."[40] As Sahli concludes, "As long as women loved each other as they did for much of the nineteenth century, without threatening the system itself, their relationships either were simply ignored by men or were regarded as an acceptable part of the female sphere."[41]

The Victorian sexologists based their conception of sex between women on a heterosexual model. One of the women had to assume the male role and, as such, was the invert. She was more easily recognizable. Consequently, she was described, derided, and disposed of as sick with greater frequency by the experts than was her "feminine" partner. Her visibility made her more vulnerable to exposure, but what is astonishing is that she does not make her appearance historically with such regularity until she is "discovered" by the sexologists. This does not deny the existence of aggressive or homosexual women before the Victorian era, nor do I claim that the nineteenth century experts created these "masculine" women. Indeed, I agree with Chauncey that "such assumptions attribute inordinate power to ideology as an autonomous social force; they oversimplify the complex dialectic between social conditions, ideology and consciousness which produced gay identities."[42] However, what the Victorian sex specialists did achieve was to make accessible detailed descriptions of what they perceived as discrete, pathological behavior and to define, record, and document innumerable case histories. Their work produced a recognizable image of the "female sexual invert" that could be used by the legal profession as well as by the police. Paradoxically, the very characteristics that were supposed to distinguish homosexual women may have been adopted by the women to make it possible for them to recognize one another.

Finally, one other outcome of the work of nineteenth century sexologists was that it put an end to the belief in female passionlessness. Women were now perceived as having sexual feelings in their own right. The age of innocence was over; the denial of female sexuality had come to an end.

It must be remembered, however, that the Victorian sex experts were but mildly interested in women's sexuality as such. The concern was a much wider notion of sex, particularly as it pertained to and was practiced by men. The idea was to define and to classify as many "sexual" acts as possible and to validate these with descriptive case histories. As Jeffrey Weeks notes, "The scientific and medical speculation can be seen as a product of the tendency of social sciences to differentiate traditionally execrated and monolithic crimes against nature into discrete deviations and to map their aetiologies."[43] The current discourse began with the notion of socially accepted sex—meaning, a man and a woman engaging in sexual intercourse within marriage and for the purpose of procreation. All sexual acts that fell outside this boundary were considered deviant. They were to be studied and analyzed, presumably so that people could diagnose them, warn against their potential harm, legislate prohibitions of those considered most virulent, and formulate cures where possible or adopt preventive measures against the more advanced or congenital instances.

Researchers collected case histories, and from these, ostensibly, they were able to create a profile of people most likely to commit specific deviant sexual acts. The tendency to attach deeds to those who act them out led to the identification of individuals by their behavior. In other words, people began to be characterized by the deviant acts they committed. This move from the concept of discrete deviant acts performed by individuals to the idea of a deviant profile may have begun the trend that would eventually lead to the recognition of deviant personalities. For the moment, *homosexuality* (the term preferred since the 1890s)[44] was but one of the many deviations that made its appearance in the Victorian era. As a concept, "it corresponded to clarification and articulation of a variety of social categories: the sexual child, the hysterical woman, the congenitally inclined prostitute,"[45] each a discrete entity that was studied and analyzed, classified and/or condemned.

The beginning of the twentieth century saw female homosexuality turn into a more ominous threat to the prevailing social structure. Sexual ideologists were now promoting a more "liberal" sexual morality, even if this actually translated into sex within the rigid bounds of heterosexual intercourse. It took the form of "companionate" marriages, which suited women's increased freedom compared with the limited spheres of the Victorian period but accommodated men even more. Christina Simmons observes, "Companionate marriage represents the attempt of mainstream marriage ideology to adapt to women's perceived new social and sexual power."[46] This new "freedom" consisted of such social reforms as women's suffrage (eventually), easier divorce, legalized birth control, and the availability of sex education for the young.[47] Companionate marriage recognized that women are sexual beings, that they may enjoy sex for other than procreative reasons, and that they have a right to learn as well as to earn. Companionate marriage was an idealized notion that was to bring men and women together in marriage on equal terms (more or less) and that was to be based on friendship, sexual intimacy, and companionship. Essentially, as Simmons notes, "companionate marriage directed female sexual energies toward men and marriage."[48] The separate spheres for each sex that were the mainstay of Victorian social order were now suddenly outmoded and derided, seen as obstacles to the new concepts of heterosexual romance and camaraderie. Nevertheless, women stood to gain very little by the considerations that accompanied companionate marriages. As Jeffrey Weeks suggests, "What was at stake . . . was the notion of reciprocity in sexual pleasure, but not the obliteration of gender distinctions, or sexual libertarianism."[49]

Middle-class white women's increased education and consequent entry into some professions decidedly gave them more alternatives. They were heavily opting to remain single, to live with other women (Boston marriages), and to devote their lives to a profession. Many of these women clearly understood that, even with the recent reforms, gender inequalities were certainly not abolished and, in many ways, not even perceptibly diminished. Consequently, they often chose to remain single.[50]

The literature of the time denigrated relationships between women, Boston marriages, and spinsters. Indeed, Sheila Jeffreys argues that it was the desire to undermine women's political and social gains, which threatened traditional male access to women, that provoked a vigorous attack on spinsters, one that was aimed at discrediting them. "This threat was particularly serious when independent women were engaged in passionate friendships with each other and were in a position to form a strong female network which could bond against men."[51] Linking any choice outside of heterosexual marriages and liaisons with lesbianism, frustration, perversion, and loneliness, the prevailing ideology strongly discouraged female independence from men. Simmons concludes, "Whether female resistence to heterosexual relationships actually occurred or not, the recognition of sexual inequality engendered in the culture a male *fear* of resistance, often expressed as a fear of lesbianism."[52] There was a preponderance of articles and authoritative treatises on female homosexuality, mostly in relation to heterosexuality. It was perceived as a deviation from the "normal" primarily because women who failed to try to appeal to or pretend interest in men were presumably attempting to save face. Ostensibly, they were suffering from not having been picked by a man or from being rejected by one. Nevertheless, it was frequently seen as potential female subversion or as possible opposition to heterosexuality, as Simmons observes. As such, it presented "a cultural meaning that homosexuality had not carried in the nineteenth century."[53]

The decades between 1910 and 1930 produced much of the popular literature that promulgated such stereotypical notions of female homosexuality as an immature choice, a lack of responsibility, and a degrading alternative to heterosexuality. It was also an era when eroticism pervaded the culture and when words and phrases that earlier had had no particular libidinous connotations now acquired new lubricous significances. Jonathan Katz writes " 'Lesbian', which through the teens in the dominant culture meant, simply, one from Lesbos, by the 1930s referred specifically to woman-to-woman eroticism."[54] Katz claims that the eroticization of the word *lesbian* can be traced from medical reports to the *New York Times* book reviews of the period.

The word *lesbian,* used to relate to female homosexuals, refers to the poet Sappho, who lived on the island of Lesbos approximately between 612 and 558 B.C. and who wrote love poems addressed to young women. These popular poems were celebrated in her era throughout the Greek world. She was a teacher, a poet, and a well-known figure in her day, yet what remains of her poetry are fragments recovered after her work was destroyed by fire at two different historical times and places. Her love songs to women condemned her to centuries of obscurity, disgrace, disrepute, denial, and even infamy. She embodied all that was threatening to men/critics, who felt excluded from her poetry, slighted by her subject matter, and ignored by her choice of love object. She was ridiculed in her day, Dolores Klaich maintains, not for her love of women, but because she was attached to no man as was customary for all decent Athenian women. It was not until the Romans that her sexuality became an issue.[55] Perhaps because of the sheer beauty of her poetry, or maybe just through miraculous chance, she survived until our time.

At the turn of the century her name was appropriated and came to denote a sexual preference. "Sapphic love" described the erotic attraction and intimacy that developed between two women. In addition, Sappho's beloved island gives its name today to women who love women. This was started in the 1930s when the word *lesbian* began to appear synonymously with euphemistic expressions or diagnostic terms such as *intermediate sex, sex variant, invert,* and *deviant.* A considerable body of mainstream writing warned against and declared "unnatural" all forms of same-sex attachments. The easy accessibility, mostly to the white middle class, of such admonishing literature, often published in women's magazines, was seen as necessary in the face of perceived increases in the incidence of lesbianism. While the medical profession was producing a large discourse disparaging any hint of female independence (sexual or economic) from men, bourgeois women were producing a literature of their own covertly (and sometimes overtly) legitimating their new-found relative freedom.[56] But this was also the era of the much-publicized condemnation and eventual censorship of Radclyffe Hall's *The Well of Loneliness* (1928). The book, declared obscene in a court of law, was banned in England. It was also the period when the "scandalous" lives of American ex-patriates living in Paris became well known, discussed, and "envied." These women, Natalie Barney, Djuna Barnes, Renée Vivien, and others, contemporaries of but not in the same league as Gertrude Stein and Alice B. Toklas, were all artists, notorious or famed in their heyday. At the same time, in London, Vita Stackville-West, the Bloomsbury group, and various published authors (Foster, Woolf, and H.D., to name a few) were discretely involved with members of their own sex.[57] As Simmons observes succintly, it was an interval in history when "lesbianism represented women's autonomy in various forms—feminism, careers, refusal to marry, failure to adjust to marital sexuality."[58]

By the 1930s, the sexual ideologues had finally established that female homosexuality was an unacceptable deviation, that women's sexuality in general, although recognized, should be channeled within the narrow confines of heterosexuality with a view toward marriage and family, and that lesbians were frustrated, unfulfilled, lonely drifters forever deprived of the joys of heterosexual matehood.

The interwar years, although not very different from the previous two decades, were marked by conflicting moral ideologies that existed side by side. On the one hand, there was an emphasis on sexual harmony and pleasure for both partners in marriage, an increased awareness of female sexual needs, and a growing interest in sex education. On the other hand, there was the inveterate middle-class Christian beliefs of the sanctity of the family, the ideal permanence of marriage, and the inviolate roles of each gender. "Purity, familism, public decency remained the social norms which the apparatus of formal moral regulation sought to uphold."[59] The social climate dictated a particular mode of behavior, and whatever diverged from the norm was perceived as deviant. Later, during the World War II years, there is evidence, cited by Ruth Roach Pierson, that, at least in the United States, the war was "interpreted as liberating for lesbian women in the sense of living and working away from home and in same sex communities [which] provided a better opportunity for discovery and/or expression of their sexual preference."[60]

Jeffrey Weeks mentions a tendency articulated during the interwar years that was becoming increasingly significant. This was the growing acceptance of the medical model by psychiatrists, psychologists, and sexologists. "Vice and moral turpitude could be replaced by 'psychological disorders' as the explanatory mode," says Weeks. He goes on to show that, consequently, moral norms did not need to be changed, that "indeed they could be reinforced by new conceptualizations."[61] By the 1950s, the medical model took a firm hold as the dominant sexual ideology. Mental health experts defined, described, and proscribed behavior in the sexual sphere according to "normal," "natural" standards and deviations thereof.

The prevailing opinion was that women's function was to produce and rear children within the confines of marriage and under the financial and protective care of a man. Women who did not conform to this view were "normally deficient in the quality of womanliness and the particular physical and mental attributes of their sex."[62] Given these authoritative assertions, there was very little room for behavior that differed from normative order. Homosexual women were pathological and with proper treatment could and should be cured.

In 1955, Frank S. Caprio wrote what was, for a long time, considered a definitive work on female homosexuality. He wrote, "Psychoanalysts are in agreement that all women who prefer a homosexual way of life suffer from a distorted sense of values and betray their emotional immaturity in their attitude toward men, sex, and marriage."[63] Caprio believed, as did most of his contemporaries, that homosexuality was a symptom of maladjustment. To him, there were two kinds of lesbians, the overt (self-acknowledged, predominently homosexual) and the latent (the unconscious homosexual). He assumed that experienced lesbians seduced innocent women. He claimed that lesbians shared certain qualities that were typical of their immature personalities:

1. Strong reactions of jealousy.
2. Definite sado-masochistic trends characterized by behavior actions of hostility alternating with feelings of self-pity. All lesbians invariably display marked feelings of ambivalence toward themselves, their partners, their parents and people in general.
3. Strong feelings of guilt whether they are overtly admitted or manifested via hysterical conversion phenomena such as a multiplicity of health complaints.
4. Pronounced sense of insecurity.[64]

Caprio and his contemporaries did not attempt to question the source of such feelings of guilt and inadequacy. Women's behavior was not placed in context, and there was little effort to understand the role of social, economic, or political elements or what other factors may have contributed to the low self-esteem, the insecurity, and the various complaints that seemed to have been prevalent in the women they diagnosed.

A plethora of books and articles appeared in response to or as an explanation of the statistical picture that appeared with the publication of Kinsey's (et al.) *Sexual Behavior in the Human Female* in 1953. The report's findings left no doubt as to the incidence of female homosexuality, and many authorities turned their attention to the problem of clarifying this phenomenon. The discourse focused on why people become sexually and/or psychologically inverted, what cure there is for such behavior, whether the condition is congenital or acquired, and how homosexuals differ from "normal" people. The aetiological debates raged and theories abounded. It was presumed that if the causes could be isolated, homosexuality could be prevented and homosexuals restored to "health." Thus vigorous energy was spent tracking down the causes of this and other pathologies. No agreement was reached. However, identifiable characteristics did emerge as illustrated by D. J. West, who wrote in 1955:

> Lesbianism and male homosexuality probably spring from the same roots. In both cases neurotic family background, typified by sexual maladjustment and marital discord, colours most of their personal histories. All the most important factors concerned in the inhibition of heterosexuality—Oedipal conflict, fear of sex, guilty feelings, sense of inferiority—occur in women as well as men.[65]

West believed that lesbians were more disturbed than their male counterparts, that they tended toward aggressiveness and tomboyishness in childhood, and that they experienced feelings of rejection by the opposite sex. He summed it up with the following: "One psychological characteristic of many lesbians that all observers seem to agree about is rebellion against their sexual status, but . . . the inferior position of women in our culture provides a partial explanation for this reaction."[66] Unfortunately, this surprising insight was ignored by West and his contemporaries as they continued their search for causes and cures.

West's views are not uncommon. They are peculiar to the discourse of his time. His assertions on the topic differ slightly from the conceptualizations that emerged in the next two decades. As late as in 1972 (post-Stonewall, the 1969 riots which mark the beginning of the gay liberation movement in the U.S.), Jack H. Hedblom wrote an article (still considered significant in some psychological and sociological circles) entitled "The Female Homosexual: Social and Attitudinal Dimensions." In it he summarizes the main explanatory models of homosexuality, which he classifies under three approaches. The first is the medical model, which "assumes that homosexuality is the result of an underlying psychological or physiological pathology."[67] Hedblom does not agree or disagree with this model: he presents it as the dominant one in the literature. The second approach is the psychoanalytic one, which Hedblom accurately refutes because it "precludes the possibility of there being a psychologically healthy homosexual."[68] Hedblom bases his criticism on the 1957 ground-breaking study by Evelyn Hooker, in which she matched thirty well-adjusted homosexual men with thirty well-adjusted heterosexual men in age, IQ, and education. Judges who were asked to distinguish between the sets of people were unable to do so.

Another positive picture came from the English Wolfenden Report at that time. It stated that homosexuality was not pathological, that "normal" behavior was culturally biased, and that homosexual persons were virtually indistinguishable in everything but their sexual preference from nonhomosexuals. It also recommended that criminal penalties be removed from private consensual acts between adults.[69]

Finally, the third approach Hedblom mentions is the Family Interaction Model, which held that homosexuality was due to early parental influences on the child. Although Hedblom criticizes this view initially, he seems seduced by many of its arguments. He sums up his own preference: "Given the inherent weakness of each model, a combination of models must be used to locate the etiology of inverted psychosexual identity in the role structure of the family and the social support for the ongoing homosexual activity in the specialized community of the lesbian."[70]

Hedblom's views typify the pre–gay liberation conceptualizations about homosexuality. He writes in 1972, after the Stonewall riots, which marked the birth of the current North American movement, and yet he seems untouched by the events. His study is situated in the lesbian subculture but he does not seem aware of any lesbian social or political organizations such as the Daughters of Bilitis[71] or contemporary publications such as The Ladder.[72] Despite his shortcomings, his views seem almost refreshing after the proscriptive literature of the first half of the twentieth century, although his perceptions are steeped in the thinking of his time. Like his contemporaries, his work is impervious to the historical events that give a context to the "cases" he reports. Women did not live in a vacuum then any more than they do now. Pre-Stonewall accounts by mental health authorities and social scientists isolated their reports of "deviant" behavior, rarely considered the consequences of such obvious and overt persecution as the McCarthy era in the

United States, and continued the attempt to explicate homosexuality by posing aetiological questions. Hedblom, at least, is able to admit that discrimination exists against lesbians and that their socially stigmatized identity combined with pressures to conform potentially leads to the unstable lifestyle so often reported in the literature. It took one more year beyond Hedblom's article before the American Psychiatric Association (in 1973) removed homosexuality from its list of mental disorders.

Mary McIntosh's "The Homosexual Role"[73] is one of the most significant articles written at this time. Published in 1968, it paved the way for current discourses by arguing that "the homosexual should be seen as playing a social role rather than as having a condition."[74] The emphasis was beginning to be placed on society and how it constructed stigmatized identities of homosexuals. Over a decade later, Robert Padgug wrote, "To 'commit' a homosexual act is one thing, to *be* a homosexual is something entirely different."[75] But the concept of a gay identity was not widely recognized. Until it would be, homosexuals would be understood to suffer from "deviant" personalities, the profiles of which were well described and documented. Only homosexual identity could permit the potential achievement of a gay liberation. Being seen as "sick" is not only isolating; it tacitly blames the individual weakness for contributing to the sickness. An identity (even if stigmatized) by definition implies belonging to a group—in this case, a large number of people who would be eventually propelled into the radical politics of the sixties with its understanding of oppression as socially instigated and not a personal character trait peculiar to a "deviant" person.

The discourse shifted with the advent of the feminist and gay liberations. Homosexuality was no more a "pathological condition" any more than it was a "sin" half a century earlier. In an interview discussing her 1968 article, Mary McIntosh was asked how the gay and feminist movements have affected her views. She replied, "I now think that what needs to be understood is heterosexuality and that you can't understand homosexuality without locating it in sexuality in general."[76]

The discourses now recognized "that the concept of 'the homosexual' is a historical creation, and that a necessary distinction has to be made between homosexual behavior, which the evidence shows is present in most cultures, and homosexual identities, which the same evidence shows to be comparatively rare, and in our own culture of fairly recent origin."[77]

The current debate seems to center on several persuasive theories. One is *symbolic interactionism,* whose adherents (Gagnon and Simon; Plummer) view "homosexuality as a process emerging through interactive encounters (part of which include potentially hostile reaction) in an intersubjective world."[78] As Weeks points out, this viewpoint has been unable to explicate why sexual variations occur, "nor has it been able to conceptualize the relations between possible sexual patterns and other social variables, nor explain why there are constant shifts in the location of historical taboos on sexuality."[79] In fact, Weeks continues, symbolic interactionism stops at the point of historical determination and ideological structuring in the creation of subjectivity, considered essential in current theorization.[80] With respect to lesbians specifically, Gagnon and Simon argue that a central contention of their work rests on their belief that "the female homosexual follows conventional feminine patterns in developing her commitment to sexuality and in conducting not only her sexual career but her nonsexual career as well."[81] Faraday's critique of Gagnon and Simon stresses a feminist perspective. She takes exception to their assertion, as well as to the title of their chapter ("A Conformity Greater than Deviance: The Lesbian"). She claims that implicit in Gagnon and Simon's analysis is the notion that only men can be deviant. Since lesbians are similar to and conform with heterosexual women in their sexual patterns of development, Gagnon and Simon see fit to explain them away in terms of their "femininity." Thus "they describe 'the lesbian' in terms of 'a conformity greater than deviance' because of her 'essential femininity.' "[82]

With the increasing influence of psychoanalytic and postmodern discourses, French influence surfaced with the views of several thinkers, of whom two in particular seem to touch the English-speaking debate. The first is Guy Hocquenghem, who relies on Jacques Lacan's reinterpretation of Freud to argue that homosexual desire, like the heterosexual, "is an arbitrary division of the flux of desire, which in itself is polyvocal and undifferentiated so that the notion of exclusive homosexuality is a 'fallacy of the imaginary,' a misrecognition and ideological misperception. Nevertheless homosexuality has a vivid social presence, and this is because it expresses an aspect of desire which appears nowhere else."[83] Hocquenghem believes that repression came as a consequence of establishing homosexuality as a separate category. Weeks finds many flaws in Hocquenghem's arguments, not the least of which is that he still does not answer why some people choose homosexuality rather than heterosexuality. Furthermore, his work does not explain the recent liberation in attitude toward homosexuality.

The other French thinker is the late Michel Foucault. His work addresses the idea that knowledge is the basis of power. For instance, knowledge of condoned sexuality is produced in the process of the state's separation of what is delinquent from what is nondelinquent. Social institutions have been engaged in defining normative behavior based on this separation initially effected by the "disciplines." Science does not only discover and describe what goes on in society, but it also constructs the social experience in the process of articulating it. Thus, for example, in the case of sex, the definition of normative sexuality rests in the hands of those with the power to direct its definition. Foucault believed that sexuality was not defined by discourse but that it was defined *as* discourse. Talk about sex produced the uniform truth about sex. Foucault's concern was not necessarily with historical evidence regarding sexually repressive or libertarian periods, nor was he essentially interested in documenting which particular sexual acts were permitted or forbidden, when, and why. His preoccupation was with such questions as *who* does the speaking regarding sex, the positions and perspectives from which these speakers speak, and which institutions are involved in the production and dissemination of the discourses produced. Briefly, what was at issue for Foucault was, in his words, "the overall 'discursive fact', the way in which sex is 'put into discourse.' "[84] Gary Kinsman elaborates: "Sexual types and categories were socially constructed by identifiable power groups and the notion of sexuality as the truth of our identity and being was created by the power relations which simultaneously defined the meaning of sexuality."[85] Homosexuality as a form of sexuality appeared when it stopped being perceived as an act of sodomy and began to be conceptualized as an inherent part of the individual's personality. In Foucault's words, "The sodomite had been a temporary aberration; the homosexual was now a species."[86]

Foucault is controversial, and much of what he wrote remains ambiguous. He has been accused of idealism by Marxists and reviewed as too speculative or too theoretical, but for my purpose, one of the strongest critiques has come from Catherine MacKinnon:

> Although Foucault understands that sexuality must be discussed at the same time as method, power, class, and the law, he does not systematically comprehend the specificity of

gender—women's and men's relation to these factors—as a primary category for comprehending them. As one result, he cannot distinguish between the silence about sexuality that Victorianism has made into a noisy discourse and the silence that has *been* women's sexuality under conditions of subordination by and to men.[87]

Few can deny that Foucault left an imprint on contemporary thought, whatever his inconsistencies or oversights.

Whether promoted by Foucault, Lacan, Hocquenghem, the social interactionists, or the pre–gay movement authorities, most of these major theoretical frameworks, however liberating, challenging, or revolutionary, remain almost invariably male centered and male defined. They also mostly reflect white middle-class intellectual trends. In addition, for the most part, gay literature has proven to be unable to understand or explicate women's issues. Consequently, one of the most fundamental innovations of radical contemporary thinking was the early distinction between gay male and lesbian perspectives. Theoretically, much of gay male and lesbian issues may potentially be discussed simultaneously when dealing with aetiological problems or with questions of power, class, or color. However, in the final analysis, gender necessarily reorganizes the enquiry because of the shift in viewpoint.

Lesbian sexualities can only be understood within the framework of women's place in society. Contemporary feminists have reclaimed the right to articulate women's issues from where we, as women, are situated in the social organization. But they could not and did not speak for all women. It must be remembered that, concurrent with white middle-class women, and often different from them in circumstances and location, black women, women of color, Jewish women, and working-class women were living different experiences and developing histories of their own. However, as Robin Morgan reminds us, "Feminism itself dares to assume that, beneath all our (chosen or forced) diversity, we are in fact much the same— yet the *ways* in which we are similar are not for any one woman or group of women to specify, but for all of us, collectively, to explore and define—a multiplicity of feminisms."[88] Therefore, in the case of sexuality, whereas it may be claimed that homosexual oppression (male or female) stems primarily from ideological levels, lesbian oppression takes on added economic, political, and ideological expression because lesbians are women.[89] However, within the experience of being lesbian, differences are present according to race and

class. Yet, as Margaret Coulson reminds us, "In any patriarchal society the definition of women's sexuality (and men's) is embedded in
the definition of femininity (and masculinity) and both develop out
of and in relation to the sexual division of labour." Coulson believes
that the sexual division of labor constructs a social separation between the sexes and that this is both an acknowledgment and an
elaboration of the biological differences that may or may not exist
between them. It also establishes a social and economic dependence
of women on men, thus putting a premium on heterosexuality.[90] Essentially, then, as Annabel Faraday argues, it has been assumed
that because both lesbians and gay men share characteristic oppressions from mainstream society by virtue of the fact that both
are stigmatized on the basis of their sexual preference, what is *not*
recognized is that "while both lesbians and gay men are not 'heterosexual', heterosexuality itself is a power relationship of men over
women; what gay men and lesbians are rejecting are essentially polar experiences."[91] Men, whether straight or gay, share a similar position because of their gender in patriarchal societies in general and
in Western capitalist cultures in particular. Gay men are seen as
rejecting their male prerogative if they "choose" to be publicly identified as gay. A lesbian's relation to power, depending on her race
and class, her place in society, and her presumed economic dependence on men, rarely distinguishes her from her heterosexual sisters. However, in her choice to love other women she is perceived not
only as denying males their assumed claim to her body and services
but also as implicitly renouncing her gender because she violates
the expectations deemed appropriate for women. MacKinnon explains: "Sex as gender and sex as sexuality are thus defined in
terms of each other, but it is sexuality that determines gender, not
the other way around."[92] Ostensibly, a woman who asserts the pri-
macy of her own self and her needs, who reclaims the right to refuse
her sexual availability to men, or who defies the fundamental premises of patriarchal society that contain, restrain, inhibit, deter-
mine, and define women's sphere, loses the "privilege" of being a
woman. The early 1970s group called Radicalesbians expressed this
view somewhat graphically but accurately when they wrote, "A lesbian is not considered a 'real woman'. And yet, in popular thinking,
there is really only one essential difference between a lesbian and
other women: that of sexual orientation—which is to say, when you
strip off all the packaging, you must finally realize that the essence
of being a woman is to get fucked by men."[93] This notion may seem
simplistic at first glance, yet upon closer examination it articulates
much of women's history as written by men.

Lesbians, whatever their race or class, are women, women whose oppression stems from more than their sexual preference. Lesbians share with their heterosexual sisters many fundamental issues rooted in our common experience of being women. I agree with Adrienne Rich when she says:

I perceive the lesbian experience as being, like motherhood, a profoundly *female* experience, with particular oppressions, meanings, and potentialities we cannot comprehend as long as we simply bracket it with other sexually stigmatized existences. Just as the term "parenting" serves to conceal the particular and significant reality of being a parent who is actually a mother, the term "gay" serves the purpose of blurring the very outlines we need to discern, which are of crucial value for feminism and for the freedom of women as a group.[94]

In the struggle to affirm their existence, lesbians realized that they stood to gain more by joining the women's movement than they would by taking their customary minor part in the gay liberation movement. As early as 1959, at the Mattachine Society convention,[95] Del Martin,[96] infuriated by the proceedings, argued:

What do you men know about lesbians? In all your programs and your "Review" you speak of the male homosexual and follow this with—oh, yes, and incidentally, there are some female homosexuals too and because they are homosexuals all this should apply to them as well. . . . Neither organization [ONE nor Mattachine] has recognized the fact that this 20th century is the era of emancipation of women. Lesbians are not satisfied to be auxiliary members or second-class homosexuals.[97]

Of course, many lesbians did not deny or reject the gay movement. Many worked hard within it and understood its importance in the struggle to gain the right of sexual freedom. They participated (and still do) in fund-raising, demonstrations, political lobbying, and culture building and support many of the issues that touch upon gay male lives (for instance, bath raids, washroom invasions by police, AIDS). In general, lesbians see the advantage of taking a strong stand in the face of heterosexism. However, others have come to realize that, as women, with their own priorities, their concerns, their history, their loyalty, and their energy, depending on their race, and class and how they identified themselves, they stood to gain by aligning themselves with and working from within the women's movement. In addition, feminist analyses have undeniably provided them with an intellectual forum through which they may incorporate their understanding of differences in perspectives, differences based on race, class, ethnicity, religion, ability, and so forth.

Despite their sometimes problematic allegiance to the women's movement, lesbians often find themselves in a political bind. All else being equal, discrimination on the basis of sexual orientation often makes no distinctions between males or females. Moreover, lesbians also suffer injustices based on gender. On the one hand, when Canada amended the Criminal Code in 1969 and made homosexuality between consenting adults legal, lesbians were necessarily affected. On the other hand, when Ontario governments allocate minimum support for childcare facilities, lesbians as well as women in general are affected.

Although homosexuality was decriminalized in Canada,[98] in principle it is still possible to arrest and/or harass lesbians and gay men on related charges because sexual orientation is not specified in the Charter of Rights and Freedoms. Gay men are particularly vulnerable because of their more public lifestyle and are frequently accused of indictable offences referred to under the general rubric of "crimes against nature." These are "sexual deviations that were considered crimes at common law and have been carried over by statute into the Criminal Code; includes sodomy, bestiality and buggery." Male patrons of gay clubs and baths have been raided by police, who also harass men cruising in parks or public washrooms. The charges may vary, but usually they include "gross indecency," which is "an indictable offence punishable by up to five years' imprisonment."[99] Although "gross indecency" is rarely applied to women, legally a lesbian can be charged if her partner is not of legal age.

The Canadian Charter of Rights and Freedoms has not incorporated a specific guarantee of rights and freedoms based on sexual orientation. However, as mentioned previously, Quebec, Ontario, Manitoba, and the Yukon Territory have included sexual orientation in their Human Rights Code, thus securing our rights against discrimination in the areas of housing, employment, and services.[100]

2

# Women in Teaching:
# A Short History

Because of the paucity of Canadian sources, I have had, in some instances, to draw upon references and scholarly works from England and the United States with the confidence that, as with most ideologies that seem to dominate a social organization in a given historical period, those concerning and influencing the initial entry and eventual role of women in the teaching profession share similar trends and developments in the Western, English-speaking industrial nations.[1]

Given the potential breadth of the topic (women and education) and the vast discourses that have mushroomed, particularly since the recent feminist movement has identified the problematic as one that necessarily should include women's perspective, this chapter will concentrate on those issues and historical events that lead to some understanding of the situation of women teachers, their experiences and vulnerabilities. Particular emphasis will be placed on the development of some of the prevailing ideologies that affect the image of female teachers in general and lesbians in particular, or, conversely, that have been used by the latter to hide their sexual orientation within the profession.

Teaching has not always been considered a "woman's profession." It was only in the latter part of the nineteenth century that women began to trickle into that line of work. The pressures of a rapidly expanding population in Canada, as well as the demands for a trained labor force to support the developing industrial revolution, combined to necessitate an increase in the pool of teachers.[2] Women, as yet an untapped source of labor, were viewed as prime candidates. Moreover, they would be cheaper to hire since they were perceived as inferior to men, their abilities were more limited, and their work was traditionally voluntary and thus of restricted value.

Women would be only too grateful to be allowed to teach—and, predictably, they were. Their numbers increased, and by the end of the century they predominated, particularly in the lower grades, to such an extent that teaching came to be seen as "women's work." The eventual mass movement into that occupation, referred to as the "feminization of teaching," describes the large number of female teachers hired in the second half of the nineteenth century. According to Alison Prentice, women "did teach school before the middle of the nineteenth century in British North America; what they did not do, in most regions, is teach publicly (i.e., in the public school system such as it was) to any great extent."[3]

There were both economic and ideological changes that had to occur before women could be allowed to teach. Prentice sees female entry into the profession as made possible by three conditions. First, the leading educational administrators and propagandists of the day strongly promoted the idea of women teachers. Second, it was clear that women would cost less to hire than men and probably would do as good a job. The final but equally important reason was "the interest in the acceptance of their changing role by the women themselves, and by the society that financed and used the schools."[4]

The Victorian era was a time of confinement in the home for middle-class women in much of the English-speaking world. Women who needed to work—whatever their class—were allowed few choices. Those areas open for women to earn money (excluding prostitution, which was considered morally wrong) were usually an extension of their role as housewives. Domestic work is a case in point, and later women worked in teaching, nursing, clerical work, sales, service occupations, and factory jobs, notably in the garment and food-processing industries. Sheila Rothman points out that "a very special ideology defined women's proper social roles in narrow and restricted ways . . . closing off opportunities, fostering sex stereotyping of jobs, and ruling out options."[5]

The work that had to be done to promote the acceptance of females into the teaching profession revolved around two basic arguments. At the center of one was an economic reason: women could be hired at considerably cheaper rates than their male counterparts. The salary differential was justified then (and right through into the 1950s) on the basis of several premises. It was claimed by the authors of a 1950 Toronto Board of Education publication that the requirements of teachers' certificates of the late nineteenth century specified that female teachers were not compelled to include the more advanced mathematics and bookkeeping subjects. Consequently, the men, for whom these topics were compulsory, were given the senior grades to teach "and, rightly, received a higher salary."[6] It is interesting that despite the authors' initial acceptance and defense of this discriminatory practice, they do concede that "the salary differences continued, with an excessive disparity in the amounts, long after the Toronto staff consisted entirely of Normal School graduates who had all passed the same examinations."[7] An older teacher of my acquaintance remembers those days when women teachers were paid less than their male colleagues, a practice justified on the premise that men were required to accept extra supervisory duties. Women were simply not allowed similar opportunities and were, almost without exception, paid less than male teachers for the same work.[8]

Women were, at first, thankful for a job opportunity that provided relative economic independence and stability. Men traditionally viewed teaching as a stepping-stone to other career ventures and therefore had to be lured financially into the profession. Consequently, whether it was because women taught younger grades, which were allegedly easier, or whether it was because they supposedly did not have families to support, or because it was said they were not career oriented and this was to be a temporary job—whatever the reason—the fact remained that an obvious and very real salary differential put women at a disadvantage economically but, paradoxically, put them in a better position to be hired.

There were also ideological reasons that promoted the acceptance of women into the teaching profession. Teaching was viewed as an extension of women's already prescribed place in society and was therefore only an expansion of their proper sphere. Evidently this constituted another reason why women could justifiably be paid less than men: they were doing a job that came "naturally" to them—taking care of children.

Catharine Beecher was an early American spokeswoman who promoted women's entry into teaching. She always favored separate "spheres" for males and females and consequently defended women's inclusion into the profession by observing that "the school was a substitute for the domestic culture of the home."[9] Nancy Hoffman quotes Beecher as she reassured her audience that female teachers were like the ideal mother, truly feminine and working "not for money, nor for influence, nor for honour, nor ease, but with the simple, single purpose of doing good."[10] Similarly, in 1865 in Canada, the then chief superintendent Egerton Ryerson was coming around and reluctantly agreeing that women were "best adapted to teach small children, having, as a general rule, most heart, most tender feelings, most assuidy, and, in the order of Providence, the qualities best suited for care, instruction and government of infancy and childhood."[11] Even as late as 1931, Sir Fred Clarke, chairman of the Department of Education at McGill University, condescendingly dismissed teaching as "really a nursery concern, and women are its proper hierophants."[12] Despite his beliefs that women should teach, Ryerson went on to stress that they must continue to submit to their husbands in all matters and should not presume to think of themselves as gaining in any fundamental way; in his words: "Jesus forbids a woman to usurp authority over man."[13] Of course, it was understood that the ultimate goal for women should remain marriage and motherhood, their rightful place under the tutelage and protection of some man. Teaching, as Strober and Tyack put it succinctly, "was to be a procession into marriage, not a career."[14] It was therefore inevitable and justifiable for the state to make use of these "natural" tendencies that women exhibited. Consequently, it was not considered exploitation to pay them inadequate salaries to do precisely what the good Lord mandated as their vocation, duties that would be useful eventually when they were called upon to fulfill their innate calling of motherhood within a properly sanctified marriage.

When women were hired at cheaper rates, school boards were able to afford a larger male school administration, drawing men into the profession with promises of positions of power and leadership. Ryerson, among others, saw as one of the distinct advantages in hiring women a perfect opportunity to actualize his vision of teaching as a profession by paying men teachers increased salaries, thereby helping to "professionalize" their status. But, as Elizabeth Graham notes, "it was only possible to create this salary money by cutting back on the wages of those who made up the vast majority of the lower ranks—women."[15] Moreover, since women were permitted into teaching with the implied condition that it remain secondary to their first obligations of marriage and motherhood, their situation within the educational system seemed precarious. As Alison Prentice suggests, "The position of women teachers in the decades between 1845 and 1875 would not have permitted . . . a strong expression of women's rights or needs."[16]

Prentice discusses the many prejudices that women had to face at the time. I will try to summarize the ones she identifies, and I will also point out the inherent contradictions and double binds in which women were placed. According to Prentice, many of the obstacles facing women derive from male fears of female competition. Male educators maintained that women teachers, by accepting low salaries, were degrading the profession. We must keep in mind that women were hired originally because they were less costly and because a rapidly expanding school system needed a pool of cheap teachers. Nevertheless, and this was one of the double binds in which teachers were put, the criticism leveled against them was that the very cheapness of their wages devalued all educational careers. Second, it was believed that women were ill-adapted to the public classroom because of their inferior mental aptitude and/or training, but at the same time they were hardly allowed access to advanced studies. Women were also told that the demands of the public school with regards to discipline and organization were too great for them. In particular, they were rarely given charge of older grades, partly because it was said that they lacked the necessary training but also because of their alleged weakness. Finally, of course, there was the ultimate double bind: women were regularly pushed into marriage yet at the same time reproached for not making teaching a lifelong career. Martha Vicinus elaborated, using a British example: "Teachers were placed in a particularly difficult situation during these years [early twentieth century]. Just as marriage was once again being exalted as woman's happiest haven, local education authorities were routinely imposing bars on married women's teaching."[17] When men used teaching as a stepping-stone to a more profitable career, it was understandable. When women became teachers on their way to their socially determined roles of wives and mothers, however, it was taken as proof of their unreliability and fickleness.

When women were first allowed to teach, there were few options open to them. Domestic work was the principal alternative. Prentice says that evidence from upper Canada in the 1840s points to teaching and domestic work as equally low in status and wages. Teachers were seen to be "on the same (low) social and educational level as 'spinsters and household servants,' while others noted that teachers in general were no better than the 'lowest menials.' "[18] However, the aura of genteel respectability attached to teaching attracted hordes of young, unmarried women to the profession.

By the end of the nineteenth century teaching had changed in terms of status and wages. It had developed into a career in which women could enter without undue loss of self-respect. Danylewicz, Light, and Prentice report that teaching attracted great numbers of young, single women, a conclusion born out by the statistical picture, particularly in rural Ontario, where, in 1851, 7 percent of women teachers were single; this number steadily increased to 95 percent by 1881.[19] Many of these women were entering the profession as a temporary measure before they assumed their proper place in society as wives and mothers. However, for some, what they thought was a transitional stage proved to be a lifelong career. "To the schoolmistresses of the nineteenth century who remained celibate, the mission of the school was less a preparation than a substitute for woman's divine calling in the home."[20]

But there were women who saw in teaching a means of subsistence that guaranteed their independence outside of marriage. Whether by choice or because they had to find a husband, these women remained single and taught school all their lives. At least some of them *chose* a professional career over marriage, as accounts that have been unearthed by recent feminists (for example, Prentice, Rothman, Vicinus, Widdowson) show. Teaching was a haven for unmarried women, not only because it provided them with economic independence, but also because it accommodated their socially prescribed role of nurturer of children.

Toward the end of the nineteenth century women were allowed admission into institutions of higher learning. As their numbers increased, an interesting trend developed. Lillian Faderman reports that "in 1885, just as education for women was really coming into its own, there was a great public outcry when a survey revealed that more than half the graduates of women's colleges remained spinsters."[21] Many of these women were finding jobs in different levels of the teaching profession, and, according to Faderman, they must have been under considerable pressure to find themselves a man.

In the patriarchal society of the late nineteenth and early twentieth centuries, there were two inadmissible "sins" for women. The first was to be educated; the second was to remain single. Whereas education was seen as empowering men, "too much" learning was deemed unnecessary, indeed, unfeminine, for a lady. A letter written to a man by a woman who is defending the right of all women to education illustrates the prevailing misconception held around 1879, the year the letter was reprinted in the *Canada Education Monthly*.

Strong-minded independent women are perfectly horrid, you say; they wear queer clothes, and cut their hair short, and their boots are so very, very large and thick, and they talk loudly, and stand with their hands behind them, and are altogether most objectionable. Yes! Some of them are I must own, and they do a great deal of harm to the much larger class of women whose only desire . . . is "to use the reason God has given them to form a just opinion on the circumstances around them," by exciting a prejudice against what are the supposed attributes of every thinking woman.[22]

The reader should note to what extent the derogatory description of the "strong-minded, independent women" parallels the prevalent (contemporary, and, I might add, current) disparaging images of lesbians. There seemed to be an implicit fear that the education of women would lead to their autonomy, which in turn would induce a hatred of and a distancing from men. This state of affairs would inevitably provoke a tendency toward lesbian sexual preferences.

It was even argued that too much education could lead to that dreaded state of spinsterhood, as another letter, this time from British Columbia, written almost two decades earlier but current in its sentiment, states: "We never knew a man with matrimony in his eye who expressed any affection for 'blue stockings' in general."[23] Education for women, like any activity that potentially could provide them with some amount of freedom from male control, had to be fought for vigorously and later defended adamantly. Women had to deliver themselves from fears of becoming "mannish," "objectionable," and "perfectly horrid," typical male criticisms that were aimed at women who laid claim to any privilege considered "male" and that were almost always successful in keeping women in check, since women depended on male approval for their livelihood. And if learning made you "queer" and "objectionable," being single in a society where women are traditionally defined by their relationship to men must have been perceived negatively or even not understood. This is related to the then traditional view of the generally precarious and dependent situations of the spinster. Consequently, to *choose* to remain single was almost unheard of and somewhat unbelievable. Single women were categorized as "surplus," meaning they were in excess of what men could use in any given time and place. Evidently there was a certain female fear of being perceived as superfluous, and therefore it was not uncommon, even into the 1960s, for women to embark on promising careers only to drop them in favor of a wedding ring. There was a definite stigma attached to women's "spinsterhood."[24] Women alone were viewed as frustrated, bitter, and unfulfilled, not to say pathetic and unnatural.

Given the heavy stigma on both learning and spinsterhood for females in general, it is remarkable that women continued to choose to enter a career that openly demanded that they remain single. The following are a few points taken from an Ontario contract dated 1923. This document was to be signed by a female teacher who had to agree, amongst other things, to

- not get married;
- not ride in a carriage or automobile with any man except father or brothers;
- not leave town without permission;
- not smoke cigarettes or drink beer, wine or whiskey;
- not dye hair or dress in bright colors, and to wear at least two petticoats;
- keep the school room clean, scrub it with soap and water at least once a week;
- not use face powder, mascara or paint lips;
- not wear dresses more than two inches above ankles, and finally,
- not loiter downtown in ice cream parlors.[25]

It is evident from the above and other accounts of the period[26] that women teachers were not encouraged to fraternize with the so-called opposite sex. They seemed to be caught in the bind of either choosing to get married and forfeiting a career or remaining single and chancing a lifetime alone.

The bar against married teachers was resented by some women. The appropriate choice for most women continued to be marriage, but not all preferred matrimony to independence. Frances Widdowson mentions one teacher who remembers her mother warning her that, having got a well-paid job as an elementary teacher, she would be a fool to marry.[27]

The policy against engaging married teachers did not change in Ontario until the middle of the century. Married women who had previously been hired were granted special permission based on unusual circumstances, for instance, if they were widowed, separated, or had husbands who for some reason could not support the family. To teach beyond a certain age, for a woman, implied that she was disadvantaged in some way.

It was well into the 1940s before a number of boards of education in Ontario rescinded all restrictions against the employment of married women.[28] The motives behind the decision not to hire married women were presumably economic. Widdowson speculates about the prevailing reasoning that led to such policy. Popular rationale stipulated that hiring cheap and inexperienced young teachers made more profitable financial sense than allowing older, more experienced, and therefore expensive women to teach school. Since "older" presumed "married" (in accordance with the dictates of society), the said policy was sound. Ostensibly it weeded out the unwanted category. Secondly, by removing those who were married, it made room for the younger, college- or normal-school-educated and better-qualified teachers. There was also a strong belief that it was unfair for a married woman to earn a good salary if she had a husband who provided for her. Finally, it was held that married teachers would find it almost impossible to carry the dual burden of teaching and fulfilling their rightful domestic duties in the home.[29]

Once again, the traditional double binds imposed on women teachers are apparent. Whereas experience in any field ostensibly is an asset, for women it meant that they were viewed simply as more expensive, yet money was no object, it seemed, when it came to hiring young college graduates whose qualifications increased their marketable value. It was deemed unfair that married women with salaried husbands should still be allowed to work. However, there was no need to defend the inherent discrimination, since it was a man's inalienable right to earn, while for women it was to remain either a privilege or a shameful necessity to be allowed and condoned by men. In addition, there seemed to be no obvious injustice in firing women on the assumption that they might not be able to shoulder the dual responsibilities of teaching and domestic chores. Of course, it would be decades before the second wave of the women's movement would raise the social consciousness enough to question why, in the first place, domestic duties were the domain of women only. At the turn of the century there was a need to reduce competition for teaching jobs, and, as Widdowson points out, an easy way to do so was to remove certain categories, "and women teachers who were married appeared to be a vulnerable group."[30]

However, it must be remembered that women were allowed into the teaching profession in the first place because of their "natural" ability to nurture. It was for this reason that male administrators were able to justify lower salaries for women. On the one hand, a marriage ban was instituted that forced women to choose between marrying or continuing to earn, thus ensuring a steady flow of young, inexperienced teachers who were minimally paid. On the other hand, when the ban was lifted and women were allowed to teach after marriage, especially if they could demonstrate dire circumstances that forced them to continue working, their earnings remained low because theirs was deemed "pin money" or a second (read, undeserved) salary.

The policy of hiring women for teaching only if they were unmarried paradoxically continued to generate a choice for women between marriage and a career. Thus a woman who entered the profession "realized that 80 percent of her associates would be women, a further limitation on her heterosexual interests." [31] There was no doubt, however, that to remain unmarried was proof of their inadequacy to "catch" a man. *Old maid* was a derogatory reflection on a woman's personality, and she went to great lengths to avoid the disparaging, contemptible epithets of *spinster* or *old maid*. On the one hand, female teachers had to abide by strict moral codes that dictated dress, manner, expectations, and behavior;[32] on the other hand, they were supposed to marry. "The underlying assumption seems to be a woman 'should' belong to a man, and if she doesn't for too long, something is amiss,"[33] says Patricia O'Brien. She goes on: "People disapprove of women without men, not in any overt way but by exhibiting a vague, general cautiousness toward what is not known or understood, for example, neighbours speculating about the friendship between two female schoolteachers who buy a home together."[34]

The scornful parody of the "typical" spinster teacher survived until the so-called sexual revolution removed the stigma from sexual activity outside of marriage and until the women's movement positively supported and analyzed celibacy and sexual choices that may or may not involve men.

Alison Oram explains that the stigma surrounding "spinster" teachers in England during the interwar years was due, in part, to the link made be sexologists between perversion and women who remained unmarried and economically independent of men. She maintains that some spinster teachers may have been lesbian and for that reason chose to teach rather than to marry, but that the accusations against *all* spinster teachers, regardless of their sexual orientation, affected their status and tainted their respectability with equal disparagement as it did that of lesbians. As with the latter, spinsters were perceived as warped, repressed, and deviant.[35]

Despite the social resistance to single teachers, there were enough of them who chose this ridiculed state to warrant Mary Holman's description in 1950 of the typical female in the profession as "in her middle thirties and [one who] has taught between thirteen and fourteen years. She has the growing realization that she may never marry, and a desire for a home which will make up in part for what she has missed."[36] Holman then makes an interestingly ambiguous point: "Many women who enjoy each other's companionship have worked out a plan for shared living. However, the public often frowns on this, especially if the arrangement is a happy one."[37]

One of the most recognizable and prevalent stereotypes is that of the spinster teacher. At her worst, she is usually portrayed as severe, lacking a sense of humor, short-haired, and masculine. At best, she is most of the above except that she may be dedicated to her work to the point of obsession. This image was so deeply ingrained in the social imagination that Sybil Shack, writing in 1973, can easily refer to it confident in the knowledge that she is conveying a clear, comprehensible picture. She describes her teacher in the following terms: "Miss McKenzie could have served as a model for the standard caricature of the teacher, short-haired and grim looking."[38]

What developed as a consequence of men's regulation of the circumstances under which it was appropriate for women to be allowed to teach is peculiar to the history of women's work outside the home. They were first encouraged to join the ranks of teachers because of their "natural" abilities, thus continuing a preestablished association between womanhood and nurturing, as well as between mothering and care giving. In addition to justifying paying them less, this link also served to reassure those who opposed women's admission into the profession that it was merely a temporary measure until they had a chance to fulfill their "true" vocation of marriage and motherhood. However, when women chose to remain in teaching rather than to marry, the discourse changed once again to force women into what was claimed was natural for them: marriage and motherhood. It was inconceivable that a woman would freely elect not to marry; therefore, to remain single began to reflect some fundamental flaw in the woman. Consequently, the disparaging image of the "spinster" teacher had to be offset by the wholesome representation of the "mother teacher." For instance, as Alison Oram notes, in 1935, when a certain Dr. Williams attacked spinster teachers because he feared that they influenced the sexuality of the girls they taught, he declared, "The women who have the responsibility to teaching these girls are, many of them themselves embittered, sexless or homosexual hoydens who try to mould the girls into their own patterns." When the National Union of Women Teachers (NUWT) repudiated his unfair allegations, they framed their rebuttal within the discourse of the era, declaring that women's sexual impulses were maternal, or, to quote the NUWT, that "he should know that in the vast majority of cases a woman teacher's work is a complete outlet for her maternal instincts. Her womanly impulses were sublimated and diverted, but splendidly employed."[39] Both stereotypes slotted women into roles, both removed them from competing with men, but, even more importantly for the women who taught, both images seldom recognized their qualifications and their strengths as teachers outside of established clichés.

Whether married or single, women were consistently controlled by a predominantly male administration. The model pupil in pedagogical handbooks was usually "Johnny," whether brilliant, average, or academically disadvantaged.[40] Girl students were peripheral, included because of a need to reflect "liberal" beliefs in "progress," "equality of opportunity," and free public access to education for all. Capitalism demanded a pool of skilled (male) workers, and patriarchal dominance required trained housewives and women workers for service in the home and in those jobs that men rejected. Male interest came first. On the one hand, they were the ones responsible for families, they had to learn in order to earn, and their right to a job was entrenched in the social organization, protected as "natural," legitimized by religion, and regulated by the state. Women, on the other hand, were assured a place in the home of men. There was no "real need" for them to work. Their education was a "frill," a measure ultimately instrumental in benefiting the men whose "cultured" companions they were to become. Their careers and their energies were essentially and eventually to be put in the service of "volunteer," unpaid, undervalued work. Consequently, women teachers have had a long history of fighting for every improvement in their conditions of work, provisions that were considered a privilege for women but that would have been an inalienable right were they applicable to men. I am referring specifically to such policies as the prohibition of married women to continue to teach, and later, the exigencies to quit when visibly pregnant. These stipulations (which were frequently spelled out in contracts and later in collective agreements) originally were located historically in the years surrounding the Great Depression, during which time considerable pressure was put on women not to participate in the labor force. Arbus notes that mandatory retirement of women teachers upon marriage did not exist during the wars; nor was it a factor considered when boards needed cheap labor. It was instituted when the need arose to "protect" the jobs of men. "The policy of mandatory retirement was clearly based on the false premise that married teachers did not need the income."[41] Jobs were allocated by family, and men were considered the rightful breadwinners, a prerogative legitimized by the ideology that produced and supported the concept of the family wage. Women, as wives and daughters, were to be protected by and dependent upon men, whose role it was to provide for them. Even when the Depression was over—and in some cases, to this day (but excluding the war years, when female labor was sought while men were at the front)—women were believed to be taking jobs away from men whenever they were found in an occupation that was considered not solely "women's work."

Policies about marriage and pregnancy affect women's experience as teachers. For instance, many women today consider the burdens of childrearing and homemaking theirs alone, and they often shoulder the responsibilities of a full-time job in addition to working in their home. This is usually at the expense of their careers: they forfeit their place at bargaining tables, the advancement of their education (obtaining higher degrees, diversifying their certificates), exposure to extracurricular administrative work (assigned at the discretion of principals, for instance, timetabling), and the potential promotions based on a combination of these aforementioned factors. Historically, women have had to struggle long and hard for their need to be recognized by their various federations. Initially, teachers signed individual contracts with the different boards of education. Community standards dictated each teacher's behavior, and public expectations were frequently spelled out in the agreement. In addition to where they taught, for how long, and for what specific duties they were responsible, contracts included the financial allowances. These varied by board according to qualifications, sex of the teacher, and length of experience. There was no control over the conditions of the contract until the founding of the various teachers' federations, when the practice of collective agreements was introduced.

In 1885, following an informal meeting about salary differentials, a few women teachers in Ontario decided to found the Lady Teachers' Association. Women were still forbidden to vote, and the budding association became part of the same struggle as the equal suffrage movement. An account written in 1950 gives a clear contextual picture: "It took courage in those days for women to face publicity. . . . It was a time when women were called either 'females' or 'ladies' and were expected to be either inferior or superior (ideally, that is) to men, but not simply equal to them."[42]

By 1892, the name was changed to Women Teachers' Association and a more concerted effort was put into fighting for equality in salaries and working conditions. However, women were also struggling to produce some recognition of teaching as a profession and their place within it as professionals. This may be one of the reasons why, Danylewycz and Prentice suggest, Canadian women teachers, unlike their American counterparts, "were reluctant to ally themselves with working-class organizations or identify with working-class groups that had comparable problems."[43] Women teachers were not only discriminated against financially, but their responsibilities almost invariably included chores such as washing the floors of the schoolroom, cooking, cleaning, and making sure the place was heated in the winter. It was argued initially that these requirements ensured the schoolmistresses were able to look after themselves and provide the girls in their charge with a model for their later housewifely duties. However, regardless of the chores they were required to perform, women teachers felt that their work as educators placed them within the category of middle class. "Teachers saw they were not 'ladies'. Nor, however, could they fully see themselves as workers, in spite of the poor wages and difficult working conditions they endured."[44]

The Women Teachers' Association, which was to become the Federation of Women Teachers' Associations of Ontario (FWTAO) in 1915, was responsible for many changes that ameliorated the expectations and responsibilities of the female elementary public school teachers. FWTAO is one of the five teachers' federations presently existing in this province. The Ontario Secondary School Teachers' Federation (OSSTF), which was founded in 1919 (and, unlike FWTAO, included both sexes), fought a long battle to make teaching a well-paying, stable, and respected career. The others are the Ontario Public School Teachers' Federation (OPSTF, formerly the Ontario Public School Men Teachers' Federation, founded in 1921), the Ontario English Catholic Teachers' Association (OECTA), and L'Association des enseignants franco-ontariens (AEFO). All five federations are members of the Ontario Teachers' Federation (OTF), which is the official liaison between the teachers of the province and the minister of education. OTF boasts approximately 126,150 members in the five affiliated bodies (figures as of June 1990) and wields considerable power in the protection and support of teachers and their concerns.[45]

Since their entry into the profession, women teachers have long suffered restrictions that regulated their public behavior. A small example is cited by Sara Delamont, who reports that ladies in the Victorian era could not paint or draw landscapes because to do so would have meant wearing thick-soled shoes to work outside and such attire was unladylike.[46] What was customary or normative for the general female population was an unavoidable requisite for the woman teacher. She was considered, for all intents and purposes, the purveyor of morality to the young generation, the transmitter of culture (and breeding), the standard, the example, the ideal of decent womanhood. In the 1940s, a Saskatchewan writer published and article in *Chatelaine* in which she enumerated the confining constraints a young teacher suffered and from which she had recently escaped:

> For a lady teacher to be seen smoking is tantamount to throwing away her position; even in a man it is frowned on, while drinking and gambling, no matter how moderately, are simply not to be thought of. Carelessness in dress, reckless speech, anger, swearing . . . may cost a teacher her job. . . . If she attempts to pattern herself according to what is expected, a teacher is almost bound to become a fussy old maid—of either sex—careful to avoid all extremes, uncertain and hesitant about venturing to try any new thing, sapped of all initiative. She even gets to look different from other people. There is a popular joke we tell about ourselves: "That lady looks kind of queer Mama, is she a schoolteacher?" "No, Jimmy, she's just seasick."[47]

One teacher in my own study had the following memories:

> Back in the 1940s and early 1950s, teachers—and I don't care whether they were male or female—teachers were a fifth sex. There were men. There were women. There were doctors, lawyers, priests, and ministers, and then there were teachers. And teachers couldn't do things. I was reprimanded for going to a dance . . . because they sold alcoholic beverages there (even though I did not drink). When I taught in [small community in southern Ontario], on Friday nights the teachers in the community I taught in travelled forty miles to buy their booze in the next community and that community's teachers travelled forty miles to our community to buy their booze there because they couldn't be seen in public in a liquor store or a hotel. It just wasn't done.

FWTAO and later OSSTF made a deliberate effort to change the public image of the teacher, which, as mentioned above, by the

1940s and 1950s, stereotypically bordered on the quaint, if not eccentric, even if, for the most part, many individual teachers were respected. The image gradually ameliorated, although the federations cannot take full credit, given the complexity of the issues. Doris French questions, "How is a woman liberated, as our public school teacher has been from her multiple fears and doubts, from her sense of social ineptitude, the tensions of feeling herself obliged to behave like an innocuous prig?"[48] It took time and work by many women, inside and outside the profession, to make perceptible changes socially and economically in the conditions of women in general and female teachers specifically. As late as the 1960s and early 1970s, at the height of the miniskirt fashion, urban boards complained to the federation and demanded policies of "suitable dress." Even colored stockings were considered suspect by some principals. Teachers in rural areas and small communities were often required to adhere to even more rigorous standards of behavior and frequently expected to volunteer for local women's community functions or Sunday school teaching. A 1965 study by St. John found (predictably) that parents judged women teachers by a special code of conduct. They expected them not to bet, drink in public, make political speeches, run for political office, tell risqué jokes, go on strike, and teach after marriage.[49] Since by then women were allowed to teach after marriage, there were strict expectations that they leave their employment when they became visibly pregnant. This was a policy of OTF's against which FWTAO took a stand in the late 1960s, recommending that it "was an outmoded sanction since pregnancy is not something which needs to be discreetly hidden. . . . The date of leaving school should be at the discretion of the teacher and her Principal."[50] Today, maternity leaves are part of the collective agreements in most of Ontario, conditions aimed at protecting the teacher's seniority and allowing her various benefits during her leave. In addition, adoption, parental, and paternity leaves were also negotiated in the 1980s.

More recently, the conditions of work for women teachers have improved relative to the previous blatant inequities that continued well into the sixties. For instance, Arbus reports that in the mid 1930s, second-class teaching certificates were not accepted for men, yet despite FWTAO's attempt to do away with these second-class certificates altogether, the need for cheap teachers (read, women) in rural schools was a primary argument made by the Ontario provincial government for keeping them—and, by extension, a justifiable salary differential.[51] Today the teaching profession prides itself on the financial parity enjoyed by all its members, regardless of sex.

However, recent feminist research has called attention to the hidden injustices that have curtailed the careers of some women; it has exposed the ineffectuality of applying for promotions that are usually reserved for men, and has made visible how women are concentrated in the lower grades, teaching specific subjects.

When declining enrollment became an issue in the late 1970s for the publicly funded Ontario schools, Dorothy Smith, in conjunction with Marilee Reimer, Connie Taylor, and Yoko Ueda, prepared a document for the Commission on Declining Enrollments in Ontario in which they highlighted the effects and implications that particularly affect women teachers. The authors suggested that

> women and men teachers play rather different roles in the school system; that women generally occupy not just lower, but more subordinate positions; that they tend to be allocated different kinds of work; that they have less access to bases for promotions; that they have a typically different career structure; and that they have a different place in the overall "economy" of the profession.[52]

When the teaching occupation prides itself that women get paid the same as men for work of equal value, little, if anything, is mentioned of the inequities that are entrenched and essentially institutionalized in the profession and that tacitly discriminate against women teachers. For instance, traditionally women have seldom played a significant role in the secondary sector's collective bargaining. The reason usually given is that their domestic responsibilities curtail the time they can volunteer for such activities. Positions in the collective bargaining unit are elected by the membership local. The secondary teachers include approximately two-thirds more men than women, men who are more likely to entrust their career needs and aspirations to their male colleagues. Shelagh Luka reported in an OSSTF publication in 1981 that on the provincial executive, 1 out of 7, or 14.3 percent is a woman; that on the provincial council, 16 out of 63 members, or 25.4 percent are women; that of the OTF governors, 3 out of 10, or 30 percent are women; and that on the secretariat, 2 out of 22, or 9.1 percent are women.[53] One year later, another OSSTF publication printed further proof of the disparities inherent in the profession. In a small quiz aimed at the membership it was revealed that women teachers in Ontario were on the average more qualified (based on Type A certificates) than their male counterparts, that there were only 3.6 percent (21 out of 576) women high school principals, that the most common position for a woman member of a local OSSTF executive is secretary, and that there were 12 women technical directors out of 445. Laura Weintraub painted an even more depressing picture, claiming that boards of education and schools were well aware of "the rate of regression of women employed as principals in Ontario's elementary panel: from 26 percent in 1967 to 8.7 percent in 1983, although women comprise close to 70 percent of all elementary educators."[54]

Evidently, women's specific needs were seldom met in ensuing contracts. This partially explains, for example, why part-time teachers (predominantly women) have had, until recently, the worst working conditions of anyone in the profession.[55] It would be interesting to speculate why, until the early 1970s, OSSTF had a special rule that a secondary school teacher would be suspended if he or she accepted a salary scale commensurate with the lower pay schedules of the elementary school sector for teachers with the same qualifications.[56] Moreover, several boards in Ontario had an unwritten policy that the elementary sector could not "ride on the coat-tails" of an OSSTF agreement, thus ensuring that parity between them would not exist. These two policies are examples of the way elementary teachers have been perceived traditionally by their secondary counterparts. The policies are symptomatic of the prevalent but misinformed view that elementary teachers (predominantly women) are not as serious about their profession as are secondary teachers, who are mostly men (approximately two-thirds) and who are presumably supporting families.

Dorothy Smith et al. make visible in their report the various ways in which women's situation in the teaching profession was (and some claim still is[57]) structured to exclude them from administrative positions. There are at least five areas that the authors raise as problematic. Their arguments are still relevant and therefore interesting to present.

In the late 1970s, when declining enrollment began in Ontario, the profession was composed of approximately equal numbers of each sex. But whereas the secondary sector was made up predominantly of males (60 percent), in the elementary system women outnumbered men almost two to one. The 1977 statistical picture used by Smith et al. (which has not changed radically since then) showed that 65 percent of the elementary staff were women and 71 percent were full-time teachers. This representation clearly suggested that women were assigned "proportionately larger shares of teaching at the less advanced levels, less specialized by subject matter, and of younger students."[58]

Second, women were consistently "bunched" up into the more junior grades (between 94 percent and 88 percent of teachers in grades one to three were women; only 23 percent taught at the senior level). In addition to their predominance in the younger grades, women were characteristically concentrated in certain subject areas that gave them a more restricted range than men. Women's specialties were found in the arts and languages, with a marked prevalence in the three areas of home economics, office skills, and library.

In the third place, women and men teachers differed in their relation to administrative positions. Although women were approximately half of all educational staff, their percentage was proportionately small in the administration. This was particularly noticeable in the elementary sector, where, despite women's clear majority, they were not often administrators. The percentage of women unmistakably diminished as the position in the educational administrative hierarchy increased in importance (superintendents, directors). Smith et al. concretize the situation in this way: "What this means in terms of people's everyday experience is that when women teachers look around they see only a very small percentage in administrative position."[59]

A fourth problem centered on the work of theorists and researchers. Males were considered normative, the basis of a standard established by male scholars in the field of education. Consequently, women's needs were (and are often still) trivialized or discounted when they differed from those of men. Dale Spender elaborates:

What is beyond speculation . . . is the reluctance of researchers to see beyond males as the representatives of humanity and to identify women as an autonomous group with perhaps different, but no less valid patterns of behaviour. The surprise and bewilderment expressed by some researchers at the "abnormal" findings related to women has not always led them to question whether their theories apply to only half the human race. The "deficiency" has been found in women and not the assumptions of male educationalists and by continuing to treat the different behaviour of women as "deviancy" they have helped to reinforce the structural exclusion of women.[60]

In the case of teaching, men's career paths were established as the norm and women's as deviating from that norm. Smith et al. argue that women in the teaching profession were thus perceived as "less seriously committed than men, as making only short-term commitment, as less professional and as working largely not for pin money in these days but for the new suite of living room furniture—hence as uninterested in professional advancement."[61] This was largely denied by the number of women who continued to make teaching their lifelong occupation. Their professional commitment was comparable to men's, but their career paths differed from that of male teachers because they often include time taken for family responsibilities. Smith et al. remind us that "this differentiated career structure is organized on the basis of sex and not on the basis of different individual choices of direction and commitment." This meant that "it applies to women as a social category, rather than to individuals."[62] Moreover, because of the social expectations typically placed on women, the time they devoted to raising children and fulfilling their domestic duties, they often found themselves with less seniority than their male counterparts. The time taken by women for family responsibilities worked against them when promotions were considered, although the most fundamental reason for their lack of advancement was, and remains, gender bias. For instance, an FWTAO account describes the case of a well-known and respected woman principal of a large metropolitan school who admitted that she had applied and was rejected seventeen times before she was finally promoted.[63]

The typically differentiated career structure that applied to many women in teaching may be blamed in some instances on women's lack of advancement in their chosen profession, but it did not and does not take into account the surprisingly substantial number (in proportion to the population at large) of single women teachers who "have essentially placed themselves in the same situation as men, with respect to their capacity to pursue a career based on a man's life cycle, yet do not thereby gain equal access with men to opportunities for advancement."[64] The lesbians in my study are among some of them. They stated that they preferred not to be in the limelight for fear of being exposed. However, for the most part, women were not granted equal access to positions of responsibility, not just in teaching but in the labor market in general. Smith et al. write:

> The secondary status accorded to women teachers in the educational system in Ontario is not peculiar to education. It is an extension of a labour market segregated by sex. It takes ad-

vantage of the bottling up of skills and capacities resulting from the narrow range of professional and technical opportunities available to women.[65]

Women teachers were less likely to take time out for graduate degrees (although this pattern has changed). They frequently had less seniority and were therefore released first. They were not hired as often as men, ostensibly because they were less qualified, less experienced, and had more limited subject expertise. Shelagh Luka observes, "A clear example of this occurred in 1979 and again in 1980, when about 75 percent of the secondary teachers whose contracts were terminated by North York were women."[66]

Finally, Smith et al. explicate how female teachers' secondary status was institutionalized through their typically interrupted career patterns, which provided a relatively high level of skill at a lower cost than had their employment been continuous. The interrupted patterns secured male career paths. Moreover, it sustained a flexible pool of trained teachers (supply teachers, part-time teachers, and so on). These jobs carried limited (if any) fringe benefits. Smith et al. report that a number of boards in Ontario had implemented a system of "bridged seniority" whereby "they recognize seniority with the same board accumulated prior to a non-teaching interval as being continuous for the purpose of determining seniority in relation to job security."[67] In principle, this policy could have been beneficial to women teachers who took time off from teaching to raise young children as well as for men who followed a promotion to a different board. However, the tendency was to remove this practice in the face of declining enrollment. The reason was to protect those teachers whose careers were uninterrupted with the same board and to whom they (the board) owed more loyalty. Where this policy was adopted, it adversely affected women who reentered the profession after childbearing/rearing or whose careers were dependent on a husband's professional relocation.

In sum, Smith et al. argue that the issue for women teachers was one of inequities rather than discrimination. In recent years, many boards across Ontario have established affirmative action policies and appointed a coordinator to ensure their application. Women are now demanding to be heard, to be included, to be consulted. They are not satisfied with the secondary status allotted to them, with having their work with younger children devalued, with being excluded from teaching traditionally "male" subjects (math, science), and with being overlooked for promotions. Luka reports that more than half of the full-time postgraduate students are women, as are almost half of the candidates in part 1 of the principals' course.[68]

Despite establishing affirmative action committees to supervise promotion and hiring, few administrators, boards, or schools appear to be active supporters of employment equity, according to a recent article by Laura Weintraub. For her purposes, all those who fail to actively back equitable education and employment are effectively promoting antiequity.[69] Weintraub suggests that gender and race discrimination continue to prevail in hiring and promotion practices. She cites studies demonstrating that no statistically significant changes in the labor status of women have occurred, any more than in those of nonwhite or of Native Canadian peoples, despite affirmative action and race relation programs in existence, from the Ministry of Education of individual schools. Weintraub also reports that various "minority" sectors (such as women, people of color, native people) are pitted against each other, thus generating a "victim competition" syndrome. She cites an example in at least one board "where affirmative action for racial minority employees was blocked for a time by the women's affirmative action program," a situation that can be, and was, exploited by the organization.[70]

Perhaps the fundamental issue is not what is "wrong" with women teachers but what is wrong with the way they are viewed by their male colleagues. In April 1981, OSSTF's publication *Forum* printed an article that addressed the question "What do you think of women in teaching?" Of the twenty-six printable responses, a few were noncommittal ("They obviously should be teaching. If teaching is their thing, then they should be in it."); a small number were negative or unfair ("Women teachers have a tendency to panic when a class gets out of hand."); a couple asked concerned questions such as "Why aren't phys. ed. heads ever women?"; and only one was clearly positive: "Women don't need teaching as much as teaching needs women." However, the majority of the answers were simply outrageous, insulting, or biased:

- As long as they are pretty.
- They should be at home minding the house.
- They're not so special.
- Any answer I gave to that question would get me into trouble.
- That's a broad question.
- They're the cause of declining standards, increasing vandalism, and so on.

- They can't control the kids.
- Let's keep them working. They help to pay off the mortgage.
- Women have a pretty good deal. They are on the same [salary] grid as we are.
- I'm in love with my English teacher and she's a woman.
- Let's keep them around. They're colourful.
- We're stuck with them, I guess.[71]

That was ten years ago. Some women teachers claim that staff room humor has not changed since then.

Women in education face inequities that are often invisible but that are reflected in the labor market in general. Recent feminist critiques suggest unequivocally that women and nonwhite peoples face unequal treatment in this field, that the white, patriarchal social organization discriminates against them, that their imparity is concretized institutionally, and that the same ideology that operates to subordinate women and nonwhite peoples generally functions in teaching to keep them hierarchically on a lower scale than their white, male colleagues.[72]

This has been a short history of women in the area of education. However, like all histories, it has a context: its location is, for the most part, Canada. Its class concerns are, or aspire to be, mostly middle class. Its players are almost always English speaking and white. Their story is not universal or simple. Missing from the above-mentioned history are a number of players who either lacked the resources to be heard or who were "peculiarly eclipsed" (to use Dorothy Smith's expression) by more dominant accounts. These players include black women, francophone women in Quebec and in the rest of Canada, Native Canadians, Jewish people, people of color, immigrants, and, of course, lesbians and gay men. However, their stories in general, and specifically in education, are surfacing, being reclaimed and revealed to develop and advance our understanding of the histories of women and minorities in the area of education.[73] This book is one such addition.

# Theoretical Framework

"Society it seems was a father," said Virginia Woolf[1]—a father, she maintained, who would not allow his daughter to earn a living because money would grant her independence, which, in turn, would permit her to thwart his wishes and thus undermine his power over her. Woolf is but one example of a long history of feminist thinkers who recognized that women's subordination can be traced to the dominant position men have reserved for themselves by denying women equal access to economic, political, and legal privileges.

More recently, Kate Millett's *Sexual Politics* is one of the first major works to present a theoretical argument that analyzes male dominance in terms of an institutionalized phenomenon she identifies as "patriarchy." As she sees it, "If one takes patriarchal government to be the institution whereby that half of the populace which is female is controlled by that half which is male, the principles of patriarchy appears twofold: male shall dominate female, elder male shall dominate younger."[2]

The concept of patriarchy is still in use in current feminist literature, but it has developed to encompass several perspectives. For instance, as Veronica Beechey suggests, radical feminists use it to understand the system of male domination and female subordination, whereas Marxist feminists "have attempted to analyze the relationship between the subordination of women and the organization of various modes of production." [3] However, although it is applied extensively, the usefulness of the concept of patriarchy has been questioned by many feminists of different persuasions, even if most have had to concede, as McDonough and Harrison argue, that "there is agreement on one issue—there can be no understanding of the nature of contemporary capitalist society without placing the oppression of women at the center of such an analysis."[4]

Feminist scholars have also recognized that patriarchy is an ideology with a historical as well as a material base and that the way it manifests itself depends largely upon the particular society's mode of production, and its social, political, legal, and religious structures.[5] Moreover, patriarchy is reproduced in society through gender relations. In this context, the term *gender* refers to a set of culturally imposed traits and characteristics that are socially attributed to the biological sexes. In other words, whereas sex distinctions (male/female) are biologically determined, the gender dichotomy (masculinity/femininity) is socially constructed and/or discursively perpetuated. Most patriarchal societies ascribe the more "positive" and valued qualities to males, whereas as Millett wryly observes, "The limited role allotted the female tends to arrest her at the level of biological experience."[6] In addition, feminist writers (such as Millett) invalidated one of the most fundamental and prevailing patriarchal myths: the erroneous conviction that gender-specific traits are "natural." Indeed, Millett suggests that patriarchy's potency relies on "its successful habit of passing itself off as nature."[7]

Patriarchy predates capitalism. It also currently exists under almost every recognizable political and economic structure around the world. Obviously, patriarchy has persisted under capitalism, where it has taken a specific shape peculiar to that mode of production. Its structure is embedded in, but at the same time inextricably informs, the form and operation of the state, as well as the construction and application of the social, political, and economic systems.

From a materialist perspective, patriarchy prevails across all classes and races. However, the way in which it manifests itself differs according to the privileges or, disadvantages of the class or race in question. In other words, it can be said that all women are oppressed, but the extent and/or practice of their oppression is likely to conform to the class or race with which they are affiliated.

In Western capitalist societies, patriarchal ideology is made visible in the structure of the male-headed nuclear family and in the relations of each sex to the mode of production. The development of a gender-specific division of labor placed women in the home and dependent upon men within the context of the family and undermined the legitimacy of their participation in the paid labor force. Male dominance is thus entrenched in the social organization and is enforced by the economic, legal, and political institutions. As Walker and Barton elaborate, "Gender differentiation is produced and reproduced through the operation of patriarchal ideologies in places of work or production, in family life and in cultural forms and practices—all of which are themselves necessarily class specific and differentiated."[8] In sum, patriarchal ideology is inherent in the very institutions that enforce it.

The patriarchal notion of division of labor under capitalism placed women in a secondary and subordinate position in the paid labor force. At the same time, it situated them primarily in the family, unpaid and responsible for the well-being of husband and children. Essentially, women were not situated outside the labor force, but their patriarchally defined sphere located them in the home and undermined their worth as primary wage earners. For women, this had several implications: not only did they forfeit their economic independence when institutionally tied to a man, but because of their socially (and institutionally) constructed designation as wives and mothers, their right to wage labor was traditionally, at worst, denied and, at best, perceived as secondary—secondary to their primary vocation (wife/mother) and secondary to men's sanctioned entitlement to earn a living. A male was presumed to be head of a family and was granted the privileges of that position regardless of whether he was or not. The "family wage"[9] was but one example of such a male prerogative. Thus, when women were forced to work outside the home (for instance, when they actually headed a family), their earning capacity was reduced on the basis of the notion that they *should* be dependent on a man. The consequences were that women have been historically relegated to jobs that are almost extensions of their domestic duties (for example, teaching, nursing, and service and clerical occupations) and have been paid minimally because they would have performed this work in the home without pay in the first place, and because it was presumed that they had (or soon would have) a man who would support them. A fundamental effect of this division of labor was to constitute the family as woman's paramount domain and her means of survival. This, in turn, placed an inordinate premium on heterosexuality. In addition, the male's privilege within the nuclear family granted him control over female productive labor (whether she will earn in the work force, how her income will be spent in relation to his, and so forth) and reproductive labor. (The term is used here in both senses: he benefits from her unpaid domestic work in the home, and he had legal rights to the children born to that family.)

In sum, women's oppression under patriarchal capitalism is tied to a division of labor that shapes the household structure and thus determines the position of each gender to the mode of production,[10] and at the same time it is limited to women's socially prescribed dependence on male support, which gives men access to and claims upon female sexuality. As McDonough and Harrison elaborate, "If we understand patriarchy . . . to include the concept of male control of female fertility and sexuality, then it can certainly be said that patriarchy in this sense persists across all classes of women. Whether it is maintained directly by the husband as in the bourgeois family or reinforced by welfare provisions as in the proletariate family, the institution in which such control is exercised is still the patriarchal family."[11]

In Canada, as in other Western capitalist nations, the state plays a sometimes direct and often active role in promoting and encouraging a systemic control over and appropriation of female labor and sexuality. "Policies delineating everything from unemployment insurance benefits to daycare subsidies to the modalities of socialized medicine to the (lack of) abortion facilities to prosecution of lesbian mothers are all up-to-date expressions of a generic state."[12] Moreover, the state, by virtue of its patriarchally based social organization, sanctions and institutionalizes a form of heterosexuality that conceives of male sexuality as active, in control, dominant, and assuming and requiring female sexuality to be passive and submissive. As MacKinnon argues, "Sexuality, then, is a form of power. Gender, as socially constructed, embodies it, not the reverse. Women and men are divided by gender, made into the sexes as we know them, by the social requirements of heterosexuality, which institutionalizes male sexual dominance and female sexual submission."[13]

Obviously, heterosexuality is necessary for the reproduction of the species. What is not necessary is the inequality of the sexes that is perpetuated in its expression, since it is the property of patriarchally defined heterosexuality to assume hierarchical relations where the male is dominant. Burstyn sees male control over women's sexuality as a central mechanism for their appropriation of women's labor. Furthermore, she perceives a connection between what Engels calls "monogamy for women only" and compulsory heterosexuality, believing it to be "the major psycho-sexual organizing principle of gender-class society, with its attendant subordination of women's right to erotic pleasure as well as masculine control of children and property."[14]

Clearly, women's oppression is not confined, historically and geographically, to contemporary Western capitalist states. However, since this research is located within the Canadian context, and since Canada's political economy predominantly exhibits the characteristics of a capitalist mode of production, the conditions described are meant to reflect the Canadian situation.

Institutional heterosexuality, as the only form of sexual expression, particularly for procreative purposes, has been systematically encouraged by the state in this country.[15] Its very exclusivity renders all other forms of sexual expression illegitimate, and in some cases illegal. Patriarchally informed heterosexuality presumes and prescribes the subordination of women's needs to those of men. Patriarchal heterosexuality characteristically appropriates women's sexuality, denies its autonomy, and believes it to be nonexistent outside of men. To paraphrase Marilyn Frye, it is only when the penis is present that there is absolute certainty that sexual activity has occurred.[16]

Patriarchally interpreted heterosexuality, as it is expressed in a contemporary capitalist society like Canada, is a historically specific ideological construct sanctified and institutionalized by the state in the form of marriage contracts, definitions of what constitutes a family unit, and all such laws, policies, and rules that stem from or are meant to regulate relations between men and women. Even sexual relations are in some way controlled by state laws that govern who can be given marriage licenses, what sexual acts (even within marriage) are legal, the definition of common law partner, the legal age of sexual consent, and so forth. Sex is delineated and defined to fit traditional, cultural, religious, and social prescriptions that usually limit its expression to procreative functions, ensuring the renewal of generations and, by extension, the availability of and access to fresh pools of workers.

The term *heterosexuality*, as it is defined in Western capitalist societies, is a relatively new concept. Evidently, sexual acts (procreative or otherwise) between men and women have always existed (as did the condemnation of all other nonreproductive sexual acts, such as anal intercourse, masturbation, and bestiality). However, the insistence that there is a particularly acceptable, allegedly normative, legally sanctioned, and publicly approved sexual expression to be distinguished from "deviant," "unnatural" acts that are medically, legally, and socially defined is a historically modern phenomenon. According to Wayne Dynes's *Homolexis,* the term emerged in Germany as "the complement to 'homosexual' around 1869."[17] At the time of its early coinage it was part of a sexological discourse and referred, in essence, to those who were not practicing sexual acts that were deemed "abnormal." Those people identified as "heterosexual" fundamentally were not aware that they belonged to a category named "heterosexual." Therefore, it can safely be assumed that *heterosexuality* became a term of convenience to distinguish those who practiced normative sexuality from those who were, in the late nineteenth century, being "discovered" as "abnormal" or "perverted" according to definitions developed in that era. "Heterosexuality" is peculiar to Western capitalist societies only because they developed a discourse that made an issue of what was universally considered "sexuality" with no further referent.[18] Jonathan Katz reports that the earliest American usage of the terms *heterosexual* as opposed to *homosexual* originally did not signify polar experiences, symmetrically opposite in their categorizations.

In one of the earliest American uses of the term "homosexual," in May 1892, Dr. Kiernan (citing Krafft-Ebing) defined "Pure homosexuals" as persons whose "general mental state is that of the opposite sex." In the same article, "heterosexuals" were defined as those with a mental condition, "Physical hermaphroditism," in which "Traces of the normal sexual appetite are discoverable"—those with "inclinations to both sexes" (now called "bisexuals"). "Heterosexuals" were also defined as those with inclinations "to abnormal methods of gratification ("abnormal" here meaning methods unrelated to procreation, regardless of the actors' gender).[19]

However, it would be too simplistic to assume, even in the nineteenth century, that there were only two polar sexualities, homosexuality and heterosexuality. Scholars such as Michel Foucault, Guy Hocquenghem, Gayle Rubin, and Jeffrey Weeks, to name a few, have demonstrated that Western capitalist societies conceptualized discourses that were cognizant of multiple sexualities, all of which were hierarchically classified and recognized.[20]

Since heterosexuality, as it is understood in modern capitalist societies, is a historical and social construct, since it is situationally determined (in principle, the same person can be called "homosexual" or "heterosexual" according to the sex of the partner), and since it is a currently recognizable practice, it is ideological in its function. Dorothy Smith writes, "Ideology can be viewed as a procedure for sorting out and arranging conceptually the living actual world of people *so that it can be seen as we already know it ideologically.*"[21] Clearly, heterosexuality in its patriarchal form, as a term applied to a set of identifiable behaviors, "sorts out" and "arranges conceptually" our way of thinking about gender and sexuality. Prescribed ideological behavior presumes a privileged group in society in whose interest a particular ideology is promoted—in this case, men's.

Ideology is a way of thinking about the world, of conceptualizing it to make it intelligible to those who adhere to it. Ideology is transmitted. For instance, our notions of what constitutes proper behavior for each gender are learned, as are our ideas about sexuality. Much time and effort, endless prodding, constant reminders, and consistent reinforcement are necessary to produce gendered individuals. Deviance from "acceptable" gender-related conduct is at the risk of ridicule or repression. Parents, religious bodies, media, friends, schools, laws, and medicine—every facet of society—is actively involved in some way in describing, qualifying, researching, "proving," and classifying what constitutes a "man" or a "woman" and what characterizes their respective "masculinity" or "femininity." This is particularly obvious in the case of sexuality. As Michele Barrett argues, although we should reject direct connections between the socially constructed gender identities (masculinity/femininity) and their assumed (and expected) consequences for sexual behavior, we should also particularly discredit any categorical links between maleness and femaleness and a "natural" orientation to heterosexual genital sexuality. Nevertheless, Barrett warns that she does not propose a radical dissociation of the two (gender and sex) because, in her words, "there can be no doubt that the familial and general ideological processes by which the categories of masculinity and femininity are established and reproduced in our society lead, at the very least, to a disposition toward 'appropriate' forms of eroticism."[22] It is on the basis of that very "appropriateness" that heterosexuality is justified, indeed promoted, as "natural," while at the same time it is enforced (compulsory heterosexuality)[23] both institutionally (through education, family pressure, heterosexual privilege, and so forth) and culturally (from television to movies, from advertizing to popular songs, and from prose and poetry.)

Ideology works to preserve the status quo of those who have the power to enforce it. Gramsci calls this group the "hegemonic class," by which he means "a class which has been able to articulate the interests of other social groups to its own by means of ideological struggle."[24] He goes on to explain that this ideology is expressed, elaborated, and spread through an institutional structure that gives it a material base. The structure is made up of different "hegemonic apparatuses: schools, churches, the entire media and even architecture and the name of the streets. This ensemble of apparatuses is termed the ideological structure of a dominant class by

Gramsci, and the level of the superstructure where ideology is produced and diffused is called *civil society*."[25] Gramsci suggests that ideology is not a means whereby a dominant group dupes or manipulates an exploited class into behaving in a certain way or adhering to certain practices. "For him, ideology is not the mystified-mystifying justification of an already constituted class power, it is 'the terrain on which men acquire consciousness of themselves,' and hegemony cannot be reduced to a process of ideological domination."[26] In other words, for the ideology of the dominant group to become "hegemonic," it has to be accepted by people at the level of "common sense."

Gramsci's central concern is, of course, understanding class dynamics. Women are peripheral to his thinking except in his discussions of the family, "the sexual question," or how women fit into class by virtue of birth and marriage. Although he understands women's subordinate position, he is less sensitive to the implications of a gendered society. Nevertheless, his analysis can be used to appreciate how women continue to support a system that is oppressive to them, how they acquire a "consciousness of themselves" as women in a patriarchal society. Kate Millett argues that women acquire this "consciousness of themselves as women" through the process of socialization to which each sex is exposed, adding that males and females alike learn the "appropriate" behavior needed to survive in their particular culture. "Sexual politics obtains consent through the 'socialization' of both sexes to basic patriarchal politics with regard to temperament, role and status."[27] In contrast, Gramsci rejects the concept of socialization in favor of the notion of hegemony, which is primarily a political principle. Christine Buci-Gluckmann suggests that hegemony "is primarily a *strategy* for the gaining of the active consent of the masses through their self-organization, starting from civil society, and in all the hegemonic apparatuses: from the factory to the school and the family."[28] In the case of sexual politics, hegemony would be obtained through male influence and compromises that would convince women that they stand to gain from the status quo, that where their men succeed, they benefit as well, that it is their responsibility and to their advantage to advance the position of their men (husbands, sons, even brothers). Furthermore, since Gramsci argues strongly that the education of different classes is historically linked to the needs of each particular class, consequently the so-called democratic access of education to all classes equally is deceptive (that is, education does not transcend class). There is evidence today that suggests that, indeed, education does not transcend gender either, that it fundamentally reinforces gender-specific behavior and/or actively reproduces and encourages masculine conduct in males and feminine conduct in females.[29]

However, it is not the intention of this book to discuss the details of women's oppression in a capitalist society. This work has been accomplished by feminist writers whose expert examination of the problematic is available to those interested in pursuing the issue.[30] What is important is to explicate as simply and as clearly as possible in this limited space how Gramsci's concept of hegemony can be used to comprehend some of the reasons why women (in general) and lesbians (in particular) accept and often uphold a social organization that systematically (and systemically) denies them equal rights with men.

More specifically, Gramsci's concept of hegemony can be used to address sexuality. As was mentioned above, the state plays a direct role in actively encouraging heterosexual pair bonding, legitimizing it legally, socially, and economically. Heterosexuality,[31] as the dominant sexual ideology, is expressed, elaborated, and transmitted through the institutional structure, the "hegemonic apparatuses," in this case, schools, churches, media, and so forth. Heterosexuality is given a material base so that it is appealing for women to "be with a man" for financial support and social approbration as well as for sexual expression. Heterosexual privilege is a reality in a woman's life. It confers status upon her if she is married (particularly as a mother), and her "reward" is that she is "protected," "supported," and "fulfilled"; she "belongs." Indeed, she is accepted, she is approved of, and she is effecting her place in society, achieving her designated role as "helpmate," and, of course, by virtue of being with a man, she is viewed as a "real" woman. In contrast, a woman who is lesbian is perceived as acting against "nature," not because she is simultaneously rejecting her prescribed feminine sphere, but because she is also denying the hegemonic position that makes her accessible sexually (and otherwise) to some man or men.[32] Hegemonic ideology presents heterosexuality as "natural" and "normal" because it is procreative. Conversely, homosexuality is necessarily considered "abnormal" and "unnatural" since it is usually socially posited as a polar opposite to heterosexuality and since it deviates from it. The hegemonic position that equates heterosexuality with "natural" and "normal" has become "commonsense" knowledge, permeating all levels of society. It is evident in my own study in the words of the following lesbian teacher:

> I mean, I look at the way my body is made and I try to fit it together with another female body—obviously I am not a very imaginative lover—sometimes it's frustrating. You think to yourself: my god, the penis does make an enormous difference for that final union.

This woman ostensibly accepts the argument that since there is an obvious physical fit between penis and vagina, we therefore have to be limited to one expression of sexuality at the expense of all others. The strength of Gramsci's argument is evident in that, in her own view, this teacher is not being coerced in her beliefs; rather, she is influenced by what Adrienne Rich calls "the ideology of heterosexual romance" that is "beamed at her from childhood out of fairy tales, television, films, advertizing, popular songs, wedding pageantry."[33] Hegemonic ideology eventually seems, in fact, to grow out of "nature." Subsequently, involvement with a man becomes inextricably linked with being a "real" woman, being "feminine." Conversely, although women's heterosexuality is only one aspect of femininity, in a patriarchal society, the very definition of woman's (and man's) sexuality, as Coulson points out, "is embedded in the definition of femininity (and masculinity) and both develop out of and in relation to the sexual division of labor."[34]

In a patriarchally defined, heterosexually dominant culture, a woman's social being is "produced" through her heterosexuality. She is a woman because of her particular relation to a man or men. Her social form as a woman has an appearance that conceals any actual relationship between herself and a man or men and makes invisible her potential as an individual independent of men, with an autonomous sexual need. When we speak of or perceive a woman only in heterosexual terms, when we conceive of her life only in relation to a man or men, we make invisible alternative sexual preferences.[35]

Deviation from heterosexual norms is discouraged. Unlike Gramsci, Althusser believes that ideology alone is not effective in molding individuals. He suggests that there is no such thing as a purely ideological apparatus. He explains that "appropriate attitudes," a conformity to regulations, an observation of rules of morality, civic, and professional conscience, and so on, all were established by class domination. Althusser describes the Ideological State Apparatuses (ISAs), which "function necessarily and predominently *by ideology*" adding that "they also function secondarily by repression, even if ultimately . . . this is very attenuated and concealed, even symbolic."[36] The ISAs are to be distinguished from the Repressive State Apparatuses (RSAs), such as the police and the justice system, which are ultimately the most successful in inducing conformity. However, he believes that even ISAs use suitable methods of punishment, which, although they are less immediately apparent than those of the Repressive State Apparatuses, also control behavior by using suitable methods of punishment, which include expulsion, selection, suspension, and ostracism.

Like Gramsci, Althusser was not interested in how women fit into his conceptual framework. Nevertheless, his belief that even ideological apparatuses also contain repressive elements may help to explain how women who deviate from the dominant sexual norms may be chastened. Women alone are often feared and distrusted. If young and available, they are seen as potential "home breakers." If uninterested in men, they are perceived as "abnormal." If lesbian, their lives are often restricted, if not regulated, in Althusser's terms, both by the ISAs and the RSAs. For instance, lesbians who do not attempt to hide their sexuality, in some states (U.S.) and in some provinces (Canada), are frequently denied housing, arrested or harassed at bars where they congregate, and may be denied custody of their children (the courts often view them as "unfit" mothers). Their relationships are not acknowledged in any formal sense unless they are renounced or disclaimed; a lesbian union is not given legitimacy legally (consequently, a lover cannot automatically share medical or insurance plans, is not recognized as "next of kin" if her lover is dying, and so on). Lesbian couples are not given tax benefits, nor are they able to have claims on each other's property unless specified by contract or a will.

Both Gramsci and Althusser identify the education system as one of the most direct means by which the state influences new generations. Gramsci includes schools as a "hegemonic apparatus," part of the ideological structure of a dominant class. Althusser, of course, names schools as the most effective Ideological State Apparatus. He asserts that they purport to be ideologically free or neutral and yet they transmit to schoolchildren the ideology of the ruling class. Notably, he maintains that schools inherently contain bourgeois ideology but conceal this by presenting knowledge as purged of ideology. He suggests that teachers, "respectful of the 'conscience' and 'freedom' of the children who are entrusted to them (in complete confidence) by their 'parents' (who are free, too, i.e. the owners of their children) open up for them the path to the freedom, morality and responsibility of adults by their own example, by knowledge, literature and their 'liberating' virtues."[37]

More recently, Bowles and Gintis undertook a critical analysis of the U.S. educational system, noting that, in their view, the institution neither adds nor subtracts from the degree of repression and inequality that originates in the economic (capitalist) sphere. In the process of training and stratifying the work force, education reproduces and legitimates a preexisting pattern that is present in the social relations of the educational encounter. These relations "correspond closely to the social relations of dominance, subordination, and motivation in the economic sphere. Through the educational encounter, individuals are induced to accept the degree of powerlessness with which they will be faced as mature workers."[38]

The work of Bowles and Gintis is crucial in its examination of the educational system of a capitalist nation, the United States. However, like that of Gramsci and Althusser before them, their analysis must remain incomplete because they ignore the importance of gender, and thus, by extension, disregard the fact that the same social relation that perpetuates powerlessness and subordination in "the" worker operates to maintain a sexual division of labor that preserves male supremacy. As Madeleine MacDonald notes, "Any theory of education which seeks to account for the form of schooling in terms of the mode of reproduction of the work force, I would argue, must recognize the structure of male-female dominance relations as integral and not subsidiary organizing principles of the work process."[39]

In short, Gramsci, Althusser, and Bowles and Gintis, amongst others, all attempt to understand how schools reproduce the ideology of the ruling class. What they neglect to address is that patriarchal values are also reproduced by the school system, and also that these values are represented as "genderless," universal to "mankind." It took the feminist writers[40] to make visible the influence of patriarchal values, both in the school system and in the society at large. They clearly demonstrate that the same schooling that reproduces a skilled, competent, and conforming work force, possibly well versed in the exigencies of a diversified labor market, also generates a population infused with notions of what constitutes "masculinity" and "femininity," as well as which forms of sexual behavior are "normative," what befits the career expectations of each gender, and what styles of living are deemed acceptable for males or females. A good example of a feminist critique is MacDonald's work, in which she argues that gender definitions are historically specific, that they "are socially constructed categories and power relations which are contained within, and defined by, the structure of class relations. In educational institutions one is likely to find, therefore, the imposition of gender definitions which are integral to the culture of the ruling class (e.g. aristocratic or bourgeois concepts of masculinity and femininity)."[41] More recent analyses would include race in addition to gender and class in their attempt to understand the influence of ideologies in the area of education.[42]

In sum, I have argued that the capitalist mode of production as it is expressed in Canada (and other Western capitalist nations) embraces the patriarchal precepts of white male supremacy and advocates heterosexual hegemony to ensure the reproduction of its labor force. I have also suggested that the formal tax-financed, state-supported education is in part responsible for advocating and reinforcing the ideology of gender identity as an expression of what constitutes "real" men and women. Furthermore, since ideology is not only a belief system but is also a set of practices, I maintain that the school system, as the "established" transmitter of dominant ideology, not only embraces patriarchal values overtly through curriculum requirements but also implements male privilege and compels the heterosexual/marriage/family option covertly by offering the behavior of those allowed to teach and administer as examples of what is acceptable. The rest of the chapter is an elaboration of this last argument.

To begin with, in Ontario, all schooling comes under the jurisdiction of the Ministry of Education. The ministry determines what is to be taught, by whom, to whom, where, and when. The Education Act contains the written statutes of the ministry. The act defines the structure, administration, and regulations that govern any decisions pertaining to education at all levels in Ontario. Any teacher, by virtue of being employed in a publicly funded school (outside of Catholic schools, which, although state funded in Ontario, are given discreet powers that supersede the regulations that govern public schools), represents the state. Hence, while at work, teachers (and/or principals) stand in lieu of the state, which, in turn, has assumed the responsibility and authority of the parents during the school day and for school-related functions. Teachers become accountable for the welfare of each child in attendance at school. They must record and report attendance,[43] give attention to the health, comfort, and cleanliness of the pupils,[44] feed the younger children,[45] teach from the prescribed curriculum, discipline students (through reprimands, suspensions, or expulsions),[46] and encourage pupils in the pursuit of learning. Finally, it is the duty of a teacher "to inculcate by precept and example respect of religion and the principles of Judeo-Christian morality and the highest regard for truth, justice, loyalty, love of country, humanity, benevolence, sobriety, industry, frugality, purity, temperance and all other virtues."[47]

Obviously, a teacher, as a representative of the state while on duty, acts *in loco parentis;* and indeed, in some situations, her or his authority supersedes that the parents, as in the case of school attendance[48] or the immunization of children against contagious diseases. As Jenny Shaw observes of the British situation:

> Quite simply there are transfers of a social and political kind in that parents lose real control over their children. They are deemed to delegate to the school the authority to act in their stead, which includes the right physically to assault the child if the circumstances are viewed as "reasonable." They lose the opportunity of controlling other aspects of their child's life such as what books he or she reads and maybe what clothes he or she is allowed to wear.[49]

These remarks are pertinent in Ontario, although recent regulations forbid any physical reprimands against a child. Shaw also argues that "state education is often referred to as being paternalistic but, more to the point, is the underlying model of patriarchy."[50] She bases this statement on historical data that suggest that the above type of authority over a child is characteristic of the historical rights of fatherhood, and on her belief that the use of the doctrine of *in loco parentis* is in itself indicative of the patriarchal ideology on which it is modeled.

Shaw's argument advances the issue that an individual teacher embodies the state in the classroom. A teacher's power to impart knowledge, to discipline and reward pupils, is an indication of this authority. In addition, it is important to remember that this same teacher also represents the parent, and as such, becomes a model as well as an instructor. Consequently, it is not surprising that teachers are hired in conformity with certain standards of qualifications, values, personal morality, and respectability in line with the ideological goals of the state (which are both capitalist and patriarchal). For instance, student behavior that is rewarded usually conforms with white, middle-class ideals of orderliness, discipline, and values. As Bob Davis says, "Schools don't teach and rate skills, they teach and rate behavior."[51] Moreover, frequently student "choices" of whether to pursue general or advanced credit programs largely—and, I might add, suspiciously—coincide with their parents' socioeconomic status. In addition, girls and boys, white and nonwhite, despite recent policies sensitive to gender and race, are not only treated differently by their teachers but are often counseled and directed into career choices that are conventionally gender associated with their respective sexes or that may reflect racist stereotypes.

As representatives of the state in the classroom, and as surrogate parents, teachers are perceived to be purveyors of hegemonic ideologies. Consequently, they are invariably assumed to be heterosexual, typically married, preferably parents (or soon to be), and ideally young and male (particularly in the second sector). The idea of a lesbian teacher would be inadmissible, incomprehensible, a contradiction in terms. It is a notion that profoundly and fundamentally conflicts with and deviates from accepted traditional standards of "virtue" and "decency" for women in general and for female teachers in particular. The very word *lesbian* implies sexual activity and stands in direct contradiction to the characteristic image of the passionless woman and the sexless teacher. Lesbians are (wrongly) viewed as "antifamily," both in that they themselves are thought not to marry or conceive and in that their lifestyles exclude men. They are financially and sexually independent from men, conditions that are perceived as undermining the very fabric of society as men have organized it. However, the most crucial consideration is that, as teachers, lesbians are in charge of children, youngsters who are "innocent," "malleable," and "vulnerable" and for whom a teacher is a model to emulate and respect. Writing about the homosexual teacher, Willard Waller said sixty years ago, "The real risk is that he may, by presenting himself as a love object to certain members of his own sex at a time when their sex attitudes have not been deeply canalized develop in them attitudes similar to his own. For nothing seems more certain than that homosexuality is contagious."[52] Waller's views are still current. Moreover, a lesbian teacher cannot be tolerated, not just because her existence would negate the myth that female sexuality does not exist irrespective of men, not only because she represents an alternative to heterosexuality that is universally condemned yet manages to survive, but, more importantly, because, in her position of teacher, an employee of the state, her sexuality must be reflective of official ideology. For her to teach as a lesbian would be for the state to condone automatically her sexual choice.

Apple and Weis see schools as agencies of legitimation in that they are part of a complex structure through which some social groups are given legitimacy and through which cultural and social ideologies are built, recreated, and maintained. Schools tend to describe their own internal structure as meritocratic, hierarchical, but often democratic, and always moving toward social and economic justice; thus they foster the belief that they are equally responsive to sex, race, and class. However, Apple and Weis observe that since the schools themselves are also part of the political institutions of the society, part of the state, as such they must legitimate themselves as well. They must "generate consent from the governed."[53] Obviously, schools can neither afford to legitimate gay men and lesbians as a group (since that would go against the state and hegemonic ideology), nor can they gain legitimacy in the eyes of the public if they condone homosexuality by hiring visibly gay men and lesbians.

Frequently, women teachers suspected of being lesbian will be tolerated as long as they are not recognizable as lesbians or as long as it is not a matter of public knowledge. This means that they cannot afford to display their relationship to a woman—a privilege accorded most heterosexual liaisons—nor can they be seen to participate in a gay-related activity. What this means in the everyday life of a lesbian teacher is that she may not take her lover to staff functions, may not wear a ring or labrys or give any indication of her sexuality. She cannot talk openly about her weekend activities—in short, her life must remain invisible. This is in contrast to her heterosexual sister, who notes her attachment to a man by wearing a wedding (or engagement) band, who is encouraged to talk endlessly about her relationship, and whose pregnancy is celebrated as proof of his virility and her fertility.

The difference between what is tolerated as a "public" display of sexuality is particularly important since it forms the basis of how much of her sexual identity a lesbian teacher can afford to make visible before she is disciplined for "flaunting" or "publicly displaying" her sexual preference. In the United States, according to the editors of the *Harvard Law Review,* teachers may be dismissed on the basis of "immorality," the definition of which rests with either local policy or state statutes, depending on the area. Moreover, "public display," which comes under the rubric of "immorality," is often ambiguously defined and does not provide enough guidance to lesbian and gay teachers regarding what is considered permissible and what is perceived as "immoral." "A public display of homosexual conduct might be construed as same-sex cohabitation, kissing, or touching, while identical heterosexual conduct would be condoned."[54] In addition, other courts in the United States have "grappled with the issue of the relationship between sexual orientation and teaching ability by stressing a teacher's function as a role model."[55] For example in *Gaylord vs. Tacoma School District,* the Washington supreme court upheld the dismissal of a teacher for immorality based on his reputation as a "publicly known homosexual." "Even though there was no evidence that Gaylord had actually committed any sexual acts, the court argued that 'sexual gratification with a member of one's own sex is implicit in the term *homosexual,*' "[56] which the courts had previously deemed "inappropriate" as a role model for students.

As a consequence of hiding her sexuality, a lesbian teacher's life, in general, unfolds in two separate spheres. On the one hand, as a teacher, she operates in the public sphere of work. Her experiences in the classroom are part of a complex, established, and prescribed social organization. Her role of teacher locates her in a bureaucratic hierarchy. It confers upon her a certain authority and credibility that she uses in the everyday classroom. Although the term *teacher* is purported to be neutral, her gender is, like her race, definitely a crucial aspect of her position. Her lesbian identity can only surface in the private sphere. On the one hand, an identity, like a label, is not a mere description of a person. It is a term that implies a set of perconceived characteristics that are seen as "identifying," that is, as making recognizable, a certain "type" of person. However, the individual herself (or himself) is the only one who can identify with a group or groups, and through this identification creates a sense of belonging to a group of groups. On the other hand, a label attributes characteristics (frequently limiting and stereotypical) to certain individual(s) or groups by other (often dominant) individual(s) or groups, for the purpose of, at best, distinguishing themselves from the former, and at worst, of discrediting the labeled group. Thus, when a woman assumes the identity of lesbian, she is "identifying" herself as such, she is seeing herself as belonging to a group or community she recognizes as sharing a similar identity with herself. When she is labeled "lesbian," regardless of whether she identifies herself as one or not, certain (often negative) characteristics are ascribed to her. Identities are assumed by an individual; labels are imputed from the outside. Identities give strength, a sense of belonging; labels are often vehicles of discrimination against an individual or group. Identity has to do with self-definition and is not an imposition of someone else's characterization of that identity, even if he or she is of the same identity. But the moment a woman is labeled "lesbian," certain characteristics are immediately attributed to her, often superseding all other previous knowledge about her.

Because the term *lesbian* as a relevant descriptor is a feature of a conceptual substructure available to school administrators and parents, and because that same label fundamentally reveals a negatively perceived social image that places lesbians outside the acceptable, norm-defined category of teacher, a lesbian teacher has to rely on effectively concealing her sexual preference. Her invisibility is historically embedded in institutional relations that maintain this silence through such means as threat of loss of position, lack of contractual protection (except for a handful of provinces and states that protect lesbians and gays in the areas of employment, housing, and services), and assumptions that sexuality invariably and automatically refers to heterosexuality. In addition, in the performance of her job in the everyday process of the classroom, a teacher assumes a role of legitimized authority. Although, in principle, a teacher's function is to facilitate the curriculum, not question it, add to it, or modify it, in reality, as Gitlin observes, she (or he) can influence the values, attitudes, and perspectives of her students. Gitlin describes this influence as extending "from helping students function in society as it presently exists (reproductive influence) to helping them to question and transform societal relations (transformative influence)."[57] Obviously, this assumed influence poses a certain threat to a lesbian teacher because, if her sexuality were to be made public, she would certainly be perceived as abusing her position, working under false pretenses, or, possibly even being subversive, given the tacit prescription of her job as direct and official transmitter of state ideology.

Chessum suggests that a teacher's "personal and professional integrity, and her motivation to continue in her teaching role, are dependent on her concept of herself as an effective actor, within certain institutional limits."[58] For a lesbian teacher's sexuality to be known, acknowledged, or merely perceived as eccentric would undermine her authority in the classroom. Teachers, lesbian or otherwise, are strongly influenced in their thinking about their work and about themselves by ideological currents that are both dominant and widespread.[59] This is important to remember for at least two reasons. First, to be viewed as deviant by her students (whether she herself believes it or not) would threaten her credibility in the classroom. She would cease to represent the acceptable, dominant ideology. Also, as Connell, Ashenden, Kessler, and Dowsett point out, "to the extent that the teachers' authority is something which they construct in isolation and out of their own resources, it is a part and extension of themselves. To the extent that students resist, challenge or subvert their authority, so do they threaten them personally."[60] Second, often lesbian teachers themselves internalize that ideology that singles them out as deviant, and so they hide their sexuality for fear of shame and stigma as well as to protect their careers. Those women who identify as lesbian and yet continue to conceal their identity are, for the most part, obliged to live with the contradictions of their situation.

Whether a lesbian teacher would, in effect, be totally discredited or even lose her job if she came out at work is not the central issue. What is important is that all the teachers I interviewed preferred to remain "in the closet" and chose a wide range of ways to underplay, or in some instances to hide completely, their sexuality.

Lesbians have been traditionally (and still are) socially constructed as deviant, and as such are perceived (often by themselves as well) to have a stigmatized identity. Goffman uses the term *stigma* to "refer to an attribute that is deeply discrediting,"[61] adding that "normals" (those not stigmatized) tend to see a person with a stigma as not quite human. They tend to ascribe negative attributes to the stigmatized individual and furthermore "perceive his defensive response to his situation as a direct expression of his defect."[62] Goffman believes that because of the great rewards in being considered what he calls "normal," "almost all persons who are in a position to pass will do so on some occasion by intent."[63] In the case of lesbian teachers, many do attempt to pass as heterosexual, hiding their sexuality in order to cope in work or other situations that are potentially dangerous, hostile, or even just embarrassing.

Central to Goffman's argument about how a stigmatized individual is able to pass is the notion of what he calls "stigma management," which, in his words, "is an offshoot of something basic in society, and stereotyping or 'profiling' of our normative expectations regarding conduct and character."[64] In other words, stigma management *depends* on the presence of stereotypes and of the common-sense knowledge that exists in a society. To pass, it is necessary to "know" on some level the "normative expectations," and "profile," and the conduct and character presumed and/or anticipated of the stigmatized person, and to *avoid* these assiduously or as much as possible in the situations that require passing, or conversely, to emphasize them where recognition is beneficial.

When applied to the problematic at hand (lesbian teachers), Goffman's description is useful because he attempts to address the means by which people who deviate from the norm feel compelled to lead a double life. He is able to show the circumstances that allow them to pass and those where they may choose to come out. However, his analysis is incomplete because it lacks a historical specificity and a political context. Therefore, whereas Goffman is able to explicate brilliantly the situations that lead to passing, as well as how passing is achieved, using Gramsci's concept of hegemony makes visible the historical and ideological conditions that operate, first, to create the stigma, and second, to make passing possible.

Goffman's stereotyping or profiling of normative expectations regarding the conduct and character of stigmatized individuals (in this case, lesbians) comes from a commonsense knowledge available as "social information." Gramsci, also uses the notion of commonsense knowledge, which for him is an "aggregate of disparate conceptions" that are "ambiguous, contradictory and multiform."[65] However, Gramsci believes that common sense arises out of a social wisdom that is propagated to benefit a hegemonic group: "Ideas and opinions are not spontaneously 'born' in each individual brain: they have had a center of formation, of irradiation, of dissemination, of persuasion—a group of men, or a single individual even, which has developed them and presented them in the political form of current reality."[66] In other words, in the case of the stigma surrounding lesbians, it endures because a lesbian lifestyle potentially contradicts the hegemonic ideology of patriarchy. As mentioned earlier, patriarchal social organization relies on male access to women's productive and reproductive labor.

Although Gramsci intended his concept of hegemony to address class analysis, it proves a useful tool in understanding the issues and struggles that define normative sexuality at the expense of other sexual expressions. Hegemony, it must be remembered, is the process whereby subordinated groups incorporate the hegemonic ideologies of the ruling class, not because they are necessarily coerced into doing so, but because the ruling class is able to shape and win their consent. This consent of the subordinated group, in turn, gives the state legitimacy as well as a semblance of coherence and spontaneity in its ideology.[67] Similarly, when addressing the question of women's sexuality, hegemony can be used to analyze how women often adhere to dominant patriarchal ideologies for reasons that range from the sanctioned advantages of heterosexual privileges to the satisfaction of such "needs" as sex, children, love, and companionship, not to mention (given the patriarchal social structure) financial support. This is not to imply that without patriarchal hegemony all women would be lesbian. What it intends to suggest is that patriarchal hegemony limits the choice of sexual expression (for both men and women) to heterosexuality and that it benefits from the restrictions and controls.

However, despite Gramsci's very seductive and logical conceptualizations of how ideology operates, it does not explain how it works differentially on various people. How do some escape (to a certain extent) its hold? How is it that others reflect current ideologies while a few question, disregard, or are subversive to these? How do different messages work on people differently? How do we each choose to adopt, assimilate to, rebel against, or abuse the system? When we speak of ideologies, we are, in effect, placing the responsibility of how we think on a social level. However, how do individual psychologies intersect with social ideologies? Some of these questions may be answered through analyses of ideologies or through our attempts to understand the structures (macro and micro) within which individuals are transformed into social beings. We may also be able to comprehend the various ways social contexts mold individual perceptions. Finally, we may be able to discern various influences on social and individual behaviors and responses, but what ultimately seems to remain elusive is the question of how each one of us, incorporating different circumstances, living out lives within differences of gender, class, race, ability, and sexuality, can at the same time share and reject various aspects of the culture and society in which we live. How does each one of us incorporate and live out the numerous contradictions of our lives?

Lesbians thwart the established hegemonic social order. From a patriarchal perspective, they have to be repressed and suppressed. Women have to be dissuaded from expressing their sexuality in other than heterosexual terms. Thus heterosexual hegemony operates, not only by granting privileges to those who adhere to its ideology, but by negatively characterizing, that is, stigmatizing, behavior that is contrary to its prescriptions. Stigma is a repressive measure that ranges from social reproval to legal sanctions, from commonsense knowledge about the "abnormality or perversity" of certain acts and identities, to scientific, medical, sociological, and psychological reports that purport to document the specific aberration.[68]

Whereas Goffman's description of how stigma operates in a society is, to some extent, static, Gramsci's notion of hegemony as a struggle to establish and reestablish the dominance of a group and its ideology allows a more dynamic analysis of, in this case,

stigmatized forms of sexuality. In this way, the historical specificity
of the stigma against lesbianism can be grasped more readily, yet
not totally. Gramsci suggests that tension occurs between different
and rival ideologies that exist at the same moment in history and
therefore recognizes that there is a perpetual process of transformation. Boggs elaborates: "All social groups possess at least an embry-
onic world-view, with its distorted and incoherent image of reality,
their 'common sense' is never fixed and stable but is constantly
changing through the influence of new philosophical and scientific
discoveries."[69] However, Boggs believes that political content is
achieved only with the introduction of a counter-hegemonic force.
This process can be used to understand the transvaluation of lesbianism that occurred with the advent of the women's and gay liberation movements. The stigma was lifted slightly and the sexual
preference was transformed into a political act.

It would take a different book to work out the details of the
ramifications involved in linking Goffman's concept of stigma with
an adaptation of Gramsci's notions of hegemony to the issues of
sexuality.[70] My attempts are limited to an interpretation that is
presented only insofar as it may clarify the limitations of perceiving
lesbianism simply as a stigma based on a sexual deviation. It certainly contains this element, but when applied to the reality of
women's lives, the intricate dimensions become visible. We begin to
see that the stigma has a material base, that it is part of an ideology, that there is a distinct connection between the social construction of a stigmatized lesbian identity and the dominant social
organization of patriarchy and capitalism, both of which give the
stigma shape and historical context. Therefore, on the one hand, we
can see how a woman may try to pass because her job depends on
her appearing as heterosexual. On the other hand, this same
woman may feel pride in her choice given the current feminist and/
or gay literature that supports her rejection of heterosexuality and
that gives it political content. Similarly, we can appreciate how the
counter-hegemonic political consciousness that arose with the women's and gay liberation movements "transformed homosexuality
from a stigma that one kept carefully hidden into an identity that
signified membership in a community organizing for freedom."[71]
Even at the height of political persecution during the McCarthy era
in the United States, lesbians survived, their lives a testament to
the contradictions of living daily subversions while presenting
"appropriate" fronts.

In the teaching profession, although many recognize the em-
powerment achieved over the last fifteen years, and despite human

rights gains in Ontario that protect their jobs, most lesbian teachers still feel they cannot afford to disclose their sexuality. It is important to emphasize that most of the women I interviewed, especially those who have a feminist or lesbian political consciousness, did not consider themselves "stigmatized" or "deviant." They claimed that their sexuality was "not anybody's business," but, significantly, none was out intentionally, and a few made a conscious effort to conceal their sexual preference. Edwin Schur sees this as "a key indicator of persisting stigma—that most lesbians still do not openly disclose their sexual preference to all persons, but instead 'pass' as heterosexual in some situations."[72] Of course, his point is well taken. However, if we look at the dilemma using Schutz's notion of first-and second-order constructs, we may be able to grasp what is at work in this case.

Schutz refers to the commonsense experience of the intersubjective world in daily life as a first-order construct. The second-order constructs, on the other hand, are those that are produced by the social sciences to explain social reality, but that, at the same time, include a reference to the first-order constructs. For instance, the concept of stigma as used by the social scientists must "refer to the subjective meaning of the actions of human beings from which the reality originates."[73] Schutz believes that the second-order constructs "are objective ideal typical constructs and, as such, of a different kind from those developed on the first level of common-sense thinking which they have to supersede."[74] Schutz recognizes, of course, that second-order constructs are abstractions, that the "objectivity" of the social scientist is a construction of the scientific method, and that the work of a social scientist is bound by the historical moment, by the tradition of the scientific method, and so forth (current work would also add gender, race, sexuality, and class as factors).

The advent of the women's and gay liberation movements generated scholarly and popular writing that created a shift in perspective and that produced a fundamental support system in the process of reevaluating the issues dealing with women's and gay/lesbian oppression. Critical analyses of social scientific treatises that labeled homosexuality as deviant influenced how some scholars thought and wrote about the topic. The second-order constructs began to alter, inducing practical consequences such as the vote of confidence from the American Psychiatric Association in 1973 (which removed homosexuality from its list of mental disorders). First-order constructs were modified as well, mostly for those sympathetic to or politicized by the women's and/or gay movements.

Therefore, the farther (physically and/or politically) an individual or group is from the influence of either or both movements, the less affected he or she is by their impact, and the more dominated by the capitalist and patriarchal hegemonic viewpoint.

The consequence of this situation on the reality of a lesbian's life is that, although the stigma surrounding her sexuality has been somewhat dissipated, it has not done so at the same rate in all levels of society. Therefore, although official discrimination on the basis of sexual orientation may be abolished or discouraged, not everyone in the society will accept such a move to the same degree.[75] This phenomenon produces situations in which, in the case of lesbian teachers, a particular school board may have adopted a policy of nondiscrimination against lesbians and gay men but parents may continue to insist that they do not want "homosexuals" teaching their children. Or, conversely, parents and individuals in a community may be open-minded in their acceptance of a teacher's lesbianism but a school board may remain adamant in its refusal to hire a gay or lesbian teacher. The contradictions of such a situation are well illustrated in the case of *Marjory Rowland vs. Mad River Local School District:*

> Marjory Rowland, who was fired by the Mad River Local School District after telling a school secretary that she was a lesbian, intends to ask the U.S. Court of Appeal here to reconsider her case . . . [because] two of the three judges found that freedom of speech did not extend to Rowland's right to reveal her sexual identity in a private conversation.[76]

The editors of the *Harvard Law Review* mention this case and attempt to explicate the intricacies of teachers' constitutional rights versus "the unique concerns of public schools," which they claim have left lesbian and gay teachers largely unsuccessful in their attempts to challenge dismissals on the ground of free speech. This is because the Supreme Court has vested considerable discretion in local school boards to establish school curricula; therefore, if lesbian or gay teachers introduce "inappropriate" conversation in the classroom, they are infringing on the rights of local boards to decide what should be taught. Therefore, although courts have been hesitant to sanction lesbian and gay teachers for discussing their sexual orientation *outside* the classroom as private citizens, they have had "more difficulty determining which standard is applicable to faculty speech made in the workplace but outside the ambit of curricular activity. [The courts] have tended to defer to local board decisions in these cases, even though such extracurricular speech has a limited impact on the efficiency of the workplace."[77]

This example also illustrates a dilemma in which lesbians who teach often find themselves. On the one hand, they may have shed the stigma surrounding their sexuality and therefore are able to discuss their personal lives with some choice individuals and groups, but on the other hand, they may need to continue to conceal their sexual preference in some circumstances, for instance, at work.

Lesbian teachers, whatever their political commitments, are more likely to attempt to produce themselves as heterosexual or as asexual in order to avoid being questioned. Garfinkel's observations about Agnes, a transsexual, clarifies this fact: "She learned . . . how, in doing normal sexuality 'without having to think about it' [she was] able to avoid displays that would furnish sanctionable grounds for doubt that a member [of her chosen sex] was sexually what he appeared."[78] Some lesbian teachers choose to use those "background relevances" that are ascribed to each gender, to emphasize those "feminine" characteristics that are easily overlooked because they are so routinized. For instance, some women I interviewed wore makeup and lacy clothes, talked about the men in their lives (without indicating their relationship to them), and so on. These women actively produced themselves as heterosexual. Others preferred to project the image of a more practical, down-to-earth mode of dress and lifestyle, thus, in some way gently stating that they were removed from conventional existence but only harmlessly so. Both attempted to deflect suspicion, both tried to fit within some acceptable bounds, and both protected themselves by not standing out.

Reticence against "coming out" in the teaching profession is well founded. There is a particular resistance by administrators to hire gay and lesbian teachers because of a fear of "contagion." The general fear is that if young people come into contact with a gay or lesbian teacher, the young person will be molested, and/or converted, or, even worse, the youth may take the teacher's life as an example of a legitimate sexual option.

In Ontario, since Bill 7 was passed in 1986 amending the Equality Rights Statute Law and adding sexual orientation to its list of inclusions in the Human Rights Code, lesbians and gays have some protections in the areas of housing, employment, and services. However, some teachers' unions, for instance, the Ontario Secondary School Teachers' Federation, had already supported lesbian and gay rights. Indeed, the Toronto Teachers' Federation had adopted a policy on December 14, 1979, that specifically included the protection of rights of lesbians and gay teachers.[79]

All teachers of Ontario are bound by the Teaching Professional Act (1944), which makes it mandatory to belong to one of the five affiliated federations. I shall deal primarily with the OSSTF because it was the one with which I was most familiar, both because it was a focus of my research and because I belonged as an active member.

In principle, no individual's contract can be terminated on the basis of his or her sexual preference because homosexuality is legal in Canada and because employment is protected by the Human Rights Code of Ontario—unless that teacher works for a Catholic or private school board, both of which may adopt regulations specific to their religious or private needs. A teacher may not be fired except "if a matter arises that in the opinion of the Minister adversely affects the welfare of the school in which the teacher is employed."[80] The Teaching Professional Act requires each member "to achieve and maintain the highest degree of professional competence and to uphold the honor, dignity, and ethical standards of the teaching profession."[81] Gay or lesbian teachers who are convicted on criminal charges are likely to have their contracts terminated, but no more so than heterosexual teachers who may break the law. Teachers, more than those in any other profession, are held most accountable for their professional and private conduct. S. G. B. Robinson reports in a history of the first fifty years of OSSTF that very few cases of "moral turpitude" involving students ever came before the courts. "However," he continues, "perhaps in no other profession or calling does the public expect that sex offenses involving minors will be properly punished. It has the right to expect that the teacher, placed in a position of trust, shall always merit it."[82] Indeed, it is particularly interesting to point out that the vast majority of sexual offenses against minors are committed by heterosexual males against girl children.[83]

In a private telephone conversation with an official of OSSTF, he informed me that boards of education in Ontario often allege that the ability of a homosexual member to teach is impaired by her or his homosexuality. "This is discrimination," he said, "and it would not stand in a court of law." No contracts in Ontario, before Bill 7, had a protection clause other than statements that included sexual orientation in their equal opportunity policies. The Toronto Board of Education was a case in point,[85] although their policy was rescinded in 1986.

Also in Toronto, a draft report produced by several gay and lesbian groups was presented to the Toronto Board of Education's school program committee recommending that the Ontario Ministry of Education should develop manuals to help teachers raise sex-related issues, one of which would be homosexuality. The report was being considered by teachers, parents, and community groups.[86] In the same vein, in 1985, City TV (channel 57, cable 7) aired an hour-long program ("Growing Up Gay") about teenagers coming to terms with homosexuality. It stated that the Toronto Board of Education had no policy dealing with gay students and that since the board had not yet found a way to talk about the issue without condoning it and presenting it as acceptable, they preferred to remain silent. The program acknowledged a fundamental problem in dealing with homosexuality in school.[87] Even now, several years later, with AIDS a major concern for students (and adults), the subject of homosexuality remains a "sensitive" topic. In the process of interviewing lesbian students for a different project this past year, I found that one of their recurring complaints was how little information they could find regarding homosexuality in the schools they attended. For instance, the Toronto Board of Education, one of the largest and most progressive in the province, has a specific policy forbidding lesbian or gay teachers from "proselytizing" about homosexuality. Teacher and/or counselors who attempt to reassure gay teenagers about their homosexuality or direct them to organizations that could offer them support would be frowned upon because it is against board policy to speak positively about the topic. Students may choose to present lesbian- or gay-related subjects in class presentations, but the teacher may not suggest that homosexuality is a viable alternative to heterosexuality. One student in that study[88] had organized an assembly presentation on the topic of AIDS. The principal would not grant permission for the appearance of this speaker in the school until he was reassured that the subject of homosexuality would not be brought up.

In late 1981, the Halton Board of Education considered the question of whether teachers who are homosexual should be allowed to teach. They adopted guidelines for personnel decisions based upon the California supreme court (*Morrison vs. State Board of Education*) findings, which list eight factors to take into account before firing a teacher. Among these are the likelihood that the conduct may have adversely affected students or fellow teachers, the anticipated degree of such adversity, and the likelihood of recurrence.[89] What this means, in effect, is that even if homosexual teachers are allowed to teach, their "conduct" will be implicitly and explicitly perceived as deviant, and they will be assessed on a different scale than their heterosexual colleagues. Thus they will be tolerated, especially if they are not active homosexually.

The contradictions arising from a federation that will stand by and defend its gay and lesbian teachers, school boards that may discriminate against them, parents who may or may not support those teachers, and administrators who may abide by the Ontario Human Rights Code but who may make a particular gay or lesbian teacher's work situation uncomfortable enough for her or him to resign, all contribute to the dilemma facing teachers who may choose to be "out" but who cannot trust that their occupational context will support them.

Moreover, although the issue of homosexuality in the schools has been raised in recent years in Ontario, the fear surrounding it does not seem to have decreased visibly. In this era of resurging conservatism combined with an almost obsessive concern with sexuality, it is not particularly safe for a lesbian or a gay teacher to come out if she or he intends to remain in teaching. Even though homosexuality is included in the Human Rights Code, it would be very hard indeed to survive in a classroom given the extremely negative stereotypes, the prejudices, and the harassment that are likely to be part of a visibly "out" lesbian or gay teacher. However, there are women and men who, on purpose or inadvertently, have made public their sexual preference without adverse reactions. Their stories may be few, but they constitute examples of hope and potential for change.

The theories of ideology presented above and the feminist critiques of these formulations offer various explanations to some of the questions posed. Even though no single conceptualization can deal comprehensively with each of the questions I have posed or each of the situations presented, feminist perspectives are providing us with some of the most cogent tools of analysis. The following chapter is one such feminist methodology.

4

# *Methodology*

I am fourteen years old and sitting in an Irish Catholic highschool absorbing my daily dose of catechism. The nun, a teacher I greatly admire, is elaborating on the concept of soul according to church edicts: when it enters the body, how to save it, who (or what) has one and how to keep it pure. She explains: "The soul enters the body at the moment of conception, that is why abortion is considered murder by the Church." I hear those words as if in a dream. I feel a sudden rush of fear and shame because I know that my mother had had an abortion. I had never connected what my mother did with any criminal (morally sinful?) activity.

Split # 1: Cairo, Egypt: 1958.

I am a teenager. The first sexual stirrings are directed toward a woman, a teacher. This comes as the culmination of years of youthful crushes without any available understanding of the feelings involved or the means conducive to expressing them. It does not take me long to realize that my affectional interests are not considered "normal." I begin to read incessantly in an attempt to comprehend the nature of my attachments. Surreptitiously, I buy and devour books by Freud, Havelock Ellis, Krafft-Ebing, D. J. West, Frank S. Caprio, Benjamin Morse. My parents are delighted at my sudden, all-involved interest in "psychology." The books I read tell me that sexual feelings directed toward the same sex constitute a condition called "homosexuality." Most of them describe female homosexuals alternatively as mannish, ugly, able to whistle, love horses, and neurotic. It is true I can whistle, but none of the other "symptoms" apply. I am relieved. I am not a female homosexual. I am easily able to disassociate my feelings/actions from a feared, abhorred, utterly despised label.

Split #2: Cairo, Egypt.

I know without any doubt that I am a lesbian. Since it is prior to my feminist awakening and given my career in teaching, I see no need to be out to the world. I need a medical checkup and seek a female doctor. She asks: "Are you sexually active?" "Yes," I reply naively. "What kind of birth control do you use?" "I don't," I answer, anticipating the next question with rising apprehension. "Then how do you avoid pregnancy?" I am cornered and stammer, "I'm a lesbian." I feel confused and ashamed as I see her visibly cringe at my words. "Hmm," she says, "that explains it. But before I accept you as a new patient I want to say that I am happily married and have kids." Consternation. Fury. Rage.

Split # 3: Canada, mid 1970s.

It is not my intention to present those three incidents as isolated occurrences of oppression, sexism, or homophobia. I did not call them that then, and I shall not label them now. What they represent for me are illustrations of instances in my life when what I held to be knowledge of the world around me did not fit the experiences of the moment. The awareness of that disparity is what Dorothy Smith calls the "line of fault." She describes it as a "point of rupture in my/our experience as woman/women within the social forms of consciousness—the culture or ideology of our society—in relation to the world known otherwise, the world *directly* felt, sensed, responded to, prior to its social expression."[1]

The recent feminist and gay movements have produced a vast literature that articulates how and speculates why such "splits," denials, and silences surround a lesbian or woman's reality and the social world in which she functions.[2] When Dorothy Smith argues for a radical critique of sociology (as an example of any traditional man-made science), she not only explicates how women have been excluded from men's culture throughout centuries, but she also proceeds to propose a methodology that could make visible the ways by which our lives have been and are denied. I shall attempt to summarize her main arguments.

Smith begins by asserting that the points of rupture that women encounter are located in relations of power between women and men in which men dominate over women. These relations she recognizes as patriarchal. Given the hierarchical differences based on gender, it becomes evident that men will attend to and treat as significant only what other men (their equals, so to speak) say and/ or have said. "What men were doing has been relevant to men, was written by men about men for men. Men listened and listen to what one another say. A tradition is formed, traditions form, in a discourse with the past within the present."[3] In their subordinate position, women are located outside sociological discourses. Their situations are trivialized, their reality is either discredited or discounted, and their whole being is objectified. Smith's articulation of the power differential between men and women, as well as her suggestions that men's superior position hierarchically permits them to trivialize and discount women's experience, agrees with Gramsci's notion of hegemony (see Chapter 3). He maintains that hegemony operates through the cultural, political, and economic aspects of the state and that domination of one group by another is accomplished mostly through influence and consent (although he does not discount that repression and force are used as well). Smith's work on the ideological practice of sociology, of its male-based perspective, is a particular description of patriarchal hegemony. Sociology, argues Smith, is an organization of practices that structure the sociologist's relation to the group(s) under inquiry. Whereas the sociologist enters the discourse as subject, the individuals under study are constituted as objects. However, sociological practices proceed from within a conceptual framework and an epistemological assumption that presuppose a male subject, although this is fundamentally not visible until one posits (as Smith did) a sociology from the standpoint of women. The impersonal or genderless terms locating the subject of sociological assertions become manifestly male when we realize that it never quite makes sense to do a sociology of men or to suggest that we begin from the standpoint of men. Traditional sociology is already practiced from that male perspective, even by women scholars. As such, sociological discourse reflect hegemonic (patriarchal) ideology, while its methods, its conceptual base, its whole framework articulates the concerns of men and for men; it advances and supports patriarchy. The disjuncture occurs for women when they attempt to comprehend or make sense of their lives through explanations or theories formulated and developed by men. As each woman struggles to find her reality in a man's world, she consequently, in some way, dissociates herself from her sisters. Sheila Rowbotham describes the dilemma: "We were split in two, straddling silence, not sure where we would begin to find ourselves or one another. From this division, our material dislocation, came the experience of one part of ourselves as strange, foreign and cut off from the other which we encountered as tongue-tied paralysis about our own identity."[4] The experience is one of knowing ourselves as women through eyes that are not ours and through a language that does not include us. For instance, we learned to read the so-called generic "he" to include us until we found out one day that "he" is not really intended for us at all but is representative of a patriarchal dominant reality that supersedes ours. For instance, a decade ago I was a member of a negotiating team for our OSSTF district. The first suggestion agreed upon by both the board and the teachers (I was outvoted) was that we should get rid of the "encumbrance of 'he/she' " in favor of the generic "he." Although "he" was to be read to include both sexes, when it came to the clauses that dealt with pregnancy and maternity leaves, the pronouns were suddenly switched to conform to their related gender. I remarked that if there was any truth in their argument that "he" represented both sexes for the sake of clarity, then the rule should cover this particular section of the contract. The men took exception. Clearly the male membership would object to being identified with pregnancy. Without any doubt, "he" in this case referred to men. Since male secondary teachers outnumber and outvote women, since their interests supersede those of women, since most men believe in the centrality of male subjectivity, it was very natural for our negotiating team to believe in such a concept as the generic "he."

Women are only peripherally included in male discourses, and by the same token, it is only men's reality that is creditable and that is recorded. A woman either has to speak as a woman, in which case she is taken as describing her own particular reality, or she speaks by disassociating herself from her sex because "her subjectivity does not draw upon the implicit authority of the generalizing impersonal mode. [A man's] does."[5]

Insights gained through the women's movement have permitted traditional notions to be reevaluated and new perceptions to be articulated. The movement has made observable, in Smith's words, "an apparatus of social controls in part ideological in the sense of being images and symbols, and in part an organization of specialized practices."[6] Women began to understand that there was a coherent and distinguishable structure, an organizing and ruling apparatus that was entirely in the hands of men—some men, since the society is organized by hierarchy and class, as well as by race and gender.

Smith analyzes the ideology that informs the male ruling apparatus. She clarifies by stating that she means by ideology "the ideas, images, and symbols in which our experience is given social form not as that neutral floating thing called culture but as what is actually produced by specialists and by people who are part of the apparatus by which the ruling class maintains its control over the society."[7] Drawing on Marx and Engels, Smith observes that the concepts produced by a ruling class not only dominate but also inexorably penetrate the consciousness of the society at large and thus control the expression of actual experiences in the everyday world. However, whereas Marx and Engels were primarily concerned with class, Smith adds gender, without which, she shows, the analysis is incomplete. The following illustrates this position: Each one of the "splits" I described at the beginning of the chapter is informed by the ideology of the ruling apparatus. The incongruity between religious dogma and my everyday life produced a confusing picture of my mother. My mother had not changed. My consciousness of her in the light of my new "knowledge" was different. Similarly, in the second instance, my behavior and sexual attractions continued to be directed toward women. The experts' depiction of a lesbian allowed me to dissociate my feelings from my learned values. I was not a lesbian. I just loved women. In the final situation, the doctor's familiarity with ideological "scientific" knowledge concerning "typical" lesbian conduct led her improbably to fear attack (?), contagion (?), seduction (?). In each case, ideological consciousness had superseded and silenced everyday life and commonsense knowing.

Sociology, Smith asserts, is undoubtedly part of this ideological structure:

> Its themes and relevances are organized by and articulate the perspectives of men . . . as persons playing determinate parts in the social relations of this form of society, occupying determinate class positions in it, and participating in networks of relations, which link their work to that of other professionals, in the health and educational institutions of society, and its more direct practices of ruling, whether in business, in government, or elsewhere. The perspectives and interests, the experience and anxieties, that are incorporated in sociology and integrated to the sociological discourse, arise out of a determinate range of social institutions forming the governing apparatus of the society—management, government, military organization, health institutions, psychiatry, education, and the social and psychological sciences, the media, and other specialized ideological institutions which form the Marxist understanding of the "superstructure."[8]

Smith maintains that to do sociology is to know how to do sociology. It is to participate in the production of ideology, to be active in the organizing, structuring, defining process that gives form and legitimacy to the domination of a certain class and a particular gender. Ideology has a historical as well as a material specificity. It relies on the social relations that "organize and enforce the silences of those who do not participate in this process, who are outside it."[9] And women, as well as the working class, are outside it. Even females in the field can only speak as sociologists—not as women, if they want their work to be taken seriously.

The tradition of sociology constitutes a practice of suppressing the personal, inducing an objectivity that can only be achieved when the sociologist removes himself or herself from the object of research. Thus, as Smith points out, the relations between the knower and the object of her knowledge is a socially organized practice, one that concretely organizes the cognitive domain by prescribing the exact methods, tools, and conceptual frameworks available to a researcher who intends to produce sociological work.[10]

The exclusion of women from the scientific discourses, including the sociological, means that women are consistently absent from the center, concealed in the activities of men, denied and silenced in their experience.[11] Consequently, even when women participate in sociological discourses, they are forced to enter it as practitioners familiar with its organizing principles, and they function within its framework. The sociology produced in this way remains part of the ideology of the ruling apparatus. Thus, Smith argues, "by insisting that women be entered into sociology as its subjects, we find that we cannot escape how its practices transform us into objects. As women we become objects to ourselves as subjects."[12]

Smith proposes a shift from a sociology *of* women, where we are constituted as a problem to be researched and studied (there is no equivalent "sociology of men") to a sociology *for* women, where our reality is made visible, where knowledge is grounded in our experience, and where the location of the knower becomes part of the knowing. As Smith observes, in "questioning the sociological relations from the standpoint of women we find we have called into question the organization of the discourse in general, its location in the world, and the social relations organizing the positions of its subjects which its objectifying practices conceal."[13]

Smith suggests that the difficulty we might encounter in making women the center from which we begin has its origins, not only in the historical position of women in society, but in the emergence of forms of corporate capitalism that emphasize an abstracted conceptual mode of organizing in which functions become "a) differentiated as a distinct system of functions—administration, management, or aspects of professional organization; b) primarily communicative and informational . . . , c) dependent increasingly on generalized systems of planning in the same mode."[14] Smith remarks that these practices are recognized as rational administrative systems and constitute ways of organizing and conceptualizing information in the abstract, detached from the local and the particular, and entrenched in written documentary knowledge. Therefore, since traditional sociological practices are integrated in the above mode, the consciousness of the thinker is expected to be detached from particularities and from his or her (the knower's) location in the world.

As she elaborates on her proposed methodological shift, Smith reassures us that beginning from the standpoint of women does not imply a common viewpoint among women, although it does acknowledge a common exclusion from the organization of social relations. She suggests that to begin from the standpoint of women implicitly necessitates rejecting the administrative/abstract frame as an organization of social consciousness. However, she reminds us that it is not quite so simple because, in Marx and Engels' words, "the ideas of the ruling class are in every epoch the ruling ideas, i.e. the class which is the ruling *material* force of society, is at the same time its ruling *intellectual* force."[15] Therefore, to discard the dominant mode of producing knowledge and/or to identify its social base with a subordinated group in society (labor, or, in this case, women) is to invalidate it as a science. However, Smith points out, Marx clearly demonstrated that "the social organization of the forms of consciousness characteristic of a ruling class cannot be examined from the standpoint of the ruling class because that organization is not visible from that perspective or in that mode of action."[16] Marx drew attention to the intellectual idealism that disattends its essential dependence on the thinker's subsistence, and hence, consciousness, and upon the material processes of labor that produce the world in which he lives, thinks, and functions. This idealism, therefore, implicitly denies the labor of a working class (and of women), which stands "in determinate relation to a ruling class, producing not merely its subsistence, but the basic organization which the social forms of consciousness of the ruling class takes for granted."[17]

A sociologist who does not consider her existence in a material world and who takes for granted as known the social processes by which phenomena are recognized is as guilty of idealism as Marx's philosopher who is blind to the labor that makes possible his being

and his subsistence. To begin from the standpoint of women entails
that the sociologist acknowledges her existence in her body, in her
sensory experiences and her material location in the world. Her
knowledge has to encompass both the world that she experiences
directly from herself, in her body as center, and the world that is
external to herself. It must be mentioned that Smith is not merely
suggesting a phenomenological perspective where the knower is admittedly present in the knowing. This approach, she points out, continues to take for granted the material and social organization of its
bifurcated consciousness, and as such cannot render these visible.
What she is proposing is that the knower's bifurcated consciousness, the knowledge of herself as a subjectivity located in her body
as well as in a specific material and historical moment, be extended
to include her experience in the ordinary everyday world superim-
posed by a knowledge of the social organization. This, then, should
constitute the beginning of the inquiry. Smith elaborates: "Rather
than explaining behavior, we begin from where people are in the
world, explaining the social relations of the society of which we are
part, explaining an organization which is not fully present in any
one individual's everyday experience."[18]

In other words, in the examples of the "split" I gave at the beginning of the chapter, it is not enough simply to be present in my
account, nor it is sufficient to specify my sociotemporal location.
Smith's methodology would require an analysis of the social relations, the conceptual frameworks, and the position of the individuals within the social organization—in short, all factors within and
without the specific situation that would make visible the ideology
of the ruling apparatus as it is expressed (in this case) in the religious, medical, and social scientific conceptualizations and/or discourses. In so doing, we give context and are able to understand how
such an exchange or exchanges are possible.

Smith maintains that defining the everyday world as problematic guides and focuses our inquiry. It enables us to recognize that
the everyday world is neither transparent nor obvious. She observes, "Fundamental to its organization for us in this form of society is that its inner determinations are not discernible within it."
Therefore, she continues, "the conditions of our actions and experiences are organized by relations and processes outside them and beyond our power of control."[19] Smith perceives that this could occur
because capitalism—specifically, corporate capitalism—produces a
social organization wherein individuals depend upon one another,
and yet the forms of their relations become externalized as a differentiated system of relations.

In sum, I chose to adopt the methodology proposed by Smith for several reasons. The first is that it permitted me, the knower, to begin from my own experience as well as from that of the women I interviewed. It also enabled me to constitute the inquiry "in terms of the problematic arising from how it is actually organized in a social process," which in turn allowed me to "see the 'micro' and 'macro' sociological levels in a determinant relation."[20] In other words, the experiences of the interviewees and of myself form the basis of the enquiry, but only as these are located within a wider social organization that to some extent informs and controls our actions.

A second reason was that Smith's methodology provided the opportunity to question the ideas, definitions, and conceptualizations that, in traditional sociology, are taken for granted. Her argument that knowledge of society and social relations presupposes conceptual procedures and that these, in turn, serve as a boundary to inquiry rather than as a beginning is well illustrated by my research. A number of the women I interviewed initially refused to talk with me. They assumed that I had begun by defining what I meant by "lesbian teachers." The definition in and of itself creates a boundary and acts as a blueprint for including or excluding women according to whether or not they fit a particular interpretation— not only mine, but theirs as well. In addition, circumscribing the meaning of "lesbian teacher" potentially prevents the researcher from passing beyond it. Consequently, some respondents felt that they did not fit exactly into this abstract category ("lesbian teacher"), and therefore they hesitated to agree to an interview for fear of "wasting" my time. One divorced woman living with her children explained:

I thought that my information wasn't going to be very valid because . . . like I felt like saying on the 'phone "now, I relate to men, so I really don't qualify." Then I rethought that and well, I'm not sure that that really means that there isn't information that I have that would not make sense in the context of your research. And then I thought also that really what you're looking at is full-time teachers, which I'm not. So I thought— and I still do—that my story is of more limited value than other people that you might be interviewing because I'm not a full-time teacher now, and I haven't been living a lesbian existence for years—in terms of my work and so on, but that I'd come and talk to you anyway and maybe there'd be some stuff that would be of some use.

Thirdly, Smith's critique of sociology as an ideological practice was conducive to my work in that it provided a basis for questioning the traditional taken-for-granted concepts. For instance, *heterosexuality* is one example of such sociological notions. Usually, it would be recognized not only as the only acceptable form of behavior, the standard within certain social bounds, but also as the basic premise against which other sexual activities are compared. It would be, in Smith's words, the "concept which is constituted as a traditional piece of sociological currency."[21] Smith's methodology demands that we question such a concept, that heterosexuality, like any other defined sexual "category," although normative, is ideological; it has a history and it is problematic. Traditional sociological practice would treat heterosexuality as the only reality, the constant, the norm. Against its presupposed normalcy all other forms of sexual activity are compared, often rejected, and frequently labeled deviant. In Frye's words, "Being heterosexual is just being. It is not *interpreted*. It is not understood as a consequence of anything."[22] On the one hand, the same sociological practices would have no trouble identifying "homosexuality" as a "problem" to be defined, researched, and categorized. As a "condition," it would suggest an aetiology, an explanation, a cure. But few would dream of attempting to find a cause for heterosexuality. On the other hand, Smith's methodology would have us make visible how and where heterosexuality would fit in the social organization. It would give us the contextual background that would explicate how heterosexuality is used by the ruling apparatus to expropriate women's productive and reproductive labor, how it is hegemonic, and it would afford us means of understanding how individuals accept and integrate the dominant ideology in their everyday life.

This brings me to the fourth reason why I chose this particular methodology. Smith perceives ideology as those ideas, images, and symbols that are produced by specialists and others of the ruling apparatus. These ideas, images, and symbols give our experience social form and at the same time provide the means of control over society by those in a position to impose them. Consequently, to study and research ideological concepts is only to apprehend what dominant and/or formal values are promulgated in society at a particular time and place. We may also learn their potential effect on behavior and their influence on what is considered acceptable. It does not reveal what the individuals in their everyday life think, feel, modify, or accept. For instance, a traditional treatment of female homosexuality shows how and why it is condemned; it may analyze the causes and the cures, and it may even identify certain behavior characteristics that accompany the label. Often interviews with lesbians are used to legitimize and support already formulated theories and definitions. Conversely, Smith's suggestion to "begin from the standpoint of women" makes visible how the women themselves interpret their own behavior. Do they become sexually involved with women yet feel this to be an isolated (each time!) incident? Are their simultaneous involvements with a man or men and women a means of avoiding the label *lesbian*? Do they remain celibate after giving up sex with men and yet adopt a lesbian identity for political reasons? Do they accept the prevailing ideology and force themselves to become wives and mothers? Do they recognize that they are lesbian yet prefer not using that term to describe themselves? And so on.[23]

Finally, innumerable writers since the recent women's movement have proposed beginning from women's experience to validate or reject certain notions about our lives; very few have understood this experience as the culmination of absorbed ideological values as well as reflective of the position of women in general in the social organization. In other words, the experience contains its past and its present, but it also includes and reflects social relations that are external to it, but that give it form.

In sum, Smith's methodology as outlined in her "Sociology for Women" compels the researcher, that is, myself, in this case, to begin from the standpoint of women. In addition, it requires me to have knowledge of myself as a researcher, but at the same time to extend this knowledge to include my own subjectivity, my experiences and location in the everyday world. And finally, it requires me to place myself as a researcher and myself as a subject in the everyday world within the larger social organization as I would be doing for the research I am undertaking. Looking more closely at this proposition, there seems to be an inherent contradiction in placing myself as a researcher and as a subject at the same time. My role as researcher traditionally would place me outside the research. "Taking the standpoint of women means recognizing that as inquirers we are thereby brought into determinate relations with those whose experience we intend to express."[24] It also acknowledges that "determinate relation," in itself, as organized by my inquiry, is "shaped by social relations subtending it and entering into the inquiry in unseen ways."[25] Therefore, in the process of placing myself as the researcher or inquirer, I am, in effect, locating myself in the position of interpreter of the experiences of the women I interview. Even when I place my own experiences among theirs for analysis, the meaning I give what has been said remains mine, as the researcher, to interpret. In a differentiated world, where class, race, gender, and sexuality produce different experiences, how can I as one researcher, even beginning from the standpoint of women *to gather* the research, analyze the responses of the women I interview, with their multiple locations and their numerous experiences, from my perspective alone and do them justice? How can I analyze their responses except from my own standpoint—a located standpoint, but mine subjectively nonetheless? Smith responds to this dilemma by observing that multiple perspectives and versions of the world of subjects create a problem for sociology, in her words, "only when our project is to establish a sociological version superseding theirs. It is a difficulty that arises largely from grounding sociology in 'meaning', 'interpretation', 'common understandings' and the like rather than in an ongoing coordering of actual activities accomplished in definite local histories."[26] Therefore, when it is my ongoing "coordering" of activities, when it is my ontology, then it becomes my business, as Dorothy Smith remarks, "to explore the ongoing socially ordered matrices differentiating experience and the extended social relations immanent in the everyday."[27] Therefore, beginning from the standpoint of women opens the investigation to include the perspectives and experiences of those who are interviewed. It also compels the researcher to locate these in the social organization that gives meaning to the experiences from which they arise. At the same time, since I present my location within this same social organization, my ontology (which, according to Smith, is "the mode in which the social world can be conceived as existing"[28]) can be considered as part of the research and as the means by which I order and explore social relations in an ongoing way.

## Interviewer's Location

I came to teaching because I needed a job to stay in Canada as a landed immigrant. The year was 1968, I was twenty-three, and my mother was encouraging me to go back to Egypt since I did not want to continue studying for my doctorate, the reason for which I had come to Canada. My background in Egypt was very privileged, my education was in English and French, and my family had always encouraged me to study and to be independent. By the time I came to Canada I had already established (in my mind and in experience) that I was a lesbian. One of the reasons why I refused to go back to Egypt was precisely because I wanted to pursue my life without the close scrutiny of family and relatives. Although I was out to some people, I "chose" not to live as a lesbian in Egypt.

The fellowship I won to study in Canada was my ticket to independence. I survived one year in a program that did not fit my needs, but when my mother got wind of my dissatisfaction, she came to bring me home. Seeing my attachment to my adopted country, she allowed that if I found a job before we were due to leave, I could stay. I had never worked for a living. I had never even held a summer job. I had never had to care for myself. With a B.A. and an M.A. in anthropology, I was hardly marketable, especially in the small northern Ontario town where I chose to live. However, luck was on my side the day I went to submit an open application to the local board of education. I was asked to wait for the superintendent, who was busy on the telephone. It was that very call that was to change my life. The superintendent was speaking to one of the French teachers, who was informing him that she was pregnant. It was the end of August, almost a week away from the beginning of school. Because of board policy, her pregnancy forced her to take the year away from teaching. And I was about to get her job. What was to be a casual appointment with the superintendent ended up being an interview for a one-year appointment teaching French as a second language. In 1968, elementary school teachers could still be hired on a letter of permission. Except for my degrees and the fact that I was fluent in French, I was hardly qualified. When I was assigned to a junior high school I went straight home to ask my friends what age group that entailed. I had never been inside a Canadian school. The superintendent had arranged for me to follow an experienced teacher for one week, hoping that some of her skill would rub off on me. It didn't. That academic year was one of the most traumatic of my life. I had two factors going for me: I was the only Egyptian for hundreds of miles, and I was young and innocent. People around me took care of me, and whatever I lacked in teaching experience, I made up for in that those around me chose to ignore my most blatant mistakes. My present political understanding leads me to conclude that the combination of my class background and my familiarity with Canada's two official languages allowed me to be tolerably assimilated, to be perceived as not threatening and sufficiently different to be "exotic." Finally, my strongest impression of that year is the purposefulness with which I forced myself *not* to stand out and my determination to acquire the skill to teach. The next year I went to teachers' college, and for the next ten years I taught various subjects at the secondary level.

I had had my first sexual experience with a woman when I was still in Egypt. Given my privileged background, I grew up with an intellectual understanding of what constituted homosexuality—the way it was conceptualized in the late 1950s and in French literature.[29] My first and subsequent sexual experiences with women were difficult in that they were hidden, almost completely invisible and unacknowledged. In Egypt, the women I met were all as a result of my first experience. She knew a number of other "lesbians."[30] In Canada, it was up to me to develop a sensitivity to pick up "cues" that would lead me to find "like-minded" women. I became extremely adept at figuring out who was potentially interested in women, a talent which, in the 1960s and 1970s, was extremely convenient.

Even before I became a teacher I lived my sexual preference in hiding. In the early years of adapting to being in Canada, my identity was wrapped up in the combinations and contradictions of being both Egyptian and Canadian. When I became a teacher, there was no doubt that I had to "pass" as heterosexual. Even when I lived with my partner for twelve years in that northern community, we lived as two single women sharing an apartment. Therefore, once again, I seemed to combine identities, caught between presenting to my neighbors and colleagues an accepted "heterosexual" front while I lived a hidden lesbian existence. In the 1980s, when I became a feminist and began toying with the idea of coming out, I had to consider my partner, who was herself a teacher.

Finally, my place in this project is as a scholar, a researcher who is included in the Canadian academic community, who produces articles and book(s) that become part of ongoing feminist and sociological discourses. My location permits me the privilege of coming out, a privilege not automatically granted those women I interviewed. My class background and my family's material resources combined to give me the opportunity to study full-time for my doctorate, and thus to change professions in my early forties.

### Interviews: The Procedure

Beginning from the standpoint of women meant actually interviewing lesbian teachers. The essence of my problematic centers on how lesbian teachers manage to retain their jobs in a system that clearly discriminates against homosexuals in general. The term *lesbian* in this society suggests a fundamentally negative social image that places anyone labeled as such outside the acceptable and normative definitions of teacher. Consequentially, lesbian teachers have to rely on concealing their sexuality, in part by becoming more aware of the distinction between the private and the public worlds and by existing in each differently.

Since discovery means a potential loss of job and/or harassment in more subtle ways, lesbian teachers prefer to remain "in the closet," hidden, invisible. For me, it meant the difficult task of attempting to find and to interview women who, for all intents, do not exist in our society. Since I wanted interviews rather than questionnaires, it meant that each one of these teachers I contacted, whether she agreed to talk to me or not, was actually "coming out" or revealing her sexual preference. By the same token, given the choice of my topic, each woman I asked to interview surmised my sexual identity. This presented problems during the earlier stage of my research because I was still employed by a board of education as a secondary teacher, a teacher who intended to resume her profession, and therefore I could not afford the label. Nevertheless, despite my initial difficulties, I was able to find women who agreed to be interviewed, especially when I left the area where I used to teach.

All contacts made were essentially through word of mouth. Few lesbian teachers in the early 1980s frequented lesbian bars, and when they did, they wanted to remain invisible—if that was possible. Furthermore, bars and radical politics were more likely to be found in large urban centers, and many of the women I interviewed came from small towns, two of which were more like villages. In order to protect the identity of a woman who could potentially refuse to speak with me, I arranged it so that the person who suggested a particular woman would ask her to call me. For each woman I finally interviewed, at least four or five absolutely refused. One or two were so fearful of my task that they avoided my presence from then on. One woman I met at a party got up and left the room when I revealed the topic of my research. Another would not sit at the same table with me at a women's dance. Most women were sympathetic, supportive, and encouraging, whether they agreed to talk or not. However, because I only interviewed women who agreed to speak to me, and by so doing came out to me and in my work, it should be noted that those who refused me interviews ostensibly lived a much more closeted, hidden life than those women who could talk about their experiences. I recorded only one entry in my journal of a woman vice-principal who was unexpectedly rude. Although initially she had agreed to be interviewed, she demanded to know who had "approved" such a work, and didn't I realize that I "would do a lot of harm by exposing good teachers" and "making it dangerous for us who want nothing more than to continue our career in teaching?" Her attitude was not surprising. Lillian Faderman explains:

> Despite the many successes of the gay liberation movement, which has made homosexuality much more acceptable in America, middle-class lesbians often feel that activists are a real threat to them because they draw public attention to the phenomenon of lesbianism and thus create suspicion about all unmarried women. The closeted lesbian's cover could be blown. Older lesbians especially, who perfected the techniques of hiding through most of their adult lives, still cannot conceive of suddenly coming out into the open, even in what appear to be freer times.[31]

Another journal entry mentions a telephone call from a very well known Canadian artist from whom I had requested the words of a particular song. In my letter to her I mentioned who I was and what I was doing. Her call was very warm, encouraging, and supportive. She helped me in more ways than I had requested or anticipated.

Given the very real and inherent fear of reprisal experienced by almost all the women to whom I spoke about my planned topic, I saw immediately the need to protect any teacher who granted me an interview. I was therefore forced to take stringent precautions to shield each teacher from any potential threat of discovery. To protect both my rights to use the interview material and theirs to privacy was not easy because I could not obtain a signed statement permitting me to use their experiences. Signatures, as well as any record of names and addresses, can be subpoenaed in court. Therefore, I had to devise a method that afforded me protection, gave my respondents a written guarantee for their safety, and yet did not leave any trace of their identity open to formal investigation—if any should arise. I solved the problem by incorporating a guarantee that I read immediately following each interview and transcribed as part of the interview. Since we each had a copy of the completed interview, both were protected, and yet only my name appeared on the transcribed guarantee. The fact that both our copies were identical signified her satisfaction with everything included in it. Each transcribed interview was sent to the respondent by mail. A week or so later I checked that she received it safely. Some women chose to write further comments or make some alterations, which I then incorporated in the interview. None rejected any part of it.[32] For further protection, I agreed not to identify the quotations I used so that no teacher would have a continuous presence in my work and thus be recognizable to my readers.

I started out with a very structured interview schedule. I asked specific questions that obviously limited the scope and variety of the answers. One woman with whom I did some preliminary work gave me the following advice:

> You have to organize your questions and wording without being blatant about it in what answers you want. Also, don't be impatient. People will be honest with you if you give them time. In my case, when you pressed too hard, you got my back up. For instance, like your feminism—you are into something so deeply and you know what you want, but it may not be what happened. However, if you want to get some real feeling from the responses, you have to lay off the person. It is a little harder for me to formulate my ideas about lesbianism, and your pressure only succeeds in producing an opposite response. I say, "Look lady, do you want an opinion or just a response?"

I discarded the schedule in favor of an open-ended interview. I would explain to each woman what the topic was about, and she proceeded to speak without interruption. During an interview I might ask for some clarification or might remind her of some aspect she left out. My explanation at the beginning was short. It was informal in that I talked with no notes except for the list of points I wanted to cover. For instance:

> My topic is "lesbian teachers." I am interested in how you manage/d to cope in the school system given your sexual preference; whether you may have encountered any questions/ behavior which, you felt, was in any way threatening or supportive toward you. I would like you to start by talking about your background (age, parents, growing up experiences, etc.), when and how you came out, how you identify yourself and if you could relate any encounters or circumstances within the context of the school which you feel is/was relevant to your being lesbian.

As I talked I gave many examples for clarification, I was frequently interrupted, I sometimes repeated points, and the exchange between the interviewee and myself continued until we both understood what was required for my research, what was possible for her, and what was appropriate to the topic at hand. However, despite the open-endedness of the questions, the interviews were still bound by the framework of my research area, by what I was interested in making visible in the lives of the women I was interviewing. Although they had some say in the ultimate accounts that they presented, the direction of the interview remained in my hands. Furthermore, because I spoke with most women only once, consideration must be given to the problems inherent in interviews that are limited to one meeting: they bracket one moment in the life of the interviewee and the interviewer; they catch a mood, an opinion of the day. This is not to say that individuals have no consistency, but only that different days may produce a slight shift in the answers or opinions or centers of interest. Since I did send each respondent a transcribed version of the interview, there was a good chance of catching those incidents, opinions, and events they may not have mentioned the first time. Several took that opportunity to write to me regarding topics they were too embarrassed to mention face to face. Some had forgotten anecdotes that they felt would be of interest to me. Most were satisfied with our combined effort.

Because I had an insider's view (so to speak) of a lesbian teacher's everyday life, there were many instances when I could sense either inconsistencies in the speaker's narrative or else outright contradictions. For instance, one woman assured me for two hours that she behaved exactly the same way at school as she did at home. She had taught in school for so long that she did not need to hide in any way. She had never encountered anybody who asked her specifically if she was a lesbian and she did not feel it necessary to enlighten anybody. At this point I asked her if she ever went away on weekends. She did. Where? To large urban centers. Why? To go to bars and visit other lesbian friends. She said that because she lived in a small town these visits provided her and her lover with the only opportunities when they could relax totally, except when they were in their own homes and by themselves. The inconsistency was glaring and I pointed it out to her. She laughed. I expect I would have taken her words at face value had I not lived in much similar circumstances. When an individual has spent a lifetime leading a double life, one of which is consciously and elaborately hidden from public scrutiny, she finds great difficulty in disclosing or exposing her world—even when she wants to do so. These cases provided the only instances of direct intervention on my part.

## Location of Respondents

I interviewed eighteen teachers in addition to one ex-student. The average time of each interview was two hours, although some were considerably longer, and others involved more than one meeting. I transcribed each tape myself immediately, erased the tape following the transcription, and sent a copy to my respondent for her approval and her records, as per our agreement. The women ranged in age from twenty-four to sixty-one years old; most of them were between thirty-five and forty-five. All taught in Ontario boards that were both rural and urban. I spoke with women from as far north as Timmins, as southwest as London, as east as Ottawa and Kingston, and all around southern Ontario. Unfortunately, my limited means did not allow me to make contact in northwestern Ontario.

The teachers, by virtue of being in the profession, were all of middle-class income, although their personal backgrounds range from working class to upper class. In this case, class was determined by self-labeling. All were Canadian, although a few were not born in this country. One woman was from a Caribbean island, another was from a Latin American country, and a third was from a western European country. Nine of the women were white, and most of them were of Anglo-Saxon background; three were Franco-Ontarians. The remainder identified themselves as Canadian of different ethnic backgrounds. Six spoke more than one language. Their religious backgrounds included three Jewish women; the others said they were Christian and/or Catholic—practicing or nonpracticing. A number were feminist, some were apolitical, and a few were conservative, meaning traditional. One said she was a humanist. Not all accepted the label or referred to themselves as lesbian (more elaboration on this point further on in the text); some preferred "gay"; others, nothing at all.

The women's hierarchical positions in the educational system ranged from classroom teachers to heads of department, various levels of consultants, principals, and vice-principals. They specialized in English literature, mathematics, science, guidance, French, physical education, history, music and drama, Latin, and chemistry. Most had taught more than one subject. Three women taught at the elementary level; five others began as elementary school teachers but switched to secondary. The rest had only secondary school experience. The average number of years in the profession was about fifteen. One woman had taught thirty-five years; another, just a few months. No teacher from any Catholic (separate) school board was included, even though the separate board is state funded. Because those boards are not bound by state policies, and because Catholic boards are particularly sensitive to issues involving sex outside of church-sanctioned marriages, such interviews would have obscured questions of state ideology. Catholic teachers who are divorced and who cohabit with another partner in heterosexual relations are officially frowned upon, and lesbian and gay teachers are advised by their union representatives to remain invisible.

It is important to specify that these women were not intended to be a sample. They are the women who granted me an interview. They represent only themselves, and no statistical generalizations can be made from their experiences. This study is more an institutional ethnography that takes the everyday world of lesbian teachers as its problematic. In this instance, the relation of the local and particular is a property of social organization. Smith elaborates: "The particular 'case' is not particular in the aspects which are of concern to the inquirer. Indeed, it is not a 'case' for it presents itself to us rather as a point of entry, the locus of an experiencing subject or subjects, into a larger social and economic process." She continues: "The problematic of the everyday world arises precisely at the juncture of particular experience, with generalizing and abstracted forms of social relations organizing a division of labor in society at large.[33] No attempt has been made to provide exact numerical information about the informants' particular location, specialty, age, or ethnic or religious backgrounds. Each woman's experience is unique; each speaks for herself alone. Furthermore, whenever an interviewee is cited, no factor that may pinpoint her identity is given.

## Sorting and Selecting

Once the interviews were completed, the task of organizing what seemed like a monumental amount of data was daunting. First, I numbered each record of my exchange with a respondent with a letter of the alphabet, which I wrote on each consecutively enumerated page of that particular interview. I read through the interviews several times, and because I had transcribed them myself, I became extremely familiar with each one of them. In the process of rereading the transcribed interviews several times, I began noticing many areas that were common to some, and other factors seemed to stand out in others. This did not come as a surprise, because, even though the interviews were open-ended, there were essential questions of concern: I had requested each woman to locate herself, to account for her first experience with a woman, to identify herself sexually, and to relate coping practices in the school and in the classroom.

I went through each transcript (averaging twenty-five single-spaced pages) once more, this time marking in the margins the broad topic of each paragraph or combination of paragraphs. I photocopied all the interviews with my broad indicators in the margins. I then reread them, this time attempting to refine the topics and writing down each time a particular reference to a subject came up. I made a complete list of these referents, not in any particular order, but as they seemed to come up as I read. They ranged from location, to denial of lesbian experience, to effects of sexuality on their teaching.[34] The next step was to cut up each interview by topic and to paste it on 5 × 8 inch cards. I accumulated over four hundred cards, neatly classified by topic.

Finally, my use of the data depended on one factor alone: I knew I had very rich material and I wanted to incorporate every word I had worked so hard to obtain. Each interview was special; each offered distinct perspectives and different experiences. Although I came close, there were myriad subjects I had to leave out. I had chosen to limit my topic to how lesbian teachers coped at school, and I needed to use all relevant data to understand how each teacher achieved her survival in the school system. What was left out was material that I perceived as peripheral, even if interesting. For example, one interviewee lived during the McCarthy era in the United States; her stories are extraordinary, but were not directly useful to the Canadian context. However, inasmuch as her account touched upon her experiences in her job as a teacher in Canada, her words were pertinent to my project. What was left out of each interview was minimal, and the richness of the respondents' quotations attests to this fact.

# 5

# Discovering Lesbian Identity

The women I interviewed for this project ranged in age from late twenties to mid sixties. Most were between thirty-five and forty-five at the time of the interviews. This meant that more than half of them were growing up in the decades of the fifties and sixties, and at least two of them in the forties. Therefore, for the most part, the majority of the respondents were experiencing their first "lesbian" attractions before the Stonewall riots of 1969, which marked the beginning of the gay liberation movement in North America. Throughout these years, *lesbians* (and I am using the term loosely to refer to all women who were sexually or physically involved with each other) existed in all levels of society, married or single, and in most professions. Often, the conditions of this existence forced us (I grew up in the sixties) to doubt ourselves, sometimes loathing our "differentness," regularly experiencing our marginality, but surviving to find, frequently intermittently, love and support with one another.

To speak of a "lesbian identity" during those years would be to rob our history of its specificity, its complexity, and its diversity. This manner of naming would deny the struggles that are ongoing, struggles that create the opportunity to reflect simultaneously on the distinctness yet multiformity of our communities and of ourselves. We are still dealing with our terrors, discovering our internalized homophobia, and recognizing our racism. As Cherrie Moraga said more than ten years ago:

> To assess the damage is a dangerous act. I think of how, even as a feminist lesbian, I have so wanted to ignore my own homophobia, my own hatred of myself for being queer. I have not wanted to admit my deepest personal sense of myself has not quite "caught up" with my "women identified" politics. I have been afraid to criticize lesbian writers who choose to "skip

over" these issues in the name of feminism. In 1979, we talk of "old gay" and "butch and femme" roles as if they were ancient history. We toss them aside as merely patriarchal notions. And yet, the truth of the matter is that I have sometimes taken society's hatred of lesbians to bed with me. I have sometimes felt "not man enough." For a lesbian trying to survive in a heterosexist society, there is no easy way around these emotions. Similarly, in a white-dominated world, there is little getting around racism and our own internalization of it.[1]

The ways in which invisibility was embodied in the very structure of the daily lives of the lesbian teachers I interviewed produced feelings of both safety and worthlessness. There was safety in the fact that who they were was invisible to the structures within which they acted—structures that were mostly hostile to their existence. Passing as heterosexual seemed relatively easy. However, feelings of worthlessness inevitably surfaced in such a context of denial. The distressing contexts may have been shared by all the women I interviewed, although how they coped with their respective situations depended on their age, when and how they came out, their political convictions, and how these factors intersected with their culture, their race, their class, and their religious practices and whether they found themselves growing up or working in and urban or rural settings. This chapter deals with how these women, given their differences, found ways to have relationships with other women, to identify themselves using a number of socially recognized categories, and come to terms, in their own way, with their sexual orientation.

For an inquiry to begin from women's experience, it is necessary to record the words of the women themselves. The teachers' personal backgrounds varied:

I was born in Ottawa but very shortly moved to a small northern Ontario town. . . . I was brought up in this small town in what I would also describe as extraordinarily traditional circumstances, in what I would also describe as the aristocracy of this northern town. . . . I was English and Protestant at a time when to be English and Protestant, to be WASP, was definitely a social advantage.

I was born in Toronto and lived there all my life.

My father is a professional.

My parents were blue collar, labor level, not management. Dad worked with his hands. He was a railroader.

My parents had a farm and owned a butcher shop.

I come from the aristocratic class of my country. My parents had money, status, and power.

Five of the women were married initially, and three of these have children. One stayed in her marriage but continued a lesbian existence, several are divorced or separated, and a good number remained single. One woman has children but never married. All but two had had serious and/or long-term relation(s) with men prior to their involvement with women.

Many of the women related quite satisfactorily to the men in their lives (husbands and/or lovers). At least three of the women mentioned not being one bit interested in women to begin with. Their relations with their male lovers were warm and passionate, their life with their husband or lover was one of contentment, and the children that came later completed what one described as the "blissful picture." For a while. Beyond that point, the stories varied. Most of the women experienced confusion and feelings they could not understand for many years. For instance, one woman, despite an early history of being physically involved with girls when she was in boarding school and falling in love with her various women teachers, became obsessed with a man she described as "elegant, suave, and debonnaire."

I was thoroughly convinced that I was totally in love with him and wanted to get married. My letters while I was away [in Europe] were not love but obsession . . . [When he left very shortly after my return], for six to eight months I became idiotic. I would go to the town in which he was living, chase him around, try to find him at the parties, and phone him . . . Then there was another man after that. I lived with him for a while—not long, maybe six months or so. It was very much over by that time. So you see the history that I'm talking about is a very mixed bag of stuff. Extremely mixed bag of my attractions to women, my not admitting it, the occasional man in my life being important, and so on.

Another woman admitted quite readily that there were "problems around sexuality when I was married" but realized that it was because she was not particularly attracted to her husband ("he was like a brother"). However, when she left her husband, she had many different relationships with other men, three of which were important to her.

One woman mentioned that the first time she ever cared for anyone it was for the man who eventually became her husband for almost a decade. She described him as "nice, gentle, and kind" and saw the development of her ability to love as it grew in that particular relationship as directly instrumental in her later recognition of her love for women.

> What I think is ironic is that I think if I had not had that experience I would not have been ultimately free to love women the way I should, the way that was normal for me to love. Because I didn't know what was normal for me in terms of loving anyone, I sort of fell into this thinking maybe that this is what it is all about, and I'll try it. It is really through trying that that I realized something was not right . . . . I'm trying to look back and see how did I become so free that I would fall in love with a woman, actually, really. It must have been that I was in a comfortable environment, and it happened. I was free enough to love her after having some experience in articulating caring and being cared for.

At least one woman used her relationship with her husband to control her attractions to women.

> You see, when I was being made love to by my husband, I didn't get these wild crushes on girls—it's interesting. It didn't happen. I suppose it did happen but not so intensely. I was sexually satisfied. I could control this wild falling-in-love thing, you know.

Several women mention that it never crossed their mind to have "crushes on" or had never felt any attraction to women prior to their first relationship with a woman. However, the vast majority of the women I interviewed had early experiences, although few put a name to their activities. Whether they were able to acknowledge or recognize it at the time or not can only be conjectured in retrospect, usually interpreted through the wisdom of present knowledge. The following are a few recollections:

My mad crushes were always on English teachers. I didn't like phys. ed. teachers! [laughter]. Stereotypes aren't all true! [Interviewee is referring to Meg Christian's song "Ode to a Gym Teacher".][2]

Another woman remembered:

Ever since I was a little girl I had those incredible crushes every year—mostly on teachers or older girls at school, but sometimes on my mother's friends. I would harbor those secret passions which I knew, somehow, I could not share with anyone. Later, as an adolescent, these same crushes began to turn sexual and I would want to touch the person I loved. By that time I understood what I was going through. However, I was not to have my first sexual experience with a woman until I was nineteen. I had already slept with men, though.

The next three women talked about feelings for which they had no explanation, no language, and therefore they had difficulty identifying what was happening to them. This was prevalent in the society in which they grew up—North America between twenty-five and thirty years ago. Most of the women who lived then related that girls of that era were not encouraged to have any sexual knowledge. Experimentation was strictly condemned, and mention of sex was rare except for those shared "dirty secrets" between peers. Needless to say, none remembered any discussion about what was regarded as "deviant" sex. The atmosphere of secrecy surrounding the subject contributed to the lack of recognition and articulation of the feelings the girls or young women were experiencing.

I think I have had crushes—certainly on teachers, on women teachers as well as on men teachers, and I can think of particular women. A high school English teacher who was quite significant for me. Later, when I was older, a woman friend whom I was quite close to and she had a child and we were very close. And that's probably the only relationship that I would rewrite or that I would say probably I was in love with her.

One of the women started out as a nun and recalled her first crush in that context:

I remember this one young woman to whom I felt very attracted was a Junior, and I was a Junior myself. . . . Anyway,
they watched people in training even more than they watched
you when you were finally professed. It would have been a real
conscience turmoil to have even attempted anything that
would have bordered on the sexual or even the physical in
terms of articulating it. Sensing it was one thing, but articulating it was another. I'm positive that there were . . . now that
I look back, I see what were very close friendships between
women that were, I'm sure, must have gone beyond what was
so-called acceptable. But because there were no words in my
vocabulary at the time, in my feelings there were feelings, but
there were no words. I guess you need words to articulate the
feelings, to verify the feelings. So I never did explore the feelings with that particular woman.

Another woman remembered:

My first memory of being attracted to a girl . . . [was in grade
eight and grade nine.] I really felt strongly for her and in fact
that was the beginning of a real fear in me, because I never
really consciously thought of what was going on in me. I never
put it together except to know in a kind of vague and immaterial way that this was "wrong," this was "bad," this was a "no-
no." But I would do strange things, like I would pester her to
come and stay with me and she did, to my memory, only once.
I remember feeling that she was afraid of me.

From what the women are saying, many adolescent "crushes" were
not necessarily tied to later lesbian experiences. In retrospect, they
may be viewed as "the beginning" of such a history, but this cannot
be verified, particularly in view of the fact that many heterosexual
women have had crushes on women teachers and/or older girls when
they were younger. However, a number of lesbians do not recall ever
having a "crush" on or exhibiting any interest in women prior to
their coming out.

### Heterosexual Hegemony and Fear of the Lesbian Label

As one woman said above, experiencing the feelings of attraction toward a woman and articulating these feelings are two different matters. Implicit in the recognition of her preference for other

women is a woman's admission to entering a category that is socially constructed as "deviant." As Adrienne Rich observes, "The
lesbian choice—the choice of the woman-identified woman—[is de-
picted] as pathological or sinister."[3]

The denial of our history as lesbians (recognized and reclaimed
by a number of feminist writers since the current women's movement)[4] is a small reflection of the same denial that went on (goes
on?) in each one of our individual histories. Each woman who names
herself as "homosexual," "gay," or "lesbian" has undergone a process
of recognition, of "coming out," of acknowledgment that she is attracted to, is sexually involved with, or simply prefers women as
sexual partners. For many women who came out (or are coming
out) before or outside of the women's or gay movements, the process often begins in fear or denial. Moreover, "coming out" is a process which, for most, involves a reiteration of one's identity over and
over in different situations because of hegemonic presumptions of
heterosexuality.

The label *lesbian* becomes relevant when a woman is in a situation where she either has to identify with or to dissociate herself
from the socially recognized category *lesbian*. The label itself is
more than the experience of sexual involvement with a woman. It
contains within it a history, a transformation of an actual "everyday
world" act (sleeping with a woman) into an ideological classification
(lesbian). This occurs because the term is historically and ideologically specific. It has a particular connotation, a definition, a rele-
vance. It was coined by "experts," members of an intelligentsia, men
who created the word to identify women who reject, in some way,
what was or is considered "natural" and therefore "normal," thus—
not surprisingly—normative, namely, sex (etc.) with men. To appropriate the term *lesbian* involves a self-identification, a woman's
recognition of her sexual practices combined with an acceptance of
an identity that goes with the recognition. However, this process
may have involved years of denial during which women were persecuted for sexual acts that were, in various ways and to differing degrees, prohibited by society. In addition to an identity assumed by a
woman within a social context, *lesbian* can also denote a label that
may describe her whole person negatively, in some cases overriding
or superseding any other labels. In other words, often when a
woman is recognized as "lesbian" she ceases to be "woman," a
"teacher," a "wife," a "mother," and so forth.

It is relevant to remember that the professional men did not
see any threat in the "romantic friendships" of the eighteenth and

nineteenth centuries because they occurred within the private spheres of women, because they existed side by side with the more legitimate heterosexual marriages, and because they sustained women but did not threaten any property values (women and property remained with those who "owned" them—the husbands or fathers). It was when women became financially independent that romantic friendships were discouraged. They now posed a threat to the hegemony of the family and of men's rights to women.[5] As Lillian Faderman remarks, whenever historically women gained any independence from men, they were called "lesbian." Ti-Grace Atkinson and other radical feminists concluded in the early days of the women's movement that " 'lesbian' has always been a kind of code word for female resistance."[6]

Traditionally, to be a lesbian may or may not have entailed a physical involvement with another woman. It was not an act but a state of being. A relic from the sexologists, it was adopted by more recent "experts." It was a socially constructed diagnosis in line with the current professional opinion, one that was institutionally based, verified, and validated and that conformed with the hegemonic ideology. Typically, the diagnostician had a "scientific" literature and a textual or bureaucratic procedure that supported him. He would proceed to examine a woman's personal history (her sexual fantasies, her dreams, her childhood), look for physical and hormonal defects that could "cause" her "aberration," and, on the basis of a predetermined, "scientifically" defined, institutionally recognized set of "symptoms," declare her "lesbian" or not.

The term *lesbian* is socially (as well as medically, institutionally, and politically) identified as deviant. Although the recent women's and gay movements have reclaimed the word, *lesbian* remains an admission that a woman has rejected part(s) of the normative social organization. Since *lesbian* has entered our current language and is understood by almost everyone (positively or negatively), to acknowledge oneself as such is to take a stand. For women who must remain closeted, hidden because their livelihood depends of their assumed heterosexuality, to claim the identity publicly is a frightening experience, one that has few practical benefits unless the woman is politicized. Whether a woman identifies herself as lesbian with pride or with hesitation, as a teacher she always has to say it with caution. The phrase *coming out* may refer to one of several experiences. It is sometimes used to describe the first time a woman is physically involved with another. It may mean the moment of self-labeling. It also alludes to every instance a lesbian identifies herself as such. The phrase and its various meanings apply as well to men. In the following pages, *coming out* will represent the process through which the interviewees came to recognize their emotions and actions as lesbian (whether they use the specific term or not).

The "coming out" process is frequently a long one that includes initial stages of denial, panic, or elation. Each woman who recognizes and/or names her preference experiences different emotions. For some women, the process is drawn out and gradual, lasting for years, during which she may vacillate in her ability to accept or reject her feelings or behavior. Some women reacted by denying so vehemently what they felt that they forced themselves into a relationship with a man or a marriage just to "prove" that they were "normal." This woman remembered the doubts:

> There was one occasion when I found myself talking myself into liking a male and thinking about marriage. I suppose that that came as a result of pressure [by parents] being put on in very subtle or unsubtle ways. But then I recognized that that's exactly what I was doing. I was trying to talk myself into something.

Others battled with the label but eventually accepted it. Finally, some women relate a long history of actually making love with women but still completely denying what they were doing. For instance, one woman began by thinking of her feelings as an isolated experience: "I did not think I was a lesbian. I just thought for some strange reason I was in love with a girl, you know. That is how it was at first." More anguish is apparent in this woman's words:

> I would characterize my behavior as a lesbian like that [denial] for years, literally until I was in my late twenties. I behaved in this way as a lesbian, without making any conscious statement to myself about my sexual preference. I was riddled with guilt and fear about it, but I never put it into any kind of statement about myself.

After graduating in the very early sixties from the university where she had had her first lesbian experience, this next woman chose to accept a job hundreds of miles away from her lover. She explained:

> I was running away from the intensity of our relationship, perhaps recognizing that there was something "wrong" with it or

that it was creating difficulties in my life that I was just beginning to recognize. I was also getting a fair bit of pressure from my family in terms of the amount of time I was spending with this woman. I was also very conscious of the reaction of the other women that I lived with [roommates]. Although nothing was said, they were certainly aware of my comings and goings and I felt—not a condemnation, but an awareness on their part of my behavior. I'd never experienced this before. I'd never been questioned about what I was doing, questioned either through glances or someone actually making reference to it. This discomfort . . . certainly was one factor in my decision to go away.

An older interviewee (in her fifties) had had a sexual encounter with a woman even before she was aware of the label *lesbian*. Nevertheless, she was horrified at herself and her feelings. Although she had no name for her behavior, she put a stop to it because "[it] was not good and yet I liked it." She also felt she had to leave her town to escape her feelings. However, she said, "I spent four months in another community, found that I was attracted to [yet] another woman and thought THIS HAS GOT TO STOP! And it did." Another woman was in a relationship for ten years with a woman; she neither admitted this to herself nor discussed what she was doing with her partner. When questioned on the improbability of the situation, she said that one did not need to name what one was doing in order to do it. I asked her how one protects oneself if one is not even vaguely aware of the social implications of one's behavior. To this she replied pragmatically that being aware of and naming behavior are two different things.

It was extremely intense when we were first together. It continued to be intense but because we were not together a lot [since she had moved away], when we did get together, we recognized that we had a very short space of time and hence one doesn't waste time talking about things that one hasn't really given much thought to—and there didn't seem to be any need to talk. If we were getting along and happy with one another and fairly satisfied with this time period that we were spending together, there was no reason to talk. . . . I think that it is significant that you know that this woman had never been involved with any other woman. Neither had I. We never, in our ten years together, ever discussed our attraction for any other woman, either during the time we were together or what had happened in our earlier lives. It was just not a topic of discussion at all.

One woman recounts a very long history of sexual relations with women, beginning when she was about thirteen years old. At the same time she led a relatively full heterosexual life, dating men and, on one or two occasions, cohabiting with a male lover. Notwithstanding her involvements with women (which were both regular and intense), she recalls, "I would never have said the word 'lesbian' never mind said that I was a lesbian." She was almost thirty when she finally came to terms with her preference:

> Then came the big relationship of my life and a gradual admission to myself that if I was buying a house with, setting up house with, and doing things like making her the beneficiary of my life insurance policy, and at the time, sharing bank accounts, sharing money and sharing common goals and so on, that surely it was time for me to say that I was a lesbian. But even in the early years I wouldn't have used the word. I found it a repulsive word, a word that carried all that negative connotation. And I don't think that I'm adjusted to the whole thing as yet.

Several of the women I interviewed had come out to themselves under happy circumstances. One woman described it as "euphoric." Two other women relate similar emotions of joy, satisfaction, and a final discovery that made all behavior for the past years understandable. In an unpublished paper, Helena Feinstadt interviewed ten women who had "consciously changed from heterosexuality to lesbianism." Five of the women chose to become lesbian through their introduction to and involvement with feminism; the five other women's prime motivation was attraction to another woman. Feinstadt found that the latter group experienced a more traumatic process because they had no context (feminist or gay politics) that could provide them with support. On the other hand, those women whose lesbianism grew out of their feminism described their eventual choice as "very easy." "The main support for all these women was other women (both feminist and lesbian) and a sense of a women's community. Books were the main resource for raising consciousness and explicating experiences. These women did not feel the aloneness and isolation of the women discussed previously."[7] Although this may not be true for all women, the pattern certainly applies to most of the women I interviewed. Even those women whose experience was relatively tolerable or undeniably joyous related incidents where they were involved with a lover who completely denied the implications of their actions.

For instance, one married woman described her attraction to another woman who reciprocated the feelings. They spent a blissful time together, discovering their common interests and slowly becoming more involved physically with each other. Then suddenly the other woman started to back off when she realized how close they were becoming.

> She started to get really paranoid about what this really was that was going on. It was a terrible time in my life because I couldn't understand anyone who'd negate something that powerful or pretend that it wasn't what it was. And it took me an awful long time to integrate all those things and to—I guess, have compassion for where she was. I began to sense the terrible, terrible fear that she had of articulating what it was. . . . I found it hard enough to acknowledge for me, but I found that for someone like this other person, she had so many other constraints on her life and came from an era ten years beyond mine again, that it was impossible. And if for her it was impossible, it must be impossible for many other women.

The youngest interviewee also experienced a lover who had great difficulty acknowledging what was actually happening. The respondent met this older woman in a postsecondary institution before she herself became a teacher. The young woman was about nineteen; the other was in her late thirties. The latter was very kind and attentive to the younger one. She invited her to her home, lent her books, fed her. "Eventually we became lovers and I was in heaven! I couldn't believe it. And I could see that she loved me. It was absolutely wonderful . . . and it lasted nine years." It was the interviewee's first experience apart from an incident when she was fifteen with a peer. It was also the older woman's first experience for a long while. When I expressed support and asked if the relationship was a good one, the respondent observed; "No, because she wasn't a lesbian—or so she said. That's the whole thing I've been dealing with for a long time." Her answer confused me. I asked her to elaborate. She said:

... which means that she is not heterosexual because obviously a woman who ... OK. For the first year or so we slept together. She taught me. I had never heard the word *lesbian*. I had never lived it. I mean, I had never stopped to say I was a lesbian. So eventually, we made love. It was wonderful. Anyway, after a year—we were really close—she just said, "I don't want to do this." We had never said we were lesbians or anything. The only mention of lesbians was that first night when she said she was afraid of lesbianism and it was her she was afraid of. We never talked about it. We did it [made love] for about a year. For six months we did it about three times a day. It was incredible. Then it slowly stopped as she said she didn't want to. We still slept together and we slept in the same bed nude all this time. I spent eight years living with her. And then, I decided about two years ago I couldn't take it any more because I *was* a lesbian. Every time it was brought up ... like I would have affairs, go to a bar and pick up somebody ... she would get angry because she was possessive and wanted it to be only me and her. I was willing, except that this lesbianism always came up in me. And I kept crying and saying "Fine, I'll get rid of it. I won't be a lesbian." I saw psychologists. I did everything. I kept saying to her, "Don't worry, I'm not a lesbian" because she said, "Look, if you're a lesbian and you want to live it, fine, but we can't live together anymore." And I needed her.

The young woman eventually left, and by the time of the interview (her first year of teaching) she had decided she did want to be a lesbian.

This experience is an example of Dorothy Smith's "line of fault."[8] The point of rupture, in this case, lies, on the one hand, between the social scientific definition of *lesbian* as deviant, the social reproval that discourages potential deviations from heterosexuality, the terror engendered by the category, and, on the other hand, the support and privilege accorded to women who accept heterosexual hegemony. This woman refused to acknowledge her actions for fear of the dreaded label. She, too, was a teacher.

Another interviewee also rejected the word *lesbian* despite her sexual involvement with a woman. This teacher is a dedicated feminist whose denial stems from a clear, personal interpretation of the term and less from the fear of it. She took time claiming the identity, and when she did, it was only on a trial basis. After she had had one or two sexual encounters with women, this respondent remembered: "At this time I was labeling myself as woman-identified but as straight . . . because I was a straight woman who was involved . . . it was just supposed to be a sexual friendship." The other woman was a lesbian. When I asked what that meant to her, she replied, "A lesbian is a woman who chooses to sleep with women but also to relate within a lesbian lifestyle." I asked, "So you could sleep with women and still not be a lesbian?" She said, "Right! Just like you could be a lesbian and still have one relationship with a man. . . . [my lover] was a lesbian but she'd coined this word '*sexual friendship*', which meant that you were really friends but you slept together." This woman did not accept the ideological meaning of the word. She claimed the term *lesbian* and reworked it to fit the reality of her experience. She was able to do that within the context of her feminist understanding and politics.

To comprehend these two women quoted above, one must remember the historical distinction made in an earlier chapter between lesbian sex and being a lesbian. The former is an act in the continuum of human sexual expression; it is similar to oral sex, masturbation, and so forth. All are, in some way, ideologically and overtly denounced as improper or sinful or forbidden, yet all covertly tolerated in some situations. However, lesbian identity is a historically (and geographically) specific concept that includes an entire way of life, a way of being in the world, an identity chosen with a conscious political and/or social motive. Eve Zaremba clarifies this further. She observes that lesbian sex

is and always has been more prevalent than living as a lesbian. Women can be turned on by women and may have sex together without acknowledging it, without even knowing words for it. Women with female lovers can and do sometimes deny that either of them is a lesbian. Lesbian identity can be vehemently rejected. For living as a lesbian clearly involves a conscious social choice. Those who make the choice are doing more than expressing their individual preference for women as sexual partners: they are showing their personal identification with a despised social group.[9]

## Coming Out

To acknowledge that one is a lesbian is a very long-term process for many women. It may come as a sudden flash of insight or after years of denial, but finally there is a moment of recognition often accompanied by a certain fear or an unbounded joy. It is, in Adrienne Rich's words, "that first permission we give ourselves to name our love for women as love, to say *I am a lesbian*."[10]

Each woman I interviewed had a different experience that evidently depended upon the circumstances of her life, her age, her race and class, the historical time, her political convictions, and her own attitude toward women loving women. Acknowledging one's sexual preference does not necessarily mean identifying oneself as "lesbian," nor does it give one license to discuss it with others. It may merely mark the beginning of the process.

One woman clearly understood the implications of her attraction to another woman, but neither partner was able to discuss it: "I didn't put words to what was happening. It was simply that for both of us there seemed to be this intense attraction and the need to be with one another." This was occurring in the early 1960s outside the context and support of the women's and gay movements. These women may have had the words for what was happening to them, but these words would have been negative, contemptible, sick, and could not possibly have described the intensity, power, or beauty of the feelings they were experiencing. Another woman underwent a long period of confusion when she encountered her first incident:

> I was engaged in an athletic competition in a gymnasium . . . I can't remember whether it was judo or what the hell it was . . . but this woman was not behaving in quite the way the manual said she should be behaving. I was rather startled. I drew back rather rapidly. It frightened me.

She was almost twenty in the late 1940s, when her father had explained to her about (in her words) "the birds and the bees" but had left out any mention of attractions to members of her sex. Her bewilderment, her inability to comprehend what had happened, and the lack of social context to give her experience validity led her to deny it had ever happened. It was a full year later before she was able to admit her attraction to another woman.

Growing up in the fifties without the benefit of a typical teenage dating pattern, another woman recognized she was not attracted to boys, that she preferred the company of women, and that she even enjoyed holding hands with other camp counselors at night on the rocks. However, when a friend of hers later came out to her (she was a teacher by then), she responded with "Gee, really, not me, no, I don't see that as necessarily my lifestyle." But it began to make her think about her situation. She was in her twenties in the early 1960s, she had not yet fulfilled her father's wishes "to produce boyfriends, dating rings, engagement ring, wedding ring, and a grandchild," and she was reluctantly coming to realize she had no inclination to do so. She finally but cautiously let it enter her reality.

Another woman related an anguishing experience when she was a young teenager in a boarding school. She tells of a nun who touched her sexually, and although "it felt fine" for a while, she admits hating her for it. From that time on, for several years after the incident, she related sexually exclusively to men. In graduate school (in the early 1970s) she was involved with one of her male professors when she fell in love with a woman.

> I was confused and I went to see a psychoanalyst. She said to me "So, you're a woman and you're a lesbian, so what?" And then I thought, "Well, maybe I'm a lesbian" because I was enjoying the woman more than the professor.

She was brought up Catholic from an upper-class and conservative background. Initially, she resisted acknowledging her lesbian experience, but once it was validated by her analyst, she had less trouble accepting it.

Two interviewees felt they had "always been lesbian." Each accounted for her early recognition of her preference by recalling her mother's strength and wisdom, despite the "menial" tasks she accomplished within the context of the family. Both those women experimented sexually as youngsters, dated heterosexually, recognized their lack of interest in males, and finally became involved with women. The intensity of the feelings that accompanied each of their first experiences left no doubt in either woman's mind as to where her preference lay.

One older woman spent her youth having crushes on women but preferring to ignore them. She got married, became a teacher, and was taking her first summer school course when, as her female summer school professor was handing out the first assignment, "I looked up and our eyes met and wham! I was . . . both of us . . . I was madly in love after the first look, and I was in love with her for at least twenty years." It came to her, all of a sudden, that there was nothing wrong with her. She just preferred women to men. Everything fell into place and she was "delighted" with her discovery. She told her husband, who was very supportive and encouraged her to pursue this relationship. This woman was involved sexually with another woman during the McCarthy era in the U.S.[11] (Her lover was from the United States.) She realized the secrecy she had to maintain given the dire consequences if her relationship became public. Since she had a husband, and later children, she was not as threatened as she would have been had she been single. Rather, for her it was a relief to understand the pattern of attraction to girls and women she had always experienced. She also came to recognize her homosexuality at a time when lesbian relationships were usually expressed in "butch/femme" roles (modeled after gender-specific masculine and feminine roles). The fact that she and her lover were neither and both worried her: "We thought we were different. We thought we were the only two in the world. How would we know? There wasn't any literature written about it." However, on the whole, she felt better about herself.

In contrast with this woman, another interviewee, half her age, came out within the context of the women's movement. Books were not yet plentiful, but they were available. "All of sudden I found myself at the library taking out Del Martin and Phyllis Lyon, Abbot and Love, and so on. And, all of a sudden it was like a cosmic click—things started to make sense." On the whole, she spoke of her coming out process as relatively painless.

Another woman in her early thirties also came out within the context of the women's and gay movements. She had male lovers up to the point of coming out. Hers sounds more like a decision than a process. She had become acquainted with two lesbians and became curious about their lives, their sexuality—curious enough to suggest to one of the women that they "should try it" (becoming sexual). She described her doubts later: "I actually thought to myself as we were getting into bed: 'I wonder if this will make me feel sick.' And, of course it didn't. It was completely natural." Nevertheless, she did experience qualms as she went back to teaching. She wondered if everyone could tell, if everyone would somehow know that she had been involved sexually with a woman.

> I remember being in gym class and wondering if there was something that I was doing . . . I know that was very silly because you can't really tell that sort of thing, but I thought that maybe there was something that they can tell.

She got over her fears and eventually became very comfortable with her decision.

Another positive coming out process occurred also within the context of the women's movement. Although married, divorced, a mother, and currently with a male lover, this woman was a strong feminist and eventually a lesbian. She had known a number of lesbians but had never been curious or interested. It began one holiday weekend when she found herself with a group of (straight) women. Suddenly she was aware of this "electric attraction" to one of them. She found it scary. It was at least a year later before they decided to pursue it. She described their meeting as "earth-shattering."

It really happened all at once. Now, I mean, I'm aware that there was a buildup through my experience with feminism, and being at women's functions and being involved with lesbian women in talk sessions and at dances and so on. I realize there was a lot of preparatory work, but I hadn't actually thought about [it] . . . I don't think I consciously anticipated that there would be a change in me—that really happened all of a sudden [that] weekend.

Another positive note came from a woman who was married at the time of her "discovery." Her recognition came after she had met a woman and realized

pretty soon there was only one word for it: I loved this woman. At that time, for me it was euphoric. It was like walking on cloud 499! I realized that I knew what it was. I said what it was. And in the working out, I felt healthier for having done so.

### Self-Labeling

Notwithstanding how long it may have taken to come out to oneself, however joyful, painless, or earth-shattering the process, almost every woman commented on the difficulty she had accepting the label *lesbian*. Whether a woman claimed the name for political reasons or after a struggle that led to recognition, each woman adopted a category that was already socially defined to identify herself.

There are several reasons why a woman is likely or not to call herself a lesbian. Kenneth Plummer summarizes these: "the nature and the strength of the societal reaction, the visibility of the act, and the problematics of the act." He explains that the first instance depends on the relative tolerance surrounding the individual; the second, on the need to seek validation by means of being one of a group; and the third concerns Plummer's belief that "*the stronger the awareness of* [problems through hostile societal reaction], *the greater the likelihood for self-labeling.*"[12] Plummer's perceptive assertion applies to the women I interviewed. The more steeped in the politics of the women's movement, the analyses of feminism, and/or the activities and reforms of the gay communities, the more likely a woman was to claim a lesbian identity. Conversely, the more isolated she was from other lesbians, the more afraid or hesitant she was to adopt what she perceived was a negative label. Moreover, it is often more difficult to identify oneself as lesbian in a rural community, where social reproval could mean more isolation or ostracism than it would in the anonymity of a large urban center. A city is also more likely to offer support in the form of lesbian-related cultural events, groups, bars, and a larger community of visibly active or "out" women. However, none of these generalizations is always true.

In addition to race and class, the age and location (rural or urban) of the interviewee are especially significant factors. If she grew up in the forties, fifties, or sixties, she is likely to use the word *lesbian* with caution. Even for those who were later to join the women's movement, it was not easy to erase the effect of a lifetime of negative connotations attached to the word *lesbian*. For instance, in my first year of doctoral work I came out to a woman who was subsequently to become one of my best friends. Knowing that she was not lesbian, the whole process of talking about my private life became a fear-laden ordeal. Finally, I told her I had been with a woman quite a number of years and added, "I love this person a lot and she just happens to be a woman." I had learned to deny the existence of my lover for so long that even when I wanted to talk about her I needed a means to validate her to the heterosexual world. I had accepted the label *lesbian* since I was a teenager, but only privately—meaning with other women (and a couple of gay men) who were lesbian or gay themselves. Otherwise, I invariably presented myself as "straight" mostly by keeping silent, avoiding or omitting details that could hint at my preference.

When I asked the women I interviewed what word they chose to identify themselves, they inevitably commented on how much they hated labels. However, like every other aspect of their lives, each woman dealt with my question in her own unique way. One older teacher lived in a rural setting. She claimed to be a "humanist" rather than a feminist and was celibate at the time of the interview. She observed:

> No, I can't say that I am a lesbian. I will say that I have had lesbian experiences; some of them have been good, and some of them have been anything but. But then I have had experiences with men, some of which were good and some of which were not. I have come to the conclusion that sexually I am asexual. *Lesbian* brings to mind wanting to spend my life with another female. *Heterosexual* means wanting to spend my life with a male. And in my case, I don't want to spend my life with either.

A very young woman I interviewed hated the term but became reconciled to it as she understood the importance of reclaiming it. She took women's studies courses, read feminist analyses, and discovered radical politics,

> [These] made me accept the term *lesbian*. Before that I found it an ugly term. Lesbianism used to bring [to mind] something squirmy, something ugly, something—like a snake—something gushy, gucky, you know—squirmy. That's what it brought up. Especially in French—*lesbienne*. That word just makes me squirm sometimes. I only started using it and being proud of it, in a sense—not fully proud, because it is not something to be proud of—it's me, but it's not the best part of me. I didn't want to be a lesbian primarily and only. To me, a lesbian, if that's all you do—and I understand that you may want to do that because it gets so frustrating to be in a straight world so you want to do everything with lesbians and be with lesbians. I didn't want to be that. To me, it was neglecting a lot of who I was.

The next two respondents, both of whom were in their forties and taught in different but similar rural and isolated areas, did not identify themselves (at the time of the interview) as feminist. Both hated labels and found them limiting. However, when pressed, they each had an opinion:

> One word I'm still reluctant to use is *lesbian*. It's another label. It's a label like all other labels. I'm a teacher. I'm a lesbian. I'm

X (we won't even bring in the religious denominations). If I have to write something down, fine, I've got that I'm middle-aged, I'm grey. . . . Having spent so much time, I suppose, trying to deny it within myself, I'm still on "this is obviously my lifestyle, this is obviously what I prefer"—however, I prefer being a woman who prefers women rather than going to the more specific definitive *gay*. I find it [the term *gay*] offensive but totally innocuous. It's light, it has its application, but in a way, I don't know. I suppose it [gay] is easier to use, maybe because you can slide it off in the background again. . . .

Likewise, the other woman preferred *gay*. Her words are reminiscent of the experts' opinion of the "typical lesbian profile." She also seems to have internalized, in some way, many of the prevailing negative images associated with the term. Moreover, terms that apply to men [gay] seem somehow more acceptable socially.

I personally don't like labels. I'm more inclined to use the word *gay* because somehow it does not seem to carry the stigma *lesbian* does. It seems to include the notion of the right of an individual to choose her sexual orientation and it seems to suggest that it is not all doom and gloom and a rejected frustrated woman who simply had no choice.

A young woman in her twenties who taught in a large western Ontario community was categorical and clear in her remarks: "I would not choose to label myself by sexual preference. If I had to label myself, I would say "I'm a teacher" who happens to be a lesbian and a feminist." Two other women found the term divisive in their lives, and, the second one added, divisive amongst women. The first, a feminist living in a large urban center and in contact with many other lesbians, was frank about her reasons for rejecting the label:

I'm open to relationships with women, but I'm also involved with a man. . . . The problem with that [relating to women] for me is that relating to men fits better in my life—more as a mother than as a teacher—that's my primary concern right now. . . . What's happened to me as a result of that is that life has become very compartmentalized, something like a mosaic that does not have any openings between the parts to fit in. It makes me rather envious of other people who don't have to live

that way. . . . It's hard for me even to know how I want to be—
how I'd really choose to be with all avenues open because I'm
influenced by knowing that my life will be easier "if". . . .

The second woman lived in a rural area. She did not call herself a
feminist and hated any label. She felt that she was "just a person
who obviously does have an attraction to females far more so than to
males but I don't put a label on it." When asked why, she clarified
her reservations:

> [Labeling] seems to put a boundary around it when you use
> the term *lesbian*. I can't say what I see that boundary as be-
> ing, but it creates a general image which I don't think fits all
> women who are attracted to or who live with other women.

The next three women preferred the word *gay,* but for different
reasons. Each one's words give a strong indication of her context.
The first woman came out in the forties. She was retired by the time
the interview took place. Her comments lend a historical perspective to the whole issue of labels:

> We used the term *gay.* I understand men now like the term *gay*
> used for themselves. But we used to call ourselves "gay". . . . I
> guess we called it homosexual when we were young. I guess we
> knew the term *lesbian*—I don't know what else. I can't remem-
> ber that far back. I went to a psychiatrist once about this and
> she called it my "aberration," and I said, "You may call it an
> aberration, I prefer to call it love."

The next interviewee had little patience with the discussion. She
felt it did not make much difference to her what she called herself:

> I tend to use the word *gay* more often because I tend to have
> many men friends who always refer to themselves as gay. Po-
> litically, I guess, there is a difference. In my own head, there
> isn't. I'm a woman who likes women—you can call that "gay"
> or "lesbian" or "homosexual," I don't care what you call it. I
> guess it's more "with it" to say that I'm a lesbian, more polit-
> ical to say that I'm a lesbian, but I don't care what I am. I am
> just a woman who likes women.

The third respondent preferred *gay* but voiced reservations:

*Lesbian* is a different one. People—straight people—say it with so much rancor, so much fear and bitterness. It is used in the straight world as a negative statement so I have trouble with it too. *Gay*, I guess, is my preference. But even then, I don't like *gay* very much. It is so trivial, for something that is so seriously undertaken, as most of us who are middle or upperclass undertake being homosexual in a serious way. Most of us are in the closet, I would suggest, and most of us are protecting lifestyle and elegance and blah, blah, blah. You undertake living with someone of the same sex very seriously. And you don't like the whole thing trivialized. And the word *gay* is kind of trivial.

One urban-located feminist teacher who had been active in the women's movement for a number of years had time to think about the power of naming. After several years of hesitating about coming out, recently she decided to adopt the label—which, she is convinced, is reversible. She explained:

During the summer I went around asking people about their stories. I spoke to this woman who explained to me this continuum of sexuality and it really made sense to me. She talked about people being in the middle, and I think that probably I am too and that therefore you make a choice . . . and I am choosing right now, for a year, to be with women.

The following woman was involved for almost a couple of years with a woman before they tackled the issued of naming themselves. For them, it was part of the larger process of coming out and becoming comfortable with what they were doing. She remarked:

There wasn't a blinding light where we suddenly said "We are lesbian," so I don't really remember the first time. . . . I don't like the word *homosexual*. I always thought it related more to men, and also, it is a bit clinical. I always thought *gay* as relating to men, as well. . . . I know now that I use the word *lesbian* because I think of it as word relating more to women, and I am woman-identified. As well as sleeping with a woman, I identify with women.

For this next woman, labeling was part of her coming to terms with her sexual preference. When her decision was made, she called up a friend and told her the good news, using the word *gay*. Her friend asked her why she did not say "lesbian" instead, since it was the more powerful word. "Yes," she agreed, "it is a powerful word, therefore we ought to use it." However, she later had misgivings about it.

> Funnily enough, it occurred to me at the time that I could possibly be mistaken about my reservations. I could be mistaken about being a lesbian because I wanted to be one. And, of course it's always a mistake to get what you want. The old WASP[13] belief that if you got what you wanted, something's wrong! And if you like it, you've got to stop!!

Another teacher, for whom her discovery of her lesbianism was a wonderful revelation, had no qualms with the word.

> It's interesting, I feel more comfortable with *lesbian* than *gay* myself. . . . I guess the term *gay* seems less focused than *lesbian* does. *Gay* is more embracing, whereas *lesbian* directly identifies me as a woman who is gay. In a sense I prefer *lesbian* even though I don't use either of them out loud in too many contexts! My personal choice is *lesbian* because, I figure, if I don't say "lesbian" then I'm not thinking "lesbian."

A woman who taught in one of the more isolated and remote communities observed that the word *gay* had not reached the village where she taught at the time the interview was taking place, and so she said, "In my mind, I suppose, I use *lesbian* for women because the word *gay* isn't in our vocabulary yet. It is not vocabulary I use."

One woman replied succinctly and without nonsense: "They have a word for it, so why not: I am a lesbian!" This next teacher acknowledged to herself she was a lesbian, adopted the label, and finally accepted the whole identity even though she had not yet had a sexual relation with a woman.

> [I] still was not what I would call a "practicing" lesbian. But I didn't see that as necessary. You don't have to have sex with a man to know you're heterosexual. As I used to say, there are lesbian virgins! Part of the problem with women identifying themselves as lesbian is that it's identified publicly in society strictly on a sexual basis. That is, if you sleep with a woman

then you are a lesbian. And if you don't, then you're not. And since our society is very dicey about sex at the best of times, that's a difficulty.

The question arose for me as a researcher who begins from women's experience that, by including women in this project who preferred *not* to identify themselves as lesbian, I was imposing my own definitions on the women I was interviewing. The contradiction is compounded when you consider that some of the respondents had come out prior to the women's and gay movements and were therefore reluctant to have a label tagged on to them, one they perceived as, at best, not applicable to them, and, at worst, generally dangerous. How then, after hearing their words and experiences, would I involve those women in a research entitled "Lesbian Teachers"? I have two responses to my own questions: the first is that *before* I interviewed any of the women, I explained the details of the project, telling each teacher that I was describing how each coped *as a lesbian* in her teaching job. The respondents I interviewed understood fully that their stories were being used in a research about lesbian teachers. Secondly, by consenting to be interviewed, each teacher was tacitly acknowledging that, on some level, she accepted such a label, even if she did not fully identify with it.

For a teacher (and for all those women for whom it is imperative not to be known as lesbian), the process does not end at self-labeling or with the decision to assume a lesbian identity. There is still a social self that has to be presented to the world as conforming to heterosexual hegemony. It is one thing for a woman to acknowledge her lesbianism in the safety of her own private sphere, and it is quite another for someone hostile to hold that label against her. The fear of this situation arising was ever present with several of the women I interviewed:

> I personally feel that the term *lesbian* carries with it a stigma. It would make me very defensive if somebody threw that at me—not that I don't like being a lesbian, or that I don't take pride in it—but the way that they would make it dirty for me would upset me a lot. I definitely would not make it public in order for it not to become sullied. I would not want them to throw that as an insult when it is something that I take pride in.

Another woman said, "I always felt a fierce will to keep my private life my own business. There is no way it was anybody else's business what I did in my private life." One teacher was particularly vehement as she thought of and articulated the ultimate potential fear many teachers may carry:

> Definitely, I will never, ever, ever hide or cry or get nervous because somebody is going to blackmail me . . . I will fight back. I won't allow anybody to do that to me. . . . I am very protective of my job, but I'm free enough that I don't have anything to lose.

This next woman summarized the process she underwent: she acknowledged her initial fears but eventually learned to live, as she put it, as honestly as possible with the person she perceived herself to be:

> I definitely find that in the ten years that I've been teaching I've gone through changes in the way I feel about my job and the way I relate to students. I'm far more comfortable. I do not choose to do anything that is dishonest about the kind of life that I live. I do not make any attempts to create a false impression. I don't talk about men as though the relationship is something that it isn't. I don't think I'd be adverse to answering much more personal questions about my feeling about male/female relationships, my feelings about women. Certainly, I would exercise a great deal of discretion and judge both the situation and the intent of the questioner. I'm prepared to be far more open with my colleagues, but I leave it up to them to create the situation where I would choose to speak. I don't feel personally threatened. I don't feel afraid where I once did.

For those women who came out prior to the women's and gay movements, a major deterrent in their acknowledgment or adoption of *lesbian* as an identity came from the then available literature, which portrayed lesbian love as deviant. The only models of women who loved women lay in the shadowy lives of those living in the large urban centers of the Western world, secretly frequenting bars, hiding in the night, living double lives. Pictures showed tough, strong women dressed in men's clothes, defiant and daring, but decadent as well. These images were internalized by generations of women, who in turn frequently preferred to dissociate themselves from those women depicted in the media and often denied that their sexual feelings were in any way similar or related. The interviews took place before AIDS became an issue in the mainstream media; therefore, general discussions regarding lesbian or gay questions were seldom seen in other than feminist or gay literature. Another source of models for those women who came out before the seventies was the elusive tales of the lives of the famous, whether these were dead or alive. Comfort was found in the rumors that da Vinci was homosexual, or that Sappho, Rock Hudson, Michelangelo, Johnny Mathis, or Garbo preferred members of their own sex.

The following teacher's first experience was in the very early sixties. She has since taught in remote towns and villages, where she rarely comes in contact with feminists. Her words reflect the then prevailing ideology, which portrayed lesbians in negative terms:

> If one is called "lesbian," one has no interest in males at all and I don't necessarily agree with that. I suppose, in being called "lesbian," it also drags out the fear of being called "butchy" to which I have very strong objections—very mannish in a very—oh, what's the word—in very ugly ways: strong, forceful, tough, uncaring. When I use the term *mannish,* I don't mean that all males are like that. It's just the worst aspects of being male carried over to, or imposed on a female—the imitation of the very thing one might object to in a male.

Another, slightly younger teacher who also lived in an isolated area of Ontario expressed her discomfort with the term *lesbian* because of the stereotype attached to it. She described this as

> masculine, somehow lacking in warmth and feeling and, for me, at this stage, it's important to feel that I'm developing a greater warmth, a greater ability to relate to people in general. Also, man-hating, and I certainly don't feel that, although there's much about the imbalance of might between men and women that offends me and I find much masculine behavior falls between totally offensive and somewhat puzzling.

The next woman came out in the late forties, early fifties. Until the day of the interview on a day in 1984, she was not inured to the negative meanings she attached to the term *lesbian,* a word which, for her, implied and suggested everything that was "socially, morally, physically, philosophically wrong. I'm not certain that a relationship—physical, sexual relationship—between two women or between two men is acceptable behavior." She spent a lifetime fighting feelings, censoring senses. She called the effects of her final recognition of what she was experiencing "disturbing." Finally, she said,

> I became an alcoholic. I was a person who was very very hard to get along with. My moods were extremely volatile. I became quite physically dangerous at times. I did foolish, idiotic, stupid things because by that point I think I had recognized the fact that sex was not an important part of my life and yet I didn't know how to gain companionship and a sense of belonging in any other way than the use of sex. I was going through two things: trying to use sex to be a part of something, and trying to cope with the fact that I didn't want to use sex to be part of anything. . . . I . . . I, well, it got to the point where I got very, very stupid. The last relationship I had with a woman was in 1973, and thank God she disgusted me thoroughly and I was able to say: this is not what I want or need. And I walked away from it. But it still took quite a number of years before I came to my emotional senses.

Alcoholism was particularly prevalent in women coming out before or outside the women's and/or gay movement.[14] Indeed, it is still very much part of the bar scene and a means for many lesbians to overcome the negative feelings about themselves and those attributed to them by society, as well as a way of coping with the public/private split so prevalent in our lives. Of course, this is not to deny that women in general use alcohol to escape the oppressive situations and positions of their lives or to drum up courage to approach another woman; however, drinking plays an integral role in a lesbian's life. It is almost inherently part of our lifestyle, almost always present at social events. Whether we drink at bars, dances, or private parties, alcohol often provides us with the courage to approach other women, to cope with the hostility of society toward our existence, and to accept the contradiction between the negative prevailing images of lesbians and our own knowledge and interpretation of our way of life. A large proportion of all the women I interviewed had either gone through a period in their life of drinking heavily or were still battling the effects of addictions. One young

woman who is a feminist and who teaches in a large urban center
explained her situations in a letter sent after the interview:

> I don't usually talk about this much because I can't help feel-
> ing, if not ashamed, at least not very happy about the state of
> affairs, but for the sake of the enterprise, I shall talk about
> what I consider to be my worst aspect(s).
>
> Over the past couple of years, I found myself drinking
> rather more than was good for me, feeling very much out of
> control of my life. I thought it had to do with my growing dis-
> enchantment with teaching and with the public education sys-
> tem, but I suspect now that it had a lot to do with my
> dichotomous existence. . . . Feeling as I did about the system
> [very negatively] made me unwilling to put my energy into it,
> but my positive feelings about the students themselves made
> me feel guilty about not concentrating my energies on teach-
> ing. But I didn't *want* to teach the way the system made me
> because then I was teaching against myself, you see. So, in an
> attempt to escape ambivalence, guilt, and resentment, I began
> to drink.

Several women remembered their increased alcohol intake as coin-
ciding with the time they were coping with self-acceptance, with
their acknowledgment of their own sexuality. Some used alcohol to
blank out sexual overtures to other women who may not have responded or been interested. One older lesbian spoke at length about
the bar scenes (in the forties and fifties), which seemed the only
places where women could meet each other.

Not all the interviewees expressed difficulties in accepting
themselves in the face of a hostile social environment. But even
though some were clearly able to make a distinction between how
society perceived them and the legitimacy and beauty of their own
feelings and lives, they often insisted that their heterosexual sisters
had a much easier time. One woman was able to articulate why she
felt this:

> Socially, it is so much easier. If the whole social fabric allows
> you to be woven into it, it is just easier. You don't have to think
> about holding hands, linking arms, reaching out and touching
> a shoulder, just putting a little kiss on a cheek—these are all
> things that in the heterosexual world are perfectly fine. You

can do that. You can't if you're gay. You have to think through everything you do. Unless you come right out and then you don't care anymore, and then you proceed to live that way. I expect that must be very comfortable on one level, but I also know it is very uncomfortable too.

Another teacher, a feminist, thinking about how she would feel if her own daughters grew up to be lesbians, said:

The only concern . . . is that it's a harder life—in almost every way. There are still doors that are not open. There are people who do not want to be your friend. I think there are many, many problems in making a choice which is not part of the mainstream. Those would be my concerns. On the other hand, I can imagine that if one is a strong, independent kind of woman—which is what I'm hoping, of course, that they'll all be—that there is a chance of being extremely happy in a loving relationship with a woman. A much better chance than finding a good man.

The following woman had a child as well. Also a feminist, she could not deny that being a lesbian, although satisfactory and fulfilling in many ways, often it had its difficulties:

I basically like being a lesbian. It is basically fine. I have a child, and every once in a while—and it's not when things are going badly in my relationship—but every once in a while, I just think: "Oh, it would be much easier if I were straight, if I were with a man and if everything were, you know, very nicey nice," like regular, just regular. I think it's going to be hard for her [her daughter]. It's even hard for me. I'm not that out as a lesbian mother, but people know it. It's not a desire to be with a man, I don't experience it like that, like "Oh, I wish Mr. Right had come along and I would not be in this mess." It is more like "I think I have a longing for something I know doesn't really exist," because I have friends who are heterosexual, who have kids and I know what they go through. . . . But it's just sort of every once in a while—it's almost like longing for when I was a kid and Daddy puts you to bed—you know. It's all sort of on that elemental regular level. But in terms of me—as a woman—no, I don't have any, any desire at all to be anything but a lesbian.

This woman felt that she would love her daughter to be a lesbian as well, but realistically she knew that her daughter would probably grow up to be with men. Since she wanted to continue being friends with and part of her daughter's life, she said the following:

> I have to temper my feelings and know that she is going to fall in love with young men and she is going to start fucking probably when she is about however many years old, and she is going to use birth control and she is going to have creepy relationships—some of them—and all that, that in my wisdom, at my age, would not do myself. But I certainly did it . . . I might not choose that for her, but I don't want to prejudge that.

Women who expressed hopes and fears about their children were also disclosing much about their own existence that is hard to voice when one is attempting to reconcile the prevalent negative social image with the reality of our lives. Most of the women with whom I talked were relieved, happy, and content with their sexual choice, and when asked if they encountered difficulties, a few tended to deny any. If the interviewees had children, I often asked the respondents how they would feel if their child were gay or lesbian. Their answers were often significant and revealed how they felt about their own sexual choice.

Nevertheless, some women were unequivocally gratified with their sexuality. One teacher who was in a very long-term relationship tired to explain:

> I have a good job—it brings in the bacon. I have a nice partner. We've worked like dogs. We have a nice house, I mean, that's all material, but basically I think underneath all this junk, this material stuff wouldn't matter if we didn't have a nice, happy relationship. I don't have the vocabulary for this. I'm not used to talking about this. We have a good relationship. We don't fight over money. We have a good sexual relationship. We have a good living arrangement. School is sometimes tiresome, but otherwise, I can't ask for more.

The next teacher was more expressive. She had been married to a man for over a decade, a good marriage, she added, but nothing compared with their female partner. She felt that heterosexual

women missed much that is pleasant in life—not just the tender-
ness, the gentleness of sex with women, but also

> the perfect complementarity of it, the joy of it, the comfortable-
> ness of it, the not-having-to-play-games of it, the mutuality, I
> guess, the shared sensitivities. I suppose, understanding what
> the other person is sensing, is feeling in a way that you
> couldn't otherwise. I can't think of a more complete way of be-
> ing. I think you are fully acknowledged and are yourself. You
> are not thinking of yourself as a "complementing half" of any-
> body. It's two wholes—in the "w-h-" sense!! I know I couldn't
> choose anything else.

This chapter has dealt with lesbian identity. It has included
all information that locates the interviewees, their relationship
with men (if any), their children (if any), their coming out stories,
how they labeled themselves, and how they felt about themselves as
lesbians. Many of the women I interviewed had difficulty talking
about their lives, not because they were unwilling, but rather because they were not in the habit of doing so. They had spent a lifetime concealing the details of their sexual lives, and even when they
wished to explore some aspects with a stranger, often they did not
find the words. Sometimes they were unaware of how they would be
perceived as different by "straight" society. In order to make up for
the possibility of neglected details, I posed one more question that
helped circumvent difficulties in talking about their sexual preference. It is an indirect means of inquiring about their self-perception,
but it does shed light on particular aspects that are difficult to
make visible otherwise. The question was: "How do you recognize
other lesbians?"

### Recognition of Other Lesbians

Lesbians usually gain some support from the knowledge that
they are not alone in their way of life. However, since some women
feel they have too much at stake to be open about their sexuality,
they often resort to looking for clues to identify those women who
are lesbian but who, like themselves, cannot afford to be public.
Therefore, for those lesbian teachers who put so much effort into
maintaining privacy through various means of concealment, the
question was, how did they find each other? The answer revealed
both how each woman may potentially have elected to hide her sexuality as well as how she may have selected to disclose her hidden

life. For instance, if a respondent said that one of the clues she looked for in attempting to "identify" another lesbian was short hair, she herself may have chosen to wear her hair short to make visible her allegiance to a lesbian identity, or she may have kept her hair long in order to conceal her inclusion in such a negatively perceived group. However, this is not to say that every lesbian whose hair is long is hiding, or that every woman who sports a short haircut is lesbian. Individual clues can never be separated from the whole picture. The following is an example of how one woman went through the process of trying to recognize whether I was a lesbian or not. She first noticed that I wore a large watch (a good clue for her before the fashion of large watches). Secondly, she asked about my living arrangement and found that I had lived and owned a house with a woman (two strong clues). Even though I had short hair, she "really didn't think about that because you dressed kind of 'femmy'." To find out if I had been married, she asked if I had children (I don't). She then tried to ask about the woman with whom I lived, but, she said, "you were not very forthcoming with the information."

I remember the incident. While such questioning is going on, I have to assess whether or not I will choose to come out. If I feel the questioner is "safe," I give the answers that will lead her to the correct conclusion. If not, it is usually very easy to deflect suspicion through various means. However, sometimes, despite my willingness to cooperate, the hints themselves may work against me. That year I was rooming with a man. When this woman found that out she said, "That was the clue that I should leave you alone." Knowing how she understood this information, I then asked her about a local lesbian bar. She gave me the address but thought that I was a "straight" woman just curious about a women's bar. My living with a man was too strong an intimation of my "heterosexuality" in her eyes and therefore superseded all other conclusions and clouded any hint from there on.

As a group, teachers are interesting because, for the most part, they are wary of disclosing their lesbianism outside of very "safe" environments, that is, their lesbian peers. I choose to say "peers" because a number of the women I interviewed found it very difficult to come out to gay students or ex-students—and, by extension, younger women who may not appreciate the dangers of coming out in a hostile professional environment.

Each woman I interviewed had her own ways of recognizing other lesbians. Of course, it always depended on context and situation. If you meet a woman in a gay bar, there is a very good chance she is a lesbian. Conversely, women's dances, all-women weekends and events, and feminist concerts and demonstrations are not indicative of sexual orientation but rather of political commitment.

One woman I interviewed was surprised to find that many of the ways in which she was able to recognize lesbians in her circle of feminist friends did not necessarily work with a new group of professionals to whom she was introduced by her new lover—a teacher as well. When asked what signs she looked for in women, she mentioned slightly extra long moments in hugging, more direct eye contact that lingered a fraction longer than usual, jewelry, and so on. Since she was used to feminist interacting in a large urban center where hugging and touching each other was the norm, she became sensitized to clues within that particular context. Her lover, however, was part of the more closeted, nonpoliticized, urban, middle-class professional groups whose gatherings consisted of private parties to which women are specifically invited. In her words:

> I was astounded to find out that they were a totally different kind of group of women than the lesbian women I have known [who are] politically involved women . . . [and] come from a feminist background. . . . I would be able to identify [them] quite nicely on the street—sort of a dyke kind of habit that is worn, often a hairstyle. There's no makeup. Now, obviously, a lot of these things by themselves other women do as well . . . and then, of course, it is by association. . . . The other group looked like jocks. They were all into physical something or other. They were on basketball teams, women's baseball teams, they taught phys. ed. They were much more body-aware, much skinnier, much more caring for their bodies. I've noticed—I'm not talking in great numbers—but there's a disproportionate number of women in the lesbian feminist community who do not care for their bodies. They are overweight and quite sloppy looking. Whereas this group was extremely conscious of their bodies, of their strength. They did weight-lifting, they did various things like this—and they were middle-class. They were not political. They were much better dressed, much more expensively dressed, and in this context where I met them, which was a gay party . . . [they] looked really spiffy. I could well imagine that these women could put on a dress and have lunch in some fancy restaurant and not be recognizable at all . . . A lot of them did have much more middle-class kinds of work, some were doctors, some were law-

yers, some were teacher, and they did pass. And yet . . . I can see that there are different identifiable attributes, traits, that this groups shared that also seem particular to gay women. They are just different ones.

Most of the other women mentioned eye contact as an important indicator. They also mentioned clothes, body language, association with other more obvious lesbians, a firm handshake, a style of dress, short hair, toughness or strength, and a more independent look. One woman mentioned voice. She claimed that many nonfeminist heterosexual women use a very high pitch, especially when around men, that you never find in lesbian women. Another teacher felt that

> there's a sense of a shared experience or a shared way of looking at the world, or a shared set of values, but it comes out in tentative kinds of communication. For instance, I know other women, I'm positive that they're lesbians but they never said so to me and I've never said anything about myself to them, but I get along well with them, we seem to have the same views about things, male/female relationships, power, that kind of thing. There's a supportive network in operation at the level of work and helping each other and so forth, that may indicate a lesbian sense or just a family sense of solidarity. I am not sure. I know that I would be delighted to be aware of more women in this context, but I also know that saying it is something that would only happen in very, very careful circumstances.

Evidently, recognizing another lesbian is one thing, and talking about your private life to her is another. A number of women I interviewed knew of other lesbian teachers but had never come out to them. I myself was acquainted with a couple (both teachers) for ten years, but it was only after one of them asked me about the topic of my dissertation (which involved lesbians) that we were able to come out to each other. We then laughed about the wasted years, although we all knew it would not have been possible except after a decade of trust had elapsed. As one practical lesbian teacher who lives in a small town put it, "Thank God we drink because we'd never meet or say anything to anybody."

Most women who need to protect their profession are not readily forthcoming with information about their lesbian life. This

is especially true with teachers who may know of senior administrators or colleagues who keep their lives passionately private and
who do not allow any openings for self-disclosures either way. It is a
form of self-defense, self-preservation, even, for some, self-delusion,
as this woman admitted: "I am the proverbial ostrich with the head
in the sand—cannot be seen and I cannot see."

Concealing one's identity does not come naturally or easily to
anyone. It takes years of practice, as it does to recognize those who
do not wish to be open about their sexual orientation. A woman who
makes an effort to hide is more likely to be aware of the clues that
may give away the true identity of another. It takes experience to
relate stories, share weekend anecdotes in the staff room on Mon-
day mornings, recount crises or good times with one's lover or
friends, and use personal and possessive pronouns without disclosing the sex of one's companions. In addition, it takes training and
sensitivity to realize who is ready to come out, as well as who can be
trusted. In my first years of teaching I worked with a woman whose
personal insecurities led her to be very loose with the information
she shared with older students whom she wanted to impress. Although I knew she was a lesbian, she was ruled out immediately
when I decided to interview lesbian teachers. I had resigned by
then, but I still feared implicating women we knew in common.

Conversely, some women who have come out recently within
the women's or gay movements have less need or desire to conceal
their lesbianism so carefully, nor do they care to take great pains to
recognize the various clues that identify those who are closeted.
Theirs is a combination of lack of experience as well as lack of interest that sometimes leads to uncomfortable situations. Clues have
to be considered as part of the whole picture. One can never take
anything for granted. The following first-year lesbian teacher recalled incidents dating from when she first came out, which was not
long before the interview:

> When I first became a lesbian I couldn't tell who was a lesbian
> and who wasn't. I used to go to gay bars where there were a lot
> a fag-hags (these are women who want to sleep with homosex-
> ual men) and so I'd go up and ask them to dance and they'd say
> "Non, moi je ne marche pas," which means she's not a lesbian.
> I could never tell. You know, once I went to a bar and cruised a
> woman who had been doing a stage thing there, and I bought
> her a drink and found out it was a man! I went home [alone] to
> bed. I didn't go to a gay bar for so long. I said to myself, "You're
> totally lost, kid". Imagine that! I was so turned on. And I was

so angry . . . I was so shocked I left. So, I could never tell. I kept asking my lesbian friends . . . "How do you tell?"

This young woman eventually learned the signs. She emphasized that she caught on to the clues because she spent more time with lesbians socially—outside of bars and bed. She claimed she began by recognizing how lesbians dress and sit, learning how to glean information from conversations, and learning how to distinguish between basically straight women who will have sexual experiences with women from, in her words, " real lesbians." "Like, when I make love to a woman I can tell whether she is a lesbian or not." However, when questioned more closely about that particular difference, she had great difficulty elaborating.

Recognizing other lesbians is a process a woman learns only when she is aware that there are others like her out there, hiding, deflecting, and omitting. It becomes necessary for her social and/or sexual survival to distinguish clues meant to convey information and even those that are involuntary, although evident. Those generations of women who were raised when silence surrounding the topic prevailed, when the only reference to homosexuality was within the contexts of deviancy, perversion, sickness, and sin, and when lesbians read about "sexual inversion" and could not find their own experience in the descriptions—these women often went through life thinking they were the only ones in the world with such feelings. They did not necessarily look for clues in other women; they could not afford to be "discovered." Frequently, in urban centers, some learned to go to bars and to frequent the gay underworld in order to meet others like themselves. They often lived double lives, usually terrified by the consequences of being found out.[15] Others who lived in the more isolated and/or rural situations lived their needs and fantasies undisclosed, sometimes even to themselves.

This chapter has reviewed the sexual identity of all the interviewees, how they recognized their sexual preference and the process through which they came out to themselves. The chapter began by locating them; it then described the various positions they hold or held in the teaching profession; depicted their lives before coming out; explicated how each woman labeled herself and why she chose a particular term; tied self-labeling to their backgrounds, life contexts, and their realities; and discussed their particular means of recognizing other lesbians. The next chapter deals with the lesbian teacher's situation in the school system.

# 6

# *Lesbians in School*

Schools, as institutions, are part of the much larger social context of culture, politics, and the economy of this nation, Canada. Although they often reflect those factors in their internal fabric as well as in their presupposed function (knowledge dissemination), schools also reproduce some of the ideologies that dominate the policies and structure of our cultural, political, and economic life.

Although Apple and Weis have argued that cultural and economic reproduction is a complex and tentative process and that ideological hegemony "is not and cannot be fully secure,"[1] there is little doubt that the intent of state-controlled (and/or state-supported) schooling is to reproduce hegemonic ideology and to inculcate the values and precepts that conform with the needs of a capitalist mode of production. In this case, the mechanisms at work are not directly determined but are inferred subtly in hiring practices, in promoted ideals, and in popular aspirations. Schools mediate dominant ideology. They transmit it tacitly by example as well as overtly through the curriculum. Schools are seldom perceived as issuing ideology but rather as communicating practical, sensible, worthwhile values. Whether the design is fully realized or not is not the essential element because the structure is in place to reproduce the hegemonic ideology. In other words, for example, when a teacher signs a contract with a particular board of education, it is assumed that she or he will adhere to curricular requirements. In fact, the teacher is hired on the basis of certain qualifications that make her or him "suitable" for the said position. Most of those qualifications are formal and are spelled out by the Ministry of Education; they include certain degrees and certificates, fluency of language, and a proficiency in a proposed subject matter. However, there exist some tacit prerequisites, covert requirements that are almost as important and certainly frequently present in the assessment of new candidates for teaching positions. First of all, the university degree and ministry certificate restrictions limit entry into the profession on the basis of class. Even for those whose background or parents are working class, the process through which they achieve their career aims in addition to their personal aspirations to become teachers often reflects middle-class inclinations or values. More-over, such factors as gender, age, physical appearance, ethnic and religious background, and race do indeed influence the chances of a potential teacher to find and hold a job.

As I suggested in Chapter 2, teachers are hired, not only on the basis of their professional competency, but also as models of the ideological values they represent. For instance, MacDonald argues that "femininity as constructed within the school does not encourage achievement or ambition in the academic world: rather it directs the girls to external goals of good female companions to men."[2] In practice, this could mean that the women teachers who are hired would be more likely to reflect the ideology of femininity as synonymous with wife and mother than as a highly qualified professional. Their own marriage and motherhood would transmit by example specific definitions of gender, gender relations, and gender aspirations. However, there are other intersecting factors that are significant in determining how closely a woman would be expected to reflect dominant ideologies. These include whether the woman in question lives in a rural or urban setting, whether the community for whom she is teaching is conservative or liberal in its view of the world, and so on. Moreover, even if young and/or single, female teachers are often perceived (and expected) to be anticipating and planning for a matrimonial future. As such, the notion of a lesbian teacher would obviously run counter to any intended sociocultural reproduction in the school system that would perpetuate the concept of women as wives and mothers.

In the course of the everyday life of teachers there are required and expected duties outside of the classroom. These include such tasks as supervising dances (mostly in junior and high school), producing plays and musicals, coaching sports activities, organizing and attending school trips, and fulfilling other obligations that are encouraged by school administrators. Although not specified in a teacher's collective agreement, these responsibilities are perceived as an unstated but essential part of being a teacher. Moreover, these services are not only assumed to be included in the duties of classroom teachers but are often basis on which particular principals hire new candidates.

Frequently, these responsibilities are conducted after school hours or on weekends.[3] They are events that bring teachers and students together in informal settings and, as such, often allow the teachers' private lives to become more visible. Husbands and wives may show up for a play, cheer on sports activities, accompany their mate on school trips, or be invited to attend a school dance. Teachers' heterosexuality is assumed, indeed, taken for granted. Although single teachers are not likely to bring a lover to school unless they are engaged (or soon to be), classroom exchanges with students often inform and reassure the students of their teacher's sexual conformity.

A lesbian teacher is frequently in a quandary under these circumstances because, if she appears consistently alone (or single), people will often "help" her out by matchmaking, particularly if she is young or if she is perceived as "available" sexually. If she refuses yet has no obvious males in her life, she is questioned. In any case, she will usually be teased by students and colleagues about her "hidden" boyfriend or her frivolous bachelor lifestyle. Some of the interviewed women found it necessary to invent a lover, succumbing to the pressures of compulsory heterosexuality. Others danced mysteriously around the subject, implying some deep, dark romance that they were not likely to divulge. Still others preferred to hide behind a stony silence that permitted many a young student or sympathetic colleague to build an elaborate story of past disappointments, unrequited love(s), or a dead or jilting lover.

I interviewed an ex-student of one of the lesbian teachers in my study. The student was by then in graduate school and had come out to her former high school teacher. Since that teacher was in the process of granting me an interview, she enquired whether I would be interested in the student's story as well. I was. The younger woman's comments made visible one way that students construct the private lives of the single (lesbian?) teachers they admire. The teacher in question was a coach as well. The student had been part of her team.

I think the big question with most of the people on the team was why wasn't she married. We always talked about the teachers and the coaches. So, why was this attractive woman not married? And there were quite a few interesting stories going on, but none of them was because she was gay. There was one of them about that she was going out with this guy, she got dropped or something, she was so hurt that she could never go out with another!

In another case, a young teacher mentioned that her students were forever hoping that she would marry:

[They] would suggest that maybe next year I'll get married, or maybe this summer I'll meet Mr. Right. It's always said in a sense of affection, I think, because that seems to be something that they'd want to see someone that they like do.

Although most of the older teachers I interviewed preferred to keep their private life completely separate from school, one young respondent courageously took advantage of the prevailing atmosphere of tolerance created since the current women's and gay movements and saw fit to attempt to integrate both without any apparent consequences to date—but she was the only one:

I made sure that I brought [lover] around, although she was too scared to come to any staff functions with me. I made sure that if I was coaching and was at a track meet she'd come in and watch the track meet for a while and people would begin to associate me with [her]. Everybody knows that [she, lover] is a lesbian. She's older, I guess over forty now. . . . I'm sure that the man that I was working with at the time knew because he knows [lover], and he went through faculty with her and so forth. . . . But anyway, I don't really mind and nobody even mentioned it to me, so I just continued to continue.

However, when staff or students in a school are confronted with a teacher's lesbianism, the outcome is not always pleasant. One teacher whose sexual orientation became public knowledge with both students and staff because of an unfortunate incident at school found many previous extracurricular duties curtailed:

Things changed. I used to take kids to Quebec, the winter carnival or for something else, every year, and I wasn't allowed to do that anymore. I didn't get a lot of encouragement to take kids away from school [laughter]. What other things—There were a lot of things that were different. People would just watch who I was with. I had an office and it came to be very uncomfortable to go into my office with anybody, so I stopped using my office—just because people would—janitors would report to the principal sometimes.

It is precisely a fear most lesbian teachers have of being treated in the above fashion that keeps most so wary. After 1986, when sexual orientation was added to the list of "differences" protected from discrimination in the Human Rights Code of Ontario, I went back to the women I had originally interviewed and asked them if they would consider coming out at school now that they were protected by law from losing their jobs. I have documented their answers in detail elsewhere[4], but they leave no doubt that it is not fear of losing their job (which would be horrendous in itself) as much as the harassment and the loss of credibility that they would find anguishing. Finally, it is easier not to take one's mate to school-related functions such as field trips or sport activities than it is to have to explain one's relationship to this special "roommate" or "friend."

Even more uncomfortable than always appearing alone at extracurricular activities is attending staff functions without the mandatory male escort. Frequently, some women felt forced to avoid any social events with their colleagues, such as the quintessential Christmas dances, the ever-popular staff parties (which may occur several times a year), and the odd impromptu gathering at the local pub after "parents' night" or on the last day of school.

At least three women mentioned that they abhorred those social events and would not go to them even had they been heterosexual. As it was, they preferred to avoid all such gatherings that required that they show up with a "date." One particularly attractive teacher used to be asked by unattached male colleagues to those dances:

In a couple of cases I went. My refusal or acceptance in situations like these had more to do with the individual who was asking me rather than anything else. I don't—I will not go to a function just to pass. I will not accept somebody just to make it look good or make it look as if I am heterosexual, whereas in reality perhaps I'm not.

Another respondent recalled that her colleagues frequently insisted that she attend the occasional party. When she refused, as she often did, she was not challenged.

No one directly challenges and says, "Why don't you come to our party?" I went to a couple of parties. I usually tried to get them to have them on Thursday nights so I didn't have to ruin a weekend with them. . . . But no, they would never challenge me, and if I left early, they never said anything. I found people were not very direct. As a result of their not being direct, you can hide pretty well with your life.

When asked how she dealt with parties and the obligatory school socializing, one middle-aged teacher answered, "I don't do it very much anymore. I used to deal with it by getting drunk." She explained that when she taught in a northern Ontario community it was customary to meet for drinks at the local hotel and then go to parties from there. This prevented her from having to come into a gathering conspicuously single.

Another lesbian teacher pointed out that one can go to these staff gatherings only for so long alone because. "as a single person, there's not quite the sense of belonging. I've not enjoyed the occasions and I choose not to go to staff functions now simply because they are boring." Conversely, one young woman who did enjoy those social events said wistfully:

I will go [to parties] because I am like that and I will go alone and it won't bother me. I certainly won't attend them all. I would very much like to bring my girlfriend to those things, but I won't. And I can't. But I would love to.

Many of the women with whom I spoke found that they had little in common with the rest of the staff. Often there was a marked antipathy for some or most of their colleagues, but usually it expressed itself in a coolness, a distance, maybe even an avoidance of any closeness that could be threatening, at worst, or even just causing unease because of the need to hide one's private life.

I don't want to go to their parties whether I'm straight or not. I don't want to be their friend because I don't like most of them. And I don't like what they believe in. I don't like to associate with them. And the few that I do, they know about my personal life. It's terrible to say but I just couldn't—I just can't see myself seeing them every day. It would drive me crazy. I mean, forget me being lesbian, a lot of them are your typical male teacher type, believing that a woman should be home to take care of them, having babies. All that stuff drives me crazy. So I don't think that I would associate with them. That's not my kind of people.

One teacher described her relationship with her colleagues as "somewhat distant." Although she went to the staff room, she hardly even conversed with any of the staff. She also remarked that she found that her male colleagues often put pressure on her to go out with them. This was particularly uncomfortable for her when she was younger. She was perceived as single and therefore available, and in order to evade their persistent advances, she tried to remain inconspicuous by keeping silent. Another respondent had similar "problems":

> There are men on staff who, I think, view me as a bit of a challenge; in particular, men who are going through divorces, separations. I don't think it has a great deal to do with who I am as a person. I think, if anything, it is a case of being perceived as an available woman.

When questioned on how she handled these advances, she replied laughingly, "with gentle disinterest."

On the whole, most women expressed a general preference to keep to themselves, engaging rarely and then only superficially with their colleagues' social life or in what was going on in the staff room. Asked to describe her relationship with other teachers, this middle-aged woman who taught in a secondary school in a small community said:

> I would suggest that in terms of immediate day-to-day existence, I am pleasant, very easygoing, in general, quite superficial. I don't make an issue of getting involved in staff politics particularly. I regard time at school primarily as time where I get work done. I'll walk in for coffee and I'll say "Hello, how are you, chat, chat, chat" for five minutes and then I know I have a stack of papers I have to go back to. Most of the time I'm more faithful to the papers I've got to mark than sitting around exchanging views, say, at coffee break.

Even though most of the teachers with whom I spoke chose to keep to themselves, there was a general agreement amongst them that, for the most part, they were perceived as competent, efficient teachers by their peers and by the administration.

> I think they thought I was very competent in my job because I had come in having only taught one year and I was replacing somebody who had taught for many years in that position and who was very well liked in the community. It was a small town and the woman I was replacing had lived in the town and was in the midst of a rather messy divorce. . . . They thought she did a great job, so that was a difficult position to fill. I did a good job, so people respected me on that level. They had to. They saw that I was competent in my job.

Another teacher, who taught in a different part of Ontario but in a small community as well, reiterated that she kept a habitual distance from her colleagues, and maintained that dealings between her and them were "distant and cool. Very cool. I have *very* little to do with them except the immediate teachers in my department, but I think that there's mutual respect." She went on to say that she was not quite sure how the rest of the staff perceived her.

> I think I intimidate some of the other staff members. I think they have a feeling of interest that they would like to get to know me but they don't know how to approach me, and I don't encourage them to do so. I spend no time in the staff room whatsoever. When I meet teachers in the cafeteria, there's the usual exchange of small talk. . . . I use my time at school to work. I'm not particularly interested in the kind of conversation that goes on in the staff room. I don't think I have a great deal in common with many of the teachers with whom I teach.

Asked how this distance she maintained affected her everyday life with her colleagues, she admitted the following:

> There are offhand remarks or jokes about the fact that it was three years since I was last seen in the staff room; or, if I happen to walk into the staff room looking for a particular teacher, there's a general "what are you doing here?" but nothing that goes deeper than that.

Another teacher, somewhat older, who taught in a large secondary school, also felt that her colleagues perceived her as withdrawn but that they definitely saw her as hardworking and competent. She added that they might also view her as "a pushy female."

Lesbian teachers frequently assume a certain distance from the rest of the staff mostly as a protection against undue curiosity but also because many suspect that their colleagues would not be particularly tolerant of their sexual preference should it become known.

> I would not want the staff to know. . . . Our staff, although they are progressive, they can say things—like at one point they did not want to hire a woman because she was pregnant and she would have to put her kid into daycare, and they were not sure she should do that. They come up with some very unprogressive statements.

Since most of the women I interviewed preferred to keep their colleagues in the dark regarding their private life, they were very often careful about their behavior, wary that they not let slip any clues that might give them away.

One young woman who taught in a small rural community in southern Ontario felt she had to take particular precautions because she was in a relationship with another woman on the staff and they were both very conscious of the bond that may have been apparent to their colleagues. Both women felt like outsiders, although for different reasons. Hiding their respective private lives became more complicated "because it is easier to hide when you are on the outside by yourself, but when there is an alliance between two people, you get a bit worried that it shows and then people might wonder." I asked, "What do you think might make your situation obvious to your colleagues?"

> Well, sometimes, just the physical fact that we came to school together. We didn't live in the same town. So that was a little odd. Or sometimes we would go out to dinner if there was going to be a parents' night. We would go out to dinner together and then come back together. Now, there's nothing really odd about that, but when you are conscious about what you are doing, then you think, "Oh, people are going to notice this"—like why are they together? . . . [Also], in staff meetings when you would argue about something, there were two of us and you tend more to argue because you know somebody is on your side. But also, it makes you stand out more. So, in that way

"Oh, those two. . . ." Now, I don't think it would have ever occurred to them that we were lovers. In fact, I don't think it was
part of their vocabulary. I really don't. But, you wonder.

Clues may inadvertently be communicated in the normal
course of a conversation, the text of which may be innocent, but
which, given the circumstances, may be significant because of the
wider context. For instance, a young single woman who is engaged
to be married may choose to live with another woman in order to
save money for her impending matrimonial life. The same arrangement may be suspicious when the two women are in their forties,
have been living together for a while, or buy a house together—although, in this day and age, when mainstream media have made
lesbians and gay men much more visible,[5] any two women or two
men living together would arouse suspicion. When confronted by
her colleagues about some real estate she owned jointly with another teacher, one middle-aged woman I interviewed mentioned to
them that it was cheaper paying half the mortgage, although she
knew she really had not answered why she chose to buy a house in
the first place and how she could feel secure in her investment when
there was, presumably, a possibility that one of them would leave to
get married. Another woman, younger and more aggressive, was
aware that claiming to save money can be construed by some as a
weak excuse: "Let's say I did live with somebody, perhaps I would
say that I have a roommate. Eventually it would look stupid
though. You are making a lot of money, you don't need to have a
roommate." This next lesbian teacher summarized the dilemma,
giving a good example of the fine line one needs to tread when
speaking of even the most common events in one's private life.

I couldn't talk about my relationship the way they would talk
about their husband or their wife. Funny things that might
have happened in certain contexts, would be perfectly normal
in a staff room situation, but you couldn't talk about them if
these occurred between you and [another] woman. . . . [For in-
stance], if I'm walking on the beach or somewhere like that
late at night, you know, I couldn't say, "last night I was with so
and so on the beach at eleven o'clock and this happened and
such and so . . ." because they would say, "What are you doing
there at eleven o'clock?" I'm supposed to be at home in their
minds. Oh, and another interesting thing—she [lover] lived

not far from the Board Office, and in bad weather I'd stay there. I would not bother going home. Of course, I didn't want anybody knowing that I was staying with her instead of going home, you know, that I had a key, that I could just walk in the door, and so forth. So it became quite funny because there was another colleague of mine who lived further away from this person but still closer to the Board than my home and I often would stay there in previous years when the weather was bad. So, as soon as there was ice and snow, she would remind me that I could always come by. And it would be much worse than [the previous times] I would normally have stayed with her, and I'd say "Oh, it's all right, I'll be alright," or this sort of thing—not wanting to say, "Well, I'm going to sleep at so and so's house." That created a problem. I couldn't say where I was.

The most innocuous events in the everyday life of a woman seem to take on a major significance when she knows that she is a lesbian, that she must not give any indication of that fact unless the circumstances are perfectly safe and the woman in question is in relative control of the situation. A young respondent described an unexpected incident in the staff room that she found astonishingly threatening given how ordinary it would have been within any other context:

There was a column that Joanne Kates used to write in the *Globe and Mail*. I used to read it. It was every Wednesday. It was one of the highlights of my week—which shows how pitiful the teaching week was! I used to go to the staff room because we got the *Globe and Mail* . . . and I would look at what Joanne was writing every week. One week I opened the *Globe and Mail* and it was about *The Body Politic*[6] [a now defunct gay paper] trial. I remember it was in the morning and there were other people at the table. I opened it up and it was about *The Body Politic*—and I wanted to just close it and run out of the room. I didn't know what to do, because I'd made a big thing "Oh, what is Joanne doing—," you know, because that was one of the few public things I ever did, was to read Joanne Kates every week. . . . I mean, of course I wanted to read it right away to see what she had to say. But I also didn't want anyone to know what I was reading about and interested in. Like, They Would Know! [But] nobody picked up on it because people

basically left me alone. I quickly sort of skimmed it and
turned the page, read a few other things, made myself some
coffee and left.

Women mentioned meeting a lover at a restaurant rather than going with her so as not to be seen arriving together. One woman
found herself deliberately misleading a colleague she described as
"nosy." And when she was cornered by direct questions, she lied.
    However, some women found their colleagues more tolerant.
One teacher who had an administrative position in the office of a
large urban board was sure that her secretary had guessed

> because my lover and I talk to each other every day on the
> phone and she [the secretary] will say things to me like "how's
> [lover]? How are you two doing?" If she knows, she knows, if
> she doesn't, she doesn't. I don't know. She's never said any-
> thing to me, but she always asks about my lover. I guess I don't
> feel those things because I'm not in a position to hurt anybody.
> I don't deal with kids per se.

Her not being in the classroom may or may not have been relevant
to why her secretary showed some understanding under the circumstances, although other women's positive experience with some of
their colleagues lends credence to two teachers' view that it really
depends on the individual.

> Some of my colleagues I told—the close ones to me. The others,
> there was some talk. However, I never lost a friend, never lost
> anything by telling people.

> I think I taught at a kind of extraordinary school. People
> would disapprove, but they would not be obnoxious about it.

In fact, one young woman who inadvertently came out to her colleagues found eventual acceptance of her sexual orientation. They
managed to tease her and joke about her life openly:

> Colleagues are so normal now [that they know]. They are not
> unpleasant. There's a sort of acknowledgment that I'm a les-
> bian. The most common example [of double entendre jokes]
> plays on the word *straight*. I'll mention that my work is a mess

or that my office is disorganized and a staff member will say, "Well, you never could get anything straight anyway" and then they'll smile at me or I'll react to that.

What about how lesbian teachers coped with students in general within the bounds of the school itself, including the various ways the women I interviewed found to deal with the dilemma of concealing their private lives, protecting their job security, and, at the same time, attempting to present themselves as competent, warm, efficient teachers? It might be easier to avoid persistent questions by colleagues than to be confronted with the direct curiosity many young students have about their teacher. The majority of the women I interviewed explained that they attempted to keep students consistently at arm's length, avoiding any personal contact, evading situations that could inadvertently give away clues.

Children are often very inquisitive regarding their teacher's life outside the school. In small communities, where youngsters are likely to meet their teacher shopping at the local supermarket, strolling downtown on a given Saturday, or joining mothers or wives in a typically small town social event, there is little that can remain hidden. A teacher friend of mine remarked that it is very difficult or almost impossible to separate one's private life from one's public life when one lives in a village or a small town.[7] This factor may play an integrative role in making new teachers become part of the community, but much hinges, usually, on the assumed heterosexuality of the teacher in question. Married teachers' lives are perceived as so "normal" that they become totally unremarkable to their neighbors and to the local citizens. Single teachers, however, have a harder time protecting their privacy in a rural setting, and, straight or gay, may often prefer to live in a different nearby town or city if they can do so conveniently. For this reason, a number of the women I interviewed preferred to live far from the community in which they taught, needing to shield their lives from their questioning students. Many expressed their aversion to meeting their pupils outside the school.

Whereas some teachers are able to control where they will live, whether they are likely to run into their students downtown, or if they choose to meet with some of their pupils in social situations outside school hours, almost all the women I interviewed, particularly those not in administrative positions, had to deal with their students' curiosity on a day-to-day basis in the classroom. Many adopted a protective distance, a coolness, a reserve that did not encourage many students to feel at ease being personal. Asked how they thought they were perceived by their pupils, a number who taught in the secondary sector felt they came across as strict yet competent. The following are several examples taken from teachers who varied in age as well as teaching circumstances:

> Well, they know that I'm rather tough (like my nickname is Sarge), but I think they recognize that I'm fair. I think they know that I'm human. . . . I've always had a relatively good relationship with my students. (Small town. Age fifty-five.)

> I think I have a reputation for being strict, firm, in the way that I evaluate students, no-nonsense type teacher. I think students come into my class with a certain trepidation and find themselves surprised to find a human being there who has feelings and is not nearly as terrifying as her reputation leads them to believe. (Rural school. Age thirty-two.)

> I think I have a certain control in class which I think keeps students at somewhat of a distance but not an uncomfortable one. I don't think—no, as a general rule, I am not particularly close to students, although I recognize when students like me. I just don't encourage closeness particularly. (Small urban school. Age forty-three.)

> Well, there are certain cut-off points that I don't pursue. Like I said, I've got barriers that are rather firmly established. I have students who will say, "Oh, come on, where do you live?" It'll come out in a general discussion about something or other in class. "Which car is yours in the parking lot?" So I point it out. . . . But very little pursuits from the students during the year. (Very small town school. Age forty-one.)

> In the majority of cases, I would say that I have a good rapport in a give-and-take, day-to-day exchange. But it is also very surface. . . . I will chat with anybody anytime at school on school projects or programs, no problem whatsoever, but it is strictly that, give and take for the issue of the moment. I've had maybe one confidence within the past year. I don't have a very heavy track record on confidences. (Small town. Age forty-one.)

One older woman tried to explain why she kept her distance, believing that it had to do more with age, position, and relative maturity than with her attempt to conceal her private life. For this teacher, it was important to maintain a good rapport with her students, yet at the same time, she had to make sure to keep her distance for fear of revealing her sexual preference. This woman preferred to refer to herself as celibate despite several relationships with women. Her argument for maintaining distance from students reflects her thinking:

> It's a case of position in life's hierarchy, if you want to put it that way. A student is a student, a teacher is a teacher, and there is a distinct line between the two. A very young person does not know where that line is drawn particularly. We have to teach them that. If in my private life with my students I had permitted them liberties in the sense of the way they could talk to me or the way they could act around me, I couldn't expect to bring them back to the student/teacher line in the classroom. So therefore, at all times when you're dealing with students, whether in the classroom or whether in your own home, you must keep that barrier apparent to them. . . . You have to maintain a position, or I think they'd have contempt for you. There's no way that a mature adult can behave like a teenager and have the teenager think that the adult is mature . . . ; they must not step over that barrier and try and be in my world, and I must not step over that barrier and be in their world. An example of that is that none of my students have ever been permitted to call me by my first name until they have graduated. I am Miss "X" and that's it. And I expect it to be that way.

What students call a teacher often reflects the relationship established between teacher and student. Some teachers preferred to be addressed in a more formal way; others did not mind being called called by their first names. The choice depended on such factors as age, position, school/board policy, teacher self-confidence, experience, style of teaching, and so on. However, this small matter of a teacher's name during school hours may take on a different connotation if a woman is known to be a lesbian. For instance:

> They always ribbed me about it. Like one teacher in particular would say, "Somebody came looking for you," and I would say

"Yea? and he would say, "Yes, one young woman. Must be one of your *intimates*," and I'd say "What?" and he'd say, "Well, she called you by your first name."

Some interviewees felt that too much reticence on the part of a teacher could antagonize the students. Apart from breaking the rapport that should exist in the classroom, it could stimulate teenagers who are on the defensive to make life very uncomfortable for a teacher. One young woman I interviewed found this out when her excessive reticence prompted students to make unfriendly remarks when they passed her in the hallways of the school. This, in turn, made her withdraw even more:

I think at the time I tended to withdraw and really develop a kind of hard shell. I did my job in a very businesslike fashion. I feel I was much more cold, lacked the kind of warmth I feel is now happening quite naturally [as I learn to open up] and which has made teaching far, far more enjoyable for me. . . . I'm not sure whether that was a conscious choice on my part to try to offset that sort of thing, I think I just withdraw and then it was a case of the situation being so dissatisfying for me. I was not an effective teacher. I was not happy with my day-to-day routine. I think it was simply a case of making the situation better for me and the way to do it was to be simply more open and more revealing of myself as a person. It's had the effect that students like and admire me. Some don't. I'm not suggesting that it's a unanimous vote, but the majority of students, I can honestly say, respect me.

How much real danger of discovery is probable is not clear. Most teachers seemed to feel that even if some of the students could be tolerant because they might like or admire the individual teacher, public knowledge of their sexual preference would, in the long run, undermine the authority, the image, and the legitimacy of the teacher in the classroom. Many teachers (eight) felt that the teenagers they taught were self-centered and cared little for anything outside of their own private world. One teacher, at least, was inclined to believe that her students did not perceive her as lesbian,

not because of anything that I have done or said, or not done or said, but because of the fact that heterosexist bias is inherent in people. They will not see. I mean, anybody who looked at me now with an objective eye, my colleagues or my students, should at least have suspicions, if not make outright conclusions. But they don't. And they don't, not because I'm particularly feminine or because I talk about men—which I don't—but because they just don't see lesbians. They don't conceive them, they don't see them, it's not part of their experience. As far as people are concerned, lesbians probably don't exist.

Teaching teenagers is a different experience from teaching in elementary school. For secondary students, teachers have lost their mystique. They are perceived as human, often are forgiven their quirks, and sometimes are harassed in the typically subversive ways youths behave when they lose their respect for an individual teacher. Conversely, very young pupils are more likely to idolize their teacher, rarely question the reacher's authority and/or knowledge, and frequently respect a teacher's privacy since they are seldom aware that teachers have a life outside the school.

I teach grade one and grade two. I wasn't distant with them. I was quite close to them. But you don't talk very much about your personal life. And to kids that young, they are very open, so anything about you is not weird. The fact that you are not married, that didn't seem weird to them. I think probably because of the way I relate to kids, I think they would have accepted anything about me.

Another elementary school teacher (and a mother herself) discussed how younger pupils often attempt to gain their teacher's affection: "Certainly I've had little girls who wanted to be teacher's pet, they want to come in early and do things for you, and you know that you are sort of their idol. That's a crush of a young child." This type of attention exists in older children, but the quality and intensity of the "crush" varies according to the needs of the child. Often teenage girls will identify with, idolize, or "hero-worship" a particular teacher. This is in no way restricted to those youngsters who will eventually recognize themselves as lesbian, but seems to be a phenomenon that is, if not universal, at least quite prevalent in women's developing years. Many heterosexual women remember vivid "crushes" on special teachers or other adults, and, conversely, some lesbians do not recall ever having had a "crush" on an older woman.

Women teachers learn to deal with these "crushes" almost as part of their teaching responsibilities. Some popular teachers experience them more often than others; however, most women teachers will remember at least one incident in their career when a young secondary school girl followed them around, sent them anonymous notes, rang and hung up their telephone, or became blushingly inarticulate when addressed by them.

Schoolgirl "crushes" were documented in the social scientific discourse even before the women's and gay movements legitimized the experience by recording and examining its universality and its significance. Traditional pedagogical discourse acknowledged the existence of schoolgirl "crushes" and saw these as part of "normal" female development. What was often appended to such statements was that the objects of affection might themselves be homosexual and, as such, could influence the young teenager. This was often perceived as one of the "causes" of homosexuality. In addition, the "crush" itself was classically described as a "stage," and, on the rare occasions when it expressed itself physically, was seen as a period of time when a girl would be "experimenting" and readying herself for the "real thing," that is, intercourse with men.[8]

The teachers I interviewed had their fair share of student admirers. In the usual course of events this poses no problem since many teachers experience being a favorite of some teenager. Most young girls are very circumspect in their adoration, ostensibly because they would be teased mercilessly by their peers if their crush became public knowledge and also because, if they were suspected of being lesbian, those young women would certainly face harassment from their peers. However, from the point of view of a lesbian teacher, these crushes may be problematic for several reasons: (a) they may call attention to a whole area that often remains unacknowledged in the school context, namely, youth homosexuality;[9] (b) the youngster can become increasingly inquisitive about the teacher's private life; (c) the adolescent's expressions of attention are often inappropriate and may put the teacher in a vulnerable situation where the latter may be perceived as encouraging the devotion; and (d) some students are so emotionally involved that they project their feelings onto the teacher and publicize these without any concern for the consequences.

Not all the women I interviewed dealt with crushes the same way. Some felt that such admiration could be put to constructive pedagogical uses; others chose to ignore or avoid the youngsters in question. One previously married teacher felt that she was better able to handle those crushes precisely because she was a lesbian. If she had been unaware of her own lesbianism, "who knows what could have happened?" The following are a variety of responses to the issue, examples from the experiences of several teachers:

It's very flattering when it happens. There is no question that there is a very strong temptation to seek it out—not to create the relationship—but when you realize that it is happening, to foster it in some way. However, you must understand. I have very, very strong feelings about my responsibilities toward my students and a very, very clear line about the fact that I am an adult. I'm a teacher. . . . I see my job and my private life as separate and distinct.

When I was younger it [crushes] made me uncomfortable. I tended to push them [students with crushes] aside a little bit and try to ignore them as much as possible. When I got older, I just accepted the fact that this was a phase they were going through and I could handle it.

I used to have a private office in the gym and I had this kid who followed me around all the time. She used to clean and dust my office, she used to bring me unasked-for coffee—a real pain in the ass! That was my worst case because she was just a pest.

To be quite honest with you, it depends on the kid. There was one girl two years ago who developed an outrageous attraction to me and I just would have nothing to do with her. She just scared the life out of me. . . . I didn't like her particularly. I found her the kind of person who is overwhelming in her singlemindedness. There are other kids who develop crushes on you who are shy. I mean, they have a sense of proportion.

Those four different teachers all work in the secondary sector, and all but one teach in rural large schools.
    The next four interviewees described how they dealt with specific incidents of crushes. Their accounts are anecdotal and capture the predicament clearly.

I remember when I was teaching grades seven and eight there was a girl who used to write me love notes morning, noon, and night and I was really paranoid. I thought, oh my God, what do you do with somebody like that? Do you talk to them? Do you ignore them? I talked to her. I said: "Why do you send me all those notes?" She said: "I really care about you. I am confused." I said: "It's normal; I used to care about my teachers in grades

seven and eight." She was fine, I think she was just lonely, depressed, and confused.

This same teacher was adamant about her responsibilities toward
her students, adding that if she were superintendent and she ever
came across a teacher who was involved with a student she would
unequivocally fire him or her. The next teacher believed that her
lesbianism did not infringe upon her life at school. Since she lived
with her husband, no one suspected her sexual preference. However,
one very insistent young student did finally learn the truth:

> I remember [student], bless her heart. She was one girl who
> stayed in love with me for far too long a time and pursued me.
> She was a very bright girl who grew up to be a microbiologist.
> I managed to stall her, but finally, when she was twenty-two, I
> told her. I had stalled her [by telling her] I'm happily married.
> I was nice to her and I gave her a lot to do. And then, when she
> was twenty-two and she kept coming after me, I said, "There's
> something I'd better tell you. . . ."

A much younger teacher who teaches in a junior high school recalled a close call:

> One young girl I once had was madly in love with me—she still
> is, she's graduated now but. . . . By the time she got to grade
> nine, she began this sort of teasing of me. She would go skip-
> ping down the halls at the top of her lungs and say, "Miss X is
> gay, Miss X is a lesbian, Miss X is gay!" Cute, eh! I at first dealt
> with it by confronting the whole group of them. I would say,
> "Boy, you people use that word a lot, don't you? Do you know
> what it means?" And they'd say, "It's happy," or "You know."
> And I'd say, "Do you know any other meaning of the word?"
> They would giggle and titter and I'd say, "Yea, I do think you
> know another meaning of the word and it's a very unusual
> thing to want to broadcast about another person." I would just
> leave it at that. So, anyway, good old [student] kept it up. So I
> took her aside one day in my office and I said, "Why are you
> doing this to me? Why are you saying this about me? Do you
> believe it?" And she said, "no, no, of course not. I don't know
> why I'm doing it." So I asked her, "Well, are you teasing me?"
> and she said, "Yea." I said to her, "Well, it's a very dangerous

thing to say about someone, particularly a teacher. I could lose
my job if that kind of rumor got started, and I would appreciate if it stopped." She melted into tears and she never did
it again.

The fourth teacher remembered an incident a few years back that
also could have had dire consequences had she not dealt with it the
way she did:

I had a student who had been in my class the previous year
and who didn't come around in the traditional way looking for
attention, but always wanted to do things perfectly in class in
order to gain my approval. The year after I taught her, I had
occasion to receive a 'phone call from her. Her mother had died.
She had found the body and she was obviously upset. At the
point at which she called me, she was staying with her sister
and brother-in-law who lived up the street from where she and
her mother lived. My first reaction was to offer to go and see
her. She seemed very receptive to that. So I went and picked
her up and we just simply drove around and she told me what
had happened. She talked about her mother. She talked to
some degree about her feeling foolish about 'phoning me; however, I was the first person apparently that she thought of and
gradually, as she calmed down, she seemed to center in more
on why she had called me and the talk shifted a bit to her and
me as opposed to her mother. [Eventually], I took her back to
her house after she had calmed down and just before she was
to leave the car, she asked me if I would hug her. Well, needless
to say, that just about freaked me out and I said "no," that I
wasn't about to act as a second mother to her, but if she ever
needed me, she knew I was available, but no, that I would not
hug her. At which point she left. She called me after that just
to let me know how things were and at school; we didn't talk
other than for me to enquire how things were with her.

As it turned out, this incident had a sequel in that the teacher
met one of the school counselors three weeks later in the hallway
and asked her advice about the above incident. The teacher was re-
morseful that she had felt she could not grant the youngster's re-
quest. She wanted to know if the guidance teacher, an older,
grandmotherly, warm person, would have acted differently.

At that time, the guidance teacher told me that this young woman had been in to see her two or three times and had expressed to her—I don't know what you might call it—an affection for, or an attrac . . . not a physical attraction, but some kind of bond between her and me. She expressed those problems relative to her mother and how she saw in me things that she didn't see in her mother. The conversation was pretty well left at that but it made me feel a little bit easier in that someone else knew what had happened or what hadn't happened—whatever way you want to look at it.

In the same conversation, the counselor told the teacher that the student had asked her whether "Miss X would mind if I asked her for a hug." The counselor had discouraged the student and left it at that. The question was put to the counselor at least three weeks before the mother's death.

Not all the teachers I interviewed experienced these crushes, however. One woman remembered her own schoolgirl bouts of "passion" and offered these as an explanation for not ever noticing if she was the object of a girl's special attention:

I don't know how good I would be at recognizing it, knowing my own behavior as a high school student when I was having a mad crush and the kind of tremendously complicated evasions that one would think up to avoid being found out. I mean, that was the object of the game—is to have this mad crush and not be found out—if you're found out, then you've made this terrible gaffe. And I suspect that that's the way it still is. So, anyone who would have a tremendous crush on me would also, it seems to me, go through tremendous evasive tactics to avoid being found out.

If crushes present a potential problem for lesbian teachers, gay or lesbian students may pose more of a threat.[10] These students could still be in school, but are also likely to be frequenting the same bars, attending the same events, and congregating in the same areas as the teachers. This is much more likely to happen in large urban centers, where there is a more visible gay community (such as bars, "gay ghettos," political rallies, workshops, lectures, conferences, restaurants, and so on), than in rural areas or small towns, where a lesbian is likely to lead a more sheltered existence. Even then, at least one rural lesbian teacher, who taught in a French school, expressed the need to avoid bars in Ottawa for fear of running into her graduated students (likely to be enrolled in the bilingual universities of that city).

Most of the teachers I interviewed who knew of gay or lesbian students became aware of them when the student in question sought the teacher out for advice or confirmation. This in itself—namely, the recognition (or suspicion) by the student of a lesbian teacher—could be perceived as threatening. Often, however, students who are gay or lesbian themselves are sensitive to the plight of the teacher.[11] This is not always true, unfortunately, as is attested by the experience of one respondent. Her coming out to one student proved akin to a public statement. The student talked indiscriminately, boasting about her knowledge to others, and consequently jeopardized that teacher's career. Her full story will be presented in a later chapter.

However, the majority of the accounts recorded dealt with students who just needed to talk. Even that level of support seems to put pressure on lesbian teachers, particularly since it not only singled them out but also put them in a position of being potentially liable to the charge of proselytizing to a minor if their advice were ever to become public. This fear kept most of the women I interviewed wary when confronted with possibly lesbian or gay students.

Not only did the following teacher initially find herself the object of a student's attention, but as the youngster began to mature sexually and realize the implications of her feelings, she approached her ex-teacher with questions about being "gay" and how to deal with the rumors spread by peers who suspected.

> She's, I guess, fifteen. What she's finding of course, is that there is a million rumors flying around her, so that's also hard for her. And, you know, when she comes in in tears about these rumors and so forth, I tell her basically that it's nobody's business but your own, if you want to find someone to talk to you about it you can do that, you can go to your school and talk to your guidance counselor and if you are not happy with that, then you can find someone else. I know she wants to talk to me about it but to date I have not allowed that. I've given her support and sympathize with her about the rumors and how it feels, but I said in time everything is going to sort itself out. I hope the guidance counselors are looking at this.

Another teacher had a similar experience but in a high school setting. The student had come to this physical education teacher because she wanted a program to reduce her weight through weight lifting, exercise, counting calories, and so on. As the weeks passed, the diet was progressing well, but the student was becoming more depressed and sought out the teacher for advice.

> So she came with one of her friends to the office and after much hemming and hawing she finally admitted that she was different. Actually, I told her she was different because we didn't have all night to check all the problems of the world, after having done pregnancy, losing a boyfriend, being thrown out. Anyway, it came out. So, again, I told her it's no big deal. I went through the same spiel, sexual preference can be different, don't do any harm to anybody, and the whole bit. But it did not help her because she would have needed honest help and I couldn't give it to her because I couldn't admit that I knew something about it.

Pushed to elaborate on that last remark, the teacher continued:

> I talked more than I'm telling you here but couldn't—to help her really she would have had to know to whom she was talking. I mean really. Like, I would have had to be more open. I couldn't ask her questions—I'm not supposed to know about it really. The kid asked me, she said, "How come you don't think I'm wrong or queer?" Again, to use the word she used—and she's French but she used it in English—*queer*. So, I said, "I have very good friends who happen to have this different preference and I think they're nice people. I like them all, this is why I don't think you're bad, or whatever." So she thought that was great. It's not the same thing as saying "Hey, you know. . . ." Well, I couldn't talk. That's bad.

Lesbian teachers do not often feel they can afford to take these confidences lightly. One of the women told of a rift created between herself and a younger couple (both of whom were lesbian teachers as well). An ex-student (twenty-four years of age) of hers came out to her and asked her what it was like to be a lesbian and a professional in a small town. Since the older teacher was almost at the age of retirement, had been very closeted, and had preferred to be perceived as celibate, she gave the ex-student the names of her two friends—the aforementioned couple, neither of whom had taught the student. By giving the names of the two young teachers to her ex-student without their stated permission, the older teacher had, in effect, informed her ex-student of their sexual orientation. Unfortunately, since the older teacher had not bothered to ask to use their names, the two younger teachers took great offense. This incident alone created an irrevocable split in their friendship, even now, almost fifteen years later.

Ex-students are not considered "safe" by some teachers even when they have been gone from school for several years. This next woman was torn between giving support and protecting her own privacy since she lived in a small village:

> I went shopping in [nearby town]. I met her quite by accident at one point. We chatted a few minutes. Everything was fine. I went on to do some shopping and about five minutes later, we met again—this time "could you happen to have a few minutes to have coffee?" "Oh, right, OK, I can do that." After I finished shopping, we met, had coffee. I get the story of her life from the time she left school, her first question, one of her first questions, being "Did you realize in high school that I was a lesbian?" I looked at her and said, "No, There's a great deal about students' lives and attitudes that teachers in general don't know." "I've just been dishonorably discharged from the army because I've provoked the investigation into my lifestyle and. . . ." I was sitting there listening to her total case of harassment by the army once she had declared herself, and wanting to know with whom, and when, and what have you. So, I sympathized, but I made no declaration. Then I saw her again later in [home village] when I was shopping. "Could you come for coffee?" This time I proved a total coward and said "Oh, gee, no, I can't." Now, I sat back. This particular ex-student—and I'm talking ex-student—must be about twenty-six or twenty-seven now; this is not last year's student. But the immediate cowardice is a total defense. The next time I saw her I thought if I saw her again, maybe I should have coffee, enough of this guilt routine. Next time I saw her, she was waiting for her friend. She had met somebody. I haven't seen her since.

Two staunch feminist lesbian teachers I interviewed, both of whom worked in large urban centers that supported alternative schools, had very different stories to tell. Both spoke of the prevalence of lesbian and gay students in their respective schools, and both acknowledged that the strong gay presence led to some form of backlash. The two women did not work in the same school or in the same city.

One year was a very good year. There were five lesbian students. And that's quite a bit because we only have around two hundred students. So that's quite a few to have out. They didn't know each other. The first one I realized was lesbian [because I met her at a local lesbian bar]. It was cute. I was dancing with my lover when this other woman—well, we saw her and she saw us. She was mortified. I mean, she was one of my students and it never occurred to her that I was dancing there with another woman. . . . It never occurred to her that there was a reason why I was doing that. It only occurred to her that she was terribly embarrassed that she was in a lesbian bar and was seen by her teacher. That was funny. That helped me to know that she was a lesbian. And after I knew her [others came out to me]. . . . Then one of them, the one I had met in the bar, became president of the student council; then some of the others got heavily involved too. So, for one year there, we pretty well had a lesbian student council. . . . Things seemed to have a different tone that year. Everyone was pretty tolerant, the parents . . . We tried to organize some things in the school with the gay community coming in the school to talk but [we] got a terrifically bad backlash from the Board of Education, who didn't allow members of the gay community to come to the school to speak.

One student, when we were talking, ended up by saying that she had a secret. It just sounded to me that it had to do with sex. I would just ask questions that would help her clarify what it is that she wanted to talk about. One student had a crush on me and when it got beyond having a crush on me it was she thinks she might be a lesbian. Another student would just tell me about her history. You know. I have a tendency to talk to my students and, at that time, I was putting a lot of energy into my students—more so than I am now, and people just talked to me and opened up and it came up that they were lesbian. A lot of students were not sure that they were lesbian, but they thought they might be. I was really good to them in terms of telling them that they did not have to make a decision, it was just fine, suggesting places that they might go for

some help, and making it safe for them. At this time, one student had this problem with other students calling her something—dyke—that whole thing went through the school.
[There was] an antigay backlash that was going through the
school. We have general meetings and I got up at a general
meeting and talked about the school being a place where we
worked to fight against racism, sexism, and heterosexism and
how we fought against prejudice against gay people. Other students started talking after that. People became very excited
about that. It sort of quieted the backlash.

On the one hand, the first teacher was out at her school and could
give direct support to her students by being honest about her own
life. There was no ambiguity as to where she stood on issues. Her
involvement with and encouragement of the lesbian students' active
stand in the politics of the school earned her the ire but also the
respect of many of her colleagues and other students. On the other
hand, the second teacher was out as a feminist but not as a lesbian.
Despite that, she was often attacked as a "manhater," as being unfair to the male students in her class, as choosing to teach only
about women writers and women's issues, all accusations she felt
were grossly exaggerated and ultimately untrue. However, even her
colleagues who supported her point of view did not come to her defense in the general meeting.

It is difficult to assess how students and colleagues would react in a given time and at a given place to a particular teacher's homosexuality. Notwithstanding some very positive experiences by a
few teachers I interviewed who were out in the school or even to one
or two of their colleagues or students, it must be remembered that
the publicly supported school system here in Ontario (for example)
is considered *in loco parentis,* acting in lieu of the parents, who are
presumed to be heterosexual, heading a nuclear family, and adhering in other ways to the hegemonic ideology. A gay or lesbian
teacher, by definition, stands as a contradiction to the concept of *in
loco parentis* since it is always assumed that homosexuality precludes parenting. In addition, the notion of the lesbian or gay
teacher is potentially subversive in that she or he would always be
suspected of attempting to recruit or convert youngsters to a homosexual way of life and/or politics. Of course, it is true that the presence of gay and lesbian teachers in a school may influence in some
way the hidden curriculum, even if they may be helpless in changing the manifest curriculum. What teachers use as examples, the

refusal to accept heterosexist assumptions, remarks, or jokes, the material used in the classroom, and so on, are all important in conveying values. However, the only reason that that in itself could be construed as subversive is that dominant ideologies are usually perceived by those in a position to enforce them as the only legitimate ones, and any deviations from normative beliefs are interpreted as undermining those beliefs. Coming out as radically feminist or socialist may have adverse effects on the career of a particular teacher, although not quite as dramatically as if the teacher came out as gay or lesbian.

# Implications of Coming Out in the Classroom

Nowhere in the school system do teachers and students interact in a more concerted and intensive way than in the classroom situation. Although a teaching period is considered structured time, and therefore an opportunity for teachers to practice their pedagogical skills, it is also the circumstances during which both teachers and students reveal most about themselves as individuals. "For all the research and talk about schools, getting people to learn remains something of a mystery. It is certainly an extraordinarily complex business, an interplay of intellectual, emotional, and social processes so intricate that it virtually defies analysis."[1] R. W. Connell certainly captures the different tensions that constitute the teaching process. Whether in elementary school or in the secondary sector, some of the structured teaching period is spent on other than the responsibilities prescribed by the curriculum. Each teacher has her or his individual methods of teaching, of reaching the students, of creating a rapport that permits some learning to occur. Without the emotional and therefore personal content almost inherently present in the style of each teacher, without the relationships created between a teacher and her or his students, the formal part of the lesson could not exist. Connell explains the ways these connections constitute an intrinsic reality in the work of a teacher: "In a real sense these emotional relationships *are* her [the teacher's] work, and managing them is a large part of her labor process. Keeping order, and getting the kids to learn, both require operating on the emotions of the kids through the emotions of the teacher."[2]

Informal moments in the classroom emerge quite regularly. With younger children these are more prevalent but often not as deeply personal. With older elementary pupils, as well as with those in the secondary system, questions may arise that stem from general discussions pertaining to the topic at hand. Whereas young children are more likely to take a teacher's private life for granted, older students are generally very inquisitive and frequently use any opportunity to enquire directly about the various aspects of their favorite teacher's lifestyle.

> They ask me, am I engaged? Do I have a boyfriend? And so forth. And I tell them the truth! No, I am not engaged. Do I have a boyfriend? No, I don't have a boyfriend but I do see men, you know. I have friends who are men, or friends who are boys. At graduation and stuff like that when they want me to come, I always arrange to bring someone. In a way, I suppose, I project a different image.

For lesbian teachers, unexpected questions in the class situation may prove uncomfortable. Students do not necessarily mean to embarrass a teacher, but they are often curious as to why a young, attractive woman is unattached, or how a particular young teacher spends her weekends. Older teachers may be encouraged to reminisce, to explain certain unanswered issues about their personal life, or even just to talk so that the lesson is wasted and the students do not have to work.

Questions and answers are elements constituted in the dynamics of what normally goes on in a classroom. Some teachers may even become known to students by their favorite topics. As a guidance counselor in a secondary school, I often used to hear students mention fondly a particular male teacher who would entertain his class with World War II anecdotes, while another described endlessly his wine-making techniques and experiments. Teachers, as well as students, enjoy the relief of a few moments of personal exchanges, and frequently may choose to share quite intimate details with each other. Individual teachers pride themselves on how much they know about students, and students often boast about their information concerning teachers.

Given the relative prevalence of such exchanges, they are treated as inevitable by most teachers, who in turn learn how to deal with questions according to their personal style. Some cut them short, others avoid them, and a number view them as means of reaching students or of establishing classroom rapport. Most of the lesbian teachers I interviewed perceived enquiries into their personal lives as one more hurdle to overcome in an attempt to protect their sexual identity. For those women who never married, the question of why they choose (or chose) not to do so is very common. Age is an important factor in this case, since a young woman can say she is potentially waiting for Mr. Right, whereas an older teacher is likely to prefer to avoid or deflect such inquiries.

An attractive respondent found such occasions (when students probed about her unmarried status) relatively discomforting because she knew her answers did not satisfy them.

> They can't understand why it is you aren't married. Usually I say to them that it just doesn't interest me, that I have enough kids to look after at school, that the idea of a family life just doesn't interest me. Not only that—that I am too selfish to be married, and I laugh about it.

Another teacher, somewhat bolder, was more direct in her approach:

> I tell them I'm old enough to know what I want and I don't like kids. I like teaching them [teenagers], but I don't like little kids. I'm not good with them. And I just tell them, not everybody's a carpenter, not everybody's a doctor, so I don't want to be a mother. I don't mind teaching you, but I don't want to raise you.

But marriage is not necessarily motherhood, some students must have pointed out. "Yea," she admitted, "but then I laughingly tell them that you don't have to get married to have fun—laugh, ha, ha, ha, big joke!" This teacher was not embarrassed by such personal exchanges. She mentioned that she never dodged questions and was quite willing to discuss anything they threw at her.

One interviewee felt she was too old for such questions, but she would answer with jest, "I guess I'm one of the lucky ones!" She recalls that the year before a particular class was discussing recent statistics that showed single women and married men as the most satisfied with their lives. At that point, she did venture to boast that she rated number one in terms of contentment. However, usually, when pressed for a reason, she said,

> I will play lightly. "Nobody ever asked me." "Couldn't find someone I wanted." "Can't afford anyone to keep me in the lifestyle to which I've become accustomed." But again, it's a very surface response. I'll give them some answer—but no more of an answer than the surface would be.

One teacher felt that facile responses were very unsatisfactory but realized that she really could not divulge as much as she would have liked to her enquiring students. She describes her conflict:

> Still find that sticks in my throat occasionally. Because I want to say "I am" or "was." I've wanted to say that for the last three or four years. I simply wanted to say: but I am! So, the answer still sticks in my throat, because often the way I answer it is: "Don't you know that not getting married is as much of a choice as getting married? And you can make a choice not to." Also, I give the stock response "I'm having too much fun. You know. I have all my freedom; what would I do with a husband and more kids when I have all of you?"—all that sort of thing. And actually, kids have answered for me too: "What would she want with more kids when she has us?" is often the way some of them respond.

For a younger teacher, these questions were perceived as a test of the legitimacy of what she had to say about gender relations. It was with a sense of uncertainty that she admitted ruefully:

> I'm sure that some students go away questioning my credibility, wondering whether or not I have the right to make some of the judgments I make about male/female relationships as a single person, as a person who is probably gay. I found myself going through a period where I hesitated to talk as openly as I do now about feminist issues. I simply didn't bother. I think it was because I felt that my credibility and my views would be questioned or passed off as "what right does she have to speak?"

However, most teachers eventually learn to expect these unsolicited questions and to deal with them in the course of a given year as part of the learning process. Some exchanges are simply to get acquainted, others are more inquisitive, and still others may prove malicious. The women I interviewed gave anecdotal examples of each, and I shall quote their accounts at length.

Despite the willingness to answer questions, some teachers considered them intrusive, not just because they potentially pried into intimate details of their lives, but also because, as lesbians, most of the respondents felt ill at ease having to dodge, evade, or avoid some students' enquiries. One young woman indicated the tensions between how far she was willing to go and what was demanded of her:

> I talk about the fact that I live with a woman, that my roommate's a woman, and that I spend a lot of time with women. The kids know that. They've seen a lot of my friends come and give presentations to them. I feel that's enough. You know what I mean. I feel like I'm presenting myself as honestly as I can safely go. . . . It's a terrible thing to have to hide part of yourself. I hate it.

However, not all teachers shun those opportunities for informal exchanges during class time. As one young French teacher remarked, "I don't mind abandoning the *verbe être* in order to talk about sexual assault, wife battering, and so on and so forth." Although she knew she was hired to teach a specific subject, she also felt it her duty to raise the political consciousness of the students who came into contact with her.

The topic of homosexuality is not one that is mandated by the Ministry of Education guidelines. However, some teachers, particularly in the secondary schools, find they are able to include discussions about it because it may fit as a subheading of a particular subject matter. Such courses as Health, Man (or People) and Society, Sociology, Canadian Family, and Marriage and the Family all lend themselves potentially to the subject. Even with the recent obligatory discussions regarding AIDS and safe sex, homosexuality does not have to be mentioned. It is primarily left to the discretion of the teacher, although different boards of education may have different policies directing what is appropriate in their schools. However, even within a structured context, at least one teacher admitted her discomfort at having to mention the topic:

> I've often tried to make points about homosexuality and I have not done it very well because I was embarrassed in terms of dealing with it. In other words, I've taken opportunities to try to make it appear that it is a way of life, that it is just a choice that people are making, and that there is no reason for a condemnation of that choice as a way of life, but because I'm aware of the fact that some students think of me as being gay, it's difficult to carry it off.

Another teacher took advantage of a potential subject that could appropriately accommodate homosexuality in the curriculum and discussed it as openly and as positively as she could with her class:

> I say: we—oh, take away the "we" in the classroom—that people have different sexual preferences. And I explain it—I laugh because *c'est une bonne explication,* but it is dishonest— but I say: nowadays people don't all have to wear red slacks, I mean, some wear blue. So, I say, people have different sexual preferences, as long as it doesn't hurt anybody else. . . . So they bitch and say it's queer, you know, so I say, you've got to live and let live, and some still say that it's not nice, and I say, it's your privilege to think so, but that's how it is. You've got to let people live.

An older teacher recalls that she dealt well with the topic because she compartmentalized her life and did not let her lesbianism ever interfere with her work at school. The separation she felt between her responsibilities as a teacher and her social life as a lesbian made it possible for her to bring up the topic with no qualms, indeed, even to dissociate herself from her sexual identity while in the context of the school.

> I've always been able to separate my life into compartments . . . , [so that] when a thing came up in the classroom where it was possible—I would not even feel like a lesbian at the time—if it came up in poetry, or it came up where someone was homosexual, there would be an attempt at a giggle, I would say, why are you laughing? I would pursue that right down. Why would you laugh because someone else has a different way of life? You think it's funny that people want to make love in different ways? And I used to say to my students—the senior ones, of course—just imagine some total stranger from outer space sitting up there on a star or something, looking down on these tiny human bodies, with their little miniscule differences, few differences, imagine whether he'd care what we did with each other's bodies, whether it would bother him at all if one did something and the other did something else. And I would say, what people do with their own lives and their own bodies, that's their own business.

Whereas in the secondary school sector the topic may come up legitimately within the curricular contexts, in elementary classrooms children are more likely to use various words meaning "homosexual" as epithets hurled at each other in the playground or in class, if they suspect the teacher is not listening.

> With children, it's not been on any lesson at all that I've taught. They talk about so and so is gay, so and so is gay—everybody is gay. Little children, when they use that word, they don't mean gay at all. The mean "stupid," "silly." They have another term—"gaylord"—they don't know what they are talking about.

When pushed to elaborate how she could possibly know whether her pupils understood the words they were so easily tossing at each other, this particular elementary teacher mentioned that she had checked out the meaning with her own children. They told her it meant someone was ridiculous. When she informed them they were using the term incorrectly, they said, "Well, that's what it means at our school." It ended the discussion. This woman had no doubts that her own children, at least, were familiar with the current use of the word *gay* to indicate homosexuality, "but," she said, "they use it [to mean "stupid"] anyway because that's how it's used. So it's a new definition." New definition or not, the word *gay* is used to degrade someone, irrespective of the sexual connotations. However, another young teacher I interviewed supports the view that there may be "a new definition" among the elementary school children. She remembers that during the year she was practice teaching (quite recently), in one of her grade five classes, "every time they wanted to say something bad about the other, they would call him *queer* or *gay* or the big term *gaylord* kept coming up. It wasn't my class. If it had been my class, I would have pushed it further." Moreover, the experience of yet another teacher clearly demonstrates that the concept of homosexuality was not foreign to pupils in the elementary sector. Admittedly, the youngster in question was of junior high school age, but the comprehension of the term seemed to exceed the knowledge of the one particular child; indeed, it appeared to be almost common knowledge in the school:

> One time that I do remember it [homosexuality] had come up with a student. It had to do with an older student that I had who helped out in my classroom. This older student was in grade eight. And one day she came in and she was talking about this woman who used to teach my class—grade ones.

She said something like "Oh, you know about Mrs. Blah Blah and another Mrs. So and So, the wife of the factory foreman?" I said, "No, what?" because what did I know about Mrs. Blah Blah and Mrs. Blah? "Well, you know." "Really, I don't know what you are walking about." She said, "Well, people saw them kissing, everybody knows." So I must have gotten incredibly red. I was just shocked because I didn't know. So I walked right into it. I really liked this student and we had a pretty honest relationship, given the constraints of a student-teacher relationship. I really didn't know what to say to her. So I said, "What do you mean?" and she said, "Well, everybody knows that's why they got a divorce, you know." And she just went into the whole story, which I immediately thought is probably true for God's sake, and here I didn't even know. And then I thought, well, she was pretty dykey—I had thought that she was pretty trucky. So I took the real liberal copout and said, "Well, yea, you have to be careful about that sort of thing because you didn't know what something means. They could have really liked each other! This is really terrible, you know, they could have been kissing . . . and you know, people start rumors like that and it really can affect people's lives." Which was true. You can really affect people's lives but it was a copout. I mean, I didn't say, "Gay, OK" or any of that.

The element of surprise in this as well as the next account is very threatening to a lesbian teacher. Caught unaware because of the unexpectedness of the circumstances, teachers find themselves at a loss for words. The following anecdote occurred in a secondary school:

One of the kids in grade nine asked me, "Do feminists like men?" And since I cannot give a facile answer, I said, there are as many different kinds of feminists as there are women. There are some who are happily married. There are some feminists who have good relationships with men, but don't choose to get involved with them. And there are some feminists who wouldn't give men the time of day. One jerk, a male student, said, "Well, those feminists that don't have anything to do with men, what do they do for fun?" I said, "Oh, go to the theater, go to soccer games, movies, skateboard. . . . " He said, "Oh, you know what I mean!" So another kid said, "He means what do they do for sex?" And another student said, "They do it with

each other, ha,ha,ha,ha." And about three-fifths of the class
went "u-u-u-gh!" I am not saying anything in all this. And
somebody else says something about "lezzie friends," and the
girl who originally asked the question said to me, "Do you
know any lesbian?" This is my little evasion—I said, "Well, I'm
in the feminist movement and if you're asking me if there are
lesbians in the feminist movement, yes, there are." And she
said, "No, I want to know if any of your friends are lesbians."
She wasn't letting me get away with it, which is interesting. I
said "Yea." And the guy who said what-do-you-do-for-fun said,
"Oh, that's gross!" I said, "No, they're quite nice people." All the
while I'm thinking, I'm talking about myself—I'm calling myself "they." And then this girl who originally started this conversation said, "Oh, probably some of them are lesbians
because they don't get any sex from men." I was just opening
my mouth trying to think of some response which would not
incriminate me, and then she turns to me and says, "Do you
get any sex?" And then she continued, "Oh, of course you do!"
And that was the end of the discussion. I was relieved on the
one hand because I didn't have to expose myself (so to speak!);
on the other hand, I thought: if I had any guts—but again, it's
not a question of guts—I mean it is and it isn't.

Surprise was what this next teacher experienced as well, but more
at her own reaction when her student demonstrated a narrowness
and a rigidity she did not expect of him:

I can't remember what started it, but a discussion in a grade
thirteen class, which has to be my all-time favorite class, an
absolutely wonderful group of kids, sensitive and intelligent—
just super. Anyway, one of these young men whom I didn't
know all that well—some comment was made and he made the
most vicious, negative comment about homosexuality. I was so
surprised at him. I don't know why I assumed he'd be more liberal. You know, long hair and wants marijuana legalized and
so on—and I'm working on a stereotype that doesn't exist anymore—he was just vicious. So, for about fifteen minutes, he
and I sat at the back of the room and had a discussion where
I defended people's right to be who they are as long as they are
not taking machine guns out in the streets and so on—you
know, the old shtick—as long as you are not hurting somebody, your choices for yourself are valid. So he pushed a lot and

I could feel him being pretty negative still. I knew by the end of the discussion that—and I was really being emotionally manipulative—saying things like "I don't understand you! I would never have thought you could be this vicious!" and stuff like that. "You who are so sensitive in other areas, how come this. . . ?" The next day, apparently, this discussion had caused a tremendous kerfuffle among the class, and a lot of the cafeteria talk was about whether or not I had the right to do that—to defend gay people.

Once more, astonishment was in order as this next teacher gritted her teeth, gathered her courage, and confronted the issue of homosexuality head on by attempting to read to the class passages from Jill Johnston's *Lesbian Nation,* a radical lesbian feminist book, hoping to inspire a lively discussion:

I remember one time I read from Jill Johnston a section that started "all women are lesbians." I read it in my Canadian Family [course]—one paragraph. I read it to seventeen-, eighteen-, nineteen-year-olds. They all sat there. They didn't laugh. They didn't get upset, or anything. I thought I was being really courageous reading this. No reaction. I put it down and said, "Well, what do you think? Are all women lesbians?" And then one woman said "I guess so." "What do you mean?" And she said, "Well, it made a lot of sense what she said." I said, "Yes, I thought so too!" But, what it turned out was, they didn't know what the word meant. They understood from the paragraph I read that it had to do with women relating closely to each other, and that seems completely sensible to them. But the word did not have the negative connotations . . . I mean, it was amusing but surprising. These are downtown kids—they know *dyke,* but they didn't know the word *lesbian.*

Not all exchanges involving the topic of homosexuality occur during teaching periods. It depends on the personal style of the teacher whether students feel she may be approached outside the classroom with personal questions. In addition, not every student of a particular teacher is curious about or even cares to delve into the private life of the teacher. Some students feel a unique closeness with their teacher and may attempt to extricate a special piece of information that, in itself, may be seen as an acknowledgment of the bond the student (and maybe teacher) desires. Often, young girls want to know the names of their teacher's child(ren), husband, or boyfriend. They may even enquire about particular events or the details of a specific weekend. These types of questions are easily answered, although not all with the same ease. A married teacher is more likely to give information about her husband or children, whereas a young teacher might be more reticent about the name or the existence of a lover. However, when the teacher is heterosexual, her choice is whether or not she wants to safeguard her privacy (although it may mean her job in religious schools or particularly conservative times and places). When the teacher is a lesbian, her concerns are more for her whole career, in addition to freedom from harassment and potential violence—given the ideological values of this era in this country.

If confronted directly about their sexual preference, lesbian teachers are unable to answer as openly as perhaps they would like. Some find ingenious ways to deflect the questions, some laugh it off, and still others prefer to give a rational explanation that may avoid the issue temporarily. The following teacher is a good example of tactics to which lesbians resort when in difficulty.

> A student came up to me at the beginning of the year and said she wanted to ask me a question. I asked her what it was and she said something about that she heard from some students that I was—and I'm not sure she said the word *lesbian*—it just took a long time to get it out, but something about I was a lesbian. So I asked her what difference it really made to her if I was a lesbian or if I was straight. She said it didn't, but sort of wanted to know. I gave this very long answer about why it was important for women not to state what they are because it made it hard for those who were. And then I told her about the small town during the Second World War, and how Jews were supposed to wear yellow stars but the whole town came out wearing yellow stars and people could not know. I used that as an analogy, basically saying "I'm not going to tell you what I am." But again, the idea underneath all this is that I'm straight, but I'm supportive, which didn't feel fair to me. I felt guilty afterwards because I knew that I gave her that impression, although I did it in a roundabout way. I also did tell her that I could change, that sexuality wasn't static, that whatever I was now did not necessarily mean that I'd be that in five years.

However, students may choose not to confront a teacher they suspect or have reason to believe is lesbian. They sometimes use surrepticious and hurtful means to harass the teacher, making public their antagonism without regard for her feelings or reputation. The two teachers I interviewed who had come out (both inadvertently) within the school were subjected to some forms of malicious behavior, and each dealt with her incident according to the type of attack. The first teacher recalls that a student

> wrote terrible things about me all over the bathroom wall, about me being a lesbian and everything. And what had happened was that I was so enraged by it that I grabbed my principal and I dragged him into the bathroom and I said, "Look what this kid has written here." This was after the principal knew [about lesbianism]. I just said, "It's demeaning, it's disgusting, and I want something done with that kid." She was suspended from school immediately. Later, when she came back, we all three of us sat down and talked about it. Then I met with the girl's parents and talked about it. Then she came back into class and she was fine and I was fine with her.

The other woman taught older students who showed their hostility more blatantly. She also met with the same clandestine resistance, the writing on walls, the comments in the bathroom, the defacing of textbooks, but, in addition, she suffered incidents in the classroom. However, the teacher in question was well experienced and was able to deflect the antipathy to a learning situation, and could do that more readily because she taught in a large urban center.

> I've never been sort of straight out attacked other than on walls—I mean a face-to-face attack. I used to teach the grade thirteen sociology and I taught a lot about sexuality and lifestyles and family and stuff like that. Lots of times there would be friction but the feelings would never come straight out, you know. The only way I could get rid of those feelings was to have somebody else come in—like I would bring someone from LAR— Lesbians Against the Right—I have friends there. Then, all the negative feelings would be directed at her—like they wouldn't direct them at me.

For a teacher to come out in the school where she is teaching is not just having to contend with whether she is likely to lose her job, but also with the antagonism of her colleagues and her students. It was a fear expressed by almost every teacher I interviewed. One woman, who unintentionally came out to some teachers in the school, insisted that the students knew nothing of her lesbianism and preferred that they remain unaware. She was young, she was unafraid, and she courageously expected to continue her career even if her sexual preference was disclosed to her students. Here is how she anticipated it could happen:

> It is a topic of conversation with the kids every five minutes of the day. I think that most kids know because I think they can sense it, because I knew as a kid, I could sense it. I think if the kids ever found out, it would be initially difficult and I would have to make some things perfectly clear in the classroom. For instance, first of all, I only have to talk to a very small group of kids about it because I don't believe that everybody would find out all at once. I think a small group of kids could find out and then they would spread the rumor around. . . . I would just take them in . . . and say, "Look, why are you saying this about me?" And if they said, "Well, we know it's true," I would make no comment on that. I would say it is very damaging and it is a very personal subject, they have no business talking about it to anybody and please stop. I'd have to refer them to the principal.

In her case, she knew already that the principal would back her. However, not every teacher can expect to have an understanding and/or supportive principal. Although, presumably, the various federations would uphold the teacher, as do the laws that come under the Human Rights Code in some provinces, in the long run it is the discretion of the principal, the support of the staff, and the acceptance of the students that can ultimately sustain or sever relationships in the workplace.

In the course of working in the school system teachers make friends with various people they meet in that context. Some may find compatible colleagues; others develop friendships with various students after these graduate. Trust is an important factor in the choice of companions, particularly those to whom a lesbian teacher comes out. She may find that one or two of her colleagues have become especially close, she may begin to see them outside the staff room, and she may eventually become good friends with them. Any or all of these stages need to occur for her to confide in them. Each teacher finds her own time and place. At least one teacher had confidence in one of her students to be relatively honest with her. But that is unusual. In this instance, the student had asked the teacher about her sexual preference. When the teacher replied with vague statements, the young woman accused her teacher of being a "closet case—to myself, even." Insistently, the student pursued her probing, until finally the teacher realized that the curiosity was not malicious but rather was bonding:

> I just explained to her that I was open to relationships with women and that I was also open to relationships with men— and I left it at that. But this student is, in particular, someone that I would trust and she's been away from school a number of years now. At the time I was not sure, so I would not say anything else.

Apparently, it is a great responsibility to assess the integrity of the person who will be privy to such personal information. At stake is the teacher's job, and possibly her career.

Most lesbian teachers I interviewed were more likely to come out to colleagues than to a student. Whatever the reaction of the listener, disclosing one's homosexual preference is often a difficult process. This teacher told her friend, the school librarian, that she was a lesbian:

> She told me afterwards she was shocked at the time. She didn't say anything damning at the time—and never has, but she told me later that she was quite shocked. But then, on second thought, she said to herself, well, I liked her before, and she's not a different person now, so there is no reason why I should stop liking her.

Another teacher told her heterosexual male colleague. She worked in a rural secondary school and commuted from a nearby city every day with him.

> I felt that he had created openings earlier. General discussions about homosexuality had taken place and because of that particular warmth, affection, trust that I felt for him, and because I wanted a relationship that was more open, more complete, I chose to tell him. I did it after discussing it with my lover. I realized at the time that it was a risk to take. At one point I had some—not regrets, but second thoughts, and wondered whether or not I felt totally comfortable with what I'd done.

Since even with colleagues it is a calculated risk, other teachers prefer not to take it. Much depends on the relationship developed, on the perceived integrity of the colleague, on the active support engendered between two individuals. Several teachers recalled times when colleagues had approached them with direct questions regarding their lives—a curiosity that they had no intention of satisfying. The following incident is a good example:

There was one colleague in my department . . . who asked me if I knew about this "lesbian bar" that was down on Church Street and then proceeded to tell me how he'd gone in by mistake. He was walking back from a friend's place (I might say, by the way, just as a humorous aside, that the whole staff has their doubts about him; my suspicion is that if he is gay, he sure doesn't know it—I don't think heterosexual either, I mean, he falls into a nebulous in-between area). But anyway, he says he got into this bar before he realized what it was and he saw women with their arms around each other and all this sort of stuff. He decided to leave and he turned to leave and a couple of women at the bar said something like "So why are you leaving, are you afraid of us?" Now, I doubt this, to tell you the truth. I think it is a fabrication. I don't think that anyone I've ever seen there would do that kind of thing . . . and you can't find it [this bar]. I'd been there three times before I knew how to find it. Anyway, so he stayed for a beer. "So I got talking to these girls," he called them, "and strangely enough, they looked quite intelligent." And I said, "What do you mean 'strangely enough'?" And he said, "Well, I thought maybe they would not be aware of what they were doing, or something." And I said, "Oh, come off it, Ken. Listen, you can't hang around the feminist movement (I have such an excuse with the feminist movement, it's so wonderful) you can't hang around the feminist movement without coming into contact with some very intelligent lesbians." So then we talked a bit more and he said, "I told them, 'You are two very intelligent, attractive women, you could have anything,' and you know what they said to me?" I said, "No, Ken, what did they say?" He said, "They said, 'We don't want any men.' Can you believe that?" So I said, "Yea!" Then he said, "You should go sometime." I said, "Well, maybe I will." I can't remember if that was before or after he told me that the gossip around the staff room was that I was gay. Which was when I asked him what he thought and

he answered that he thought that I was straight. I said to him,
"Well, you keep on thinking that. . . ." [He is] the only individual in the school who actually spontaneously generates a conversation about lesbians—which is why I suspect that he's just
fishing around with a massive hook. Partly because he's so
confidential and wheedling when he talks to me—I mean, he's
so obvious—I'd tell the whole world before I'd tell him.

Those women who prefer not to disclose anything private about
themselves need to keep their distance. This is not an easy task in
a small staff room, where such discretion can be accomplished only
under limited circumstances. For instance, one teacher worked in a
small rural elementary school, but she did not live in the village:
she commuted to the nearby city. Moreover, she was new to the
school, and she did not intend to continue there for long. These factors, in addition to her own personality, enabled her to be reserved
without creating suspicion or antagonism.

I was very quiet. I am pretty shy, sometimes. And I was very
quiet about my personal life. People didn't ask. If you're not
married, I find, people don't ask very much, unless you are
very outgoing and obviously date a lot, they don't really ask. I
think that they probably thought that I was like a spinster. Although I really did not look like a spinster, you know, like
somebody who didn't really have anybody. In one city, I was in
a very large board. I was a new teacher and I worked very
hard. Nobody really noticed me. So it was easy to hide. There
were a lot of teachers. In my second job, it was a very small
elementary school, only ten teachers—it was not so easy to
hide. . . . I think I was studiously quiet, I wasn't just quiet. I
mean, I leaked certain aspects of my personal life—that my father was a professional, that I came from a city, that I went to
that city often because of my family, things like that. To some
extent, I created a life when I gave a reason why I went to that
city—it was not because my lover lived there. But, to some extent, there was this large wall around me and no one bothered
to go into it.

How do you know who can be trusted? Most women claimed
there was no "hard and fast rule." You relied on instinct, circumstances, depth of relationship, or a combination thereof; and, in the

final analysis, there was always a risk anyway. One urban lesbian teacher was able to clarify:

> Usually, I would check somebody out on the "gay question" in general—you know, the Bath Raids, or the demonstrations for *The Body Politic,* or say the word *lesbian* a couple of times— little check-out things—and if they seem OK, then usually I would do that [come out to them].

However, not everyone can be "tested" in that manner. Some people are not politically inclined, others may be indifferent or even negative about gay activism but may be sympathetic to individual choices, and many more are just not familiar with the feminist and/ or gay movements to recognize the issues, the obvious clues intended to validate whether or not they would be open to such information.

Most of the women I interviewed did not make it a habit to come out to any colleagues or students, even when they strongly suspected that one of them might be lesbian or gay. Indeed, in the process of attempting to contact lesbian teachers who would be willing to participate in this study, it became obvious to me to what extent lesbian teachers respected the privacy of others like themselves. Many said they knew of one or more women who taught for the same board but they would hesitate to call her (unless they were close friends or unless they knew for sure). The reasons varied from not wanting to come out to her, to realizing her need to remain hidden, to simply hesitating to approach a woman with such an intimate assumption when there may not have been any other bond between them. As one respondent suggested, "I can't just go up to her and say 'Hi, I'm so and so, and I'm a lesbian!' The fact that she may or may not be cannot in itself create a relationship between us." Given such reticence, most women preferred to remain silent if and when they recognized a lesbian colleague.

## Coming Out at School: Two Cases

Given the very well founded fears of most lesbian teachers, it is difficult to assess what the reactions would be if a teacher came out in the school. I was fortunate enough to interview two such teachers, both of whom came out inadvertently. Their circumstances are not comparable by any means, although certain similarities exist.

Before I present each of their accounts, I have to mention that although my guarantee of confidentiality to each interviewee included a clause that "[the] respondents will not exist as continuous persons in the text," both those women mentioned specifically that their respective narratives could be used in their entirety. The two teachers granted me an interview with the aim that their stories could give support and encouragement to all their sisters who cannot afford to come out in the school system. Both women identified themselves as strongly feminist. Unlike in the quotes I have included from transcripts up to this point, names will be used in this case in order to facilitate and clarify the flow of the account. However, both names and places have been changed to respect the anonymity of those involved. I have made editorial changes for the same reasons. For the sake of contextual clarity, their accounts will be presented almost in their entirety, beginning from when they came out to themselves to when they came out at school.

The first teacher, whom I shall name Gwen, was around thirty at the time of the incident. She taught at a secondary school in a large city. The school itself was small by high school standards and was considered somewhat of an alternative from the regular educational institutions. Gwen was married and had several children. She had never been attracted to a woman before this event. She recalls:

The way I came out is that a female student pursued me for several months. She was not in very good shape. She had been getting psychoanalytic help for several years, and had been involved in several suicide attempts. She felt very close to me and I got encouragement from psycho-ed. to be close because nobody else seemed to. I didn't realize that she was lesbian in the beginning, but she kept pursuing me for months and months. She wrote songs for me and poems and things like that. I wasn't very happy in my marriage at that time. . . . After several months, she wrote me a note where she told me she was a lesbian. It was kind of upsetting to me because I hadn't . . . I guess I'd never known anyone who was lesbian before. It never occurred to me as a valid lifestyle or anything like that. But I was a teacher, so I had to sort of remain cool about it. Shortly after that she told the whole school that she was a lesbian. She told quite a number of people that she was in love with me. Then she disappeared from the school for several months and she disappeared from her home for several months, but that was typical behavior for her. I felt a lot of pressure that year at the school and also in my marriage. I decided to quit around February or March—quit teaching. She heard about it and came back to school. She hadn't had a place to live for several months—she had been kind of living on the street. I suggested to her that she come home with me. So she did. I also changed my mind about quitting teaching. I guess there was a time when she was pursuing me when I said to my husband that she was attractive to me and I wished he would put a little bit more effort into our relationship because I didn't like being attracted to a woman. I didn't like particularly being attracted to a student who was quite a bit younger than me. He thought it was kind of amusing. When I brought her back home, he gave us both a couple of drinks and kind of encouraged us. And—I guess I was sort of angry with him—so she and I had sex, but I felt close to her anyway before that, but after I had sex with her, I felt really close to her and she moved in in the house with my husband—we had a really big house with lots of room—and stayed there.

The young woman, whom I shall call Lori, was in her late teens. She moved in with Gwen that spring and stayed through the summer. Gwen recalls helping Lori move out from her parents' house and being afraid that they'd challenge her. They didn't.

In November of that year, Gwen's marriage was ending as her husband was progressively left out of the women's lives. What he thought was just a diversion for his wife, he realized, was turning into her preference. When Gwen decided to move out, she forced Lori to find a place of her own. She felt that the young woman should be with people her age. They each found a place a few streets apart, although Lori spent most of her time at Gwen's. By then, Lori had decided to go back to school. She took one of Gwen's classes.

The year before we were lovers the kids at school had been talking about us being lovers. They seemed to be much more knowledgeable about homosexuality than I was. It didn't really occur to me that we could be lovers. She was my student and I had never felt emotionally tied that way to a woman before. So I just didn't see it as a possibility but the other students in the school did and so they were talking about it a fair amount. They were also—around the time that we actually became lovers—they were writing things about us on the walls of the bathroom. Really ugly stuff. I tried to take it lightly, but Lori got really upset, really emotional about the whole thing. I tried to sort of joke about it but I was obviously upset by it [too].

However, after spring was over, they spent an idyllic summer together. They both went back to school the following September. Because of Gwen's support, Lori, who had never been much of a student before, began to improve.

As our relationship progressed, she started to be more— socially acceptable, I guess—and happier. People who had known her before started to see the changes in her. They would come up to me and kind of give me the vibes that it was a good relationship. This would be mostly students, but sometimes teachers too. So that was nice. The atmosphere changed a little bit in the school. But there were other things that were not so nice. Like when the teachers would have any problems with her, they'd come and lay it on me all the time, which would mean that I would have to deal with her. It put me in a funny spot, you know, because I would have information that I shouldn't have about what she was doing with other teachers. Having her in my class was OK. It didn't bother me too much. Other people in my class knew that we were lovers. It didn't seem to bother them too much either. But having to relate with the other teachers around her when they would lay their problems on me, I didn't like that. And it caused a lot of problems between her and me because I didn't really know how to deal with it. Like, for instance, if they told me she skipped a class, I'd lay into her for skipping a class, and then—I had a lot of money when I was with my husband because he made a lot of money. I was used to a fairly high standard of living. When I left my husband, my standard of living went down, and I started to resent having to support her when I was having to support my own children. I felt like, if I was supporting her to go through school, then she had to show up to classes. I had teachers who were my friends say to me that she was skipping their classes and I would get angry. But I knew I shouldn't have known that. In a normal situation, I would not have known every time she skipped a class, came in late, or didn't do her homework, but I did. That's what it was like. So, that caused a problem between the two of us. But other than that, things seemed to be OK for about a year, a year and a half.

Bit by bit, the relationship became clear to most of Gwen's colleagues. Whereas many accepted it, others found it objectionable. One woman went to OSSTF (Ontario Secondary School Teachers' Federation) and initiated what Gwen called "a procedure." Asked to elaborate, she explained:

> Just different letters from different people, like from my principal, and some from OSSTF. They were really peculiarly worded, things like, when I'm in public or a school environment, I not only have to have concern about acting in appropriate ways, but I also have to be perceived as acting in appropriate ways, or concerned about being perceived as acting in appropriate ways. That kind of stuff. I felt that for sure I'd had it. This was before the board had decided that it was OK to be homosexual and to be a teacher, [sexual orientation protection policy], so I thought that was it. She [teacher who brought initial procedure] confronted me with it lots of times. She still does, I still see her. She stressed that by my behavior I was making our school vulnerable. Our school is an experimental school and the funds for it could dry out right away, so she felt it was necessary—I don't really understand her reasoning, but she talked to me lots of times. It wasn't as if she was so much against my lifestyle, it was that she felt that in the best interest of the school, it should be made clear that the people in the administration of the school understand what's going on.

Conversely, Gwen's principal never confronted her directly:

> He was very oblique when he was talking. He very definitely knew. But he would talk to me about what people were saying and what it looks like and things like that. He never confronted me. He gave me some opportunities to either say it was or wasn't true, but I didn't take them and he didn't pursue it. I had the sense that if I ever said it was true, that he would be obligated to go through the system of firing me. So I never said it was true. But I couldn't say it wasn't true, because I just wouldn't.

Gwen's relationship with Lori ended shortly thereafter. It was then that Gwen found it necessary to acknowledge to herself her sexual orientation. She began reading many of the books available at the time,[3] as well as frequenting the local lesbian bar to "see how I felt about the other women around me." She was not sure whether this was not just an isolated incident.

At school, there was no doubt in anybody's mind that she was lesbian. On the one hand, her rapport with most students continued to be good. They looked up to her. On the other hand, her colleagues and the administration found it necessary to curtail her activities. She was not allowed to go on field trips with students, she was forbidden coaching privileges, and she was frequently watched when alone with any teenager.

As Gwen progressively accepted that she was a lesbian, her whole attitude toward her life and her teaching changed accordingly.

> When I first started to be a lesbian, I felt it was all wrong. Not so much because being a lesbian was wrong, but because being involved with such a young woman was wrong, and being kicked out of my family was obviously wrong, and so I didn't feel too good about it all. I also didn't like to be ruled by lust—I felt I was being ruled by lust for the first time in my life. I was very reasonable at first, and then I was not making sense at all. As I filled in with my reading, I guess, and got to know more women, I started not to feel that way. I started to feel that it was terrific, it was the only sensible way to be in the kind of world it is now, with the people socialized the way they are now. It was safer and more nurturing and positive and so on. So I started to feel really good about it.

The upheaval in Gwen's life could not but be reflected in her teaching. She often raised the consciousness of her students regarding lesbian and gay issues, she forbade any degrading remarks about homosexuality, and she brought in speakers to discuss gay/lesbian rights. Consequently, she put up with some student hostility. She learned how to deal with antagonistic behavior. Eventually, she earned the respect of many of her students as well as most of her colleagues. She had realized at one point that if she were to survive in the school system as she intended and it she were to overcome the accusations and stereotypic assumptions attached to the label *lesbian teacher,* she had better excel at everything related to her work. She felt she did not want to give the administration any excuse to fire her (if they intended to) other than on the basis of her sexuality. And since this account took place before Ontario passed Bill 7 in 1986, thus prohibiting discrimination against lesbians or gays, the board for which she worked could have potentially had a case to dismiss her. Finally, there was part of her that wanted to show everyone that you *can* be a good teacher and be a lesbian at the same time.

> In the beginning, being better meant having detailed lesson plans, better testing, oral quizzes three times a week, making my own comprehension test—taking hours at night working on them, having greater props—organizational things, being more liked, you know. But later, it started to mean to me being more authentic.

Little by little matters improved for Gwen. Her colleagues began to send her all the problem students of the school, those on drugs or in some other kind of trouble. (That is often a backhanded compliment among schoolteachers.) As she explains, "There was a feeling that I was sort of fringe and that fringe people would relate to me." She remained a teacher for four or five years more in the school. She describes what it was like for her:

> In the beginning, everyone knew. It was *the* talk of the school. But as time went on, people forgot and as new people came in, they didn't know because it wasn't a big issue anymore. It was the accepted thing. It wasn't talked about. So, sometimes, especially in Canadian family [course] we would be talking about an issue and I would make a sort of aside that was referring to my sexuality and four or five people would get it and a whole bunch of people wouldn't get it. So it was kind of neat. Like somebody in the classroom would really say an antigay statement, and other people in the class would be embarrassed for me, you know, or feel a necessity to rebut it. One girl was adamant that lesbians should not be allowed to keep their children, especially girl children, and she went on and on for three classes in a loud voice about this. Lots of people were quite embarrassed but didn't say anything. Then, all of a sudden, one day she stopped talking, and shortly after this she dropped my subject. And I went and talked to her but she wouldn't tell me why she dropped the subject. I mean, it wouldn't have affected

me as far as grading and stuff like that, but I'm sure that's what she thought, when she found out.

Gwen was able to build connections with her students and with her colleagues as time went by. "For a while, when everyone knew, I would crack jokes that most of the class wouldn't get, but the ones that did, there would be grimaces and stuff; also, nice things with gay kids." Eventually, as she settled into her teaching, she found that she was quite popular with some. Her experience had made her both wary and sensitive to students who made her the object of their affection:

> When they idealize me, I don't feel good about having that kind of power over people. When I realize how much my own values have changed, how much I have changed, it doesn't feel good to me that the kids find me in one spot in time and respect me, everything about me, you know. I feel badly about that.

Gwen left the teaching profession five years later. At the time of her account, therefore, a whole generation of high school students had gone through the school. She felt she had proven to herself and to many others who had the openness to perceive her struggle that she could withstand being known as a lesbian and yet continue to be recognized as a first-rate teacher.

The second account is from a younger woman who was in her second year of teaching when she agreed to share her story. Sandy had come out while still in the university. She excelled as an athlete and was enthusiastic about her chosen field, physical education. She taught in a junior high school in an urban center. At the time of the interview, she had been involved with one of Canada's leading feminist artists. I shall call her Paula Miller (not her real name).

Sandy explained that before one of Paula's public appearances there was usually "a whole lot of press that [was] put out." This particular episode occurred when Paula was appearing in the city where Sandy taught. Paula had promised an interview to a reporter from the local paper described by Sandy as "just a trash bag" but one that is widely read. Sandy recounts in detail:

> We were on the road and coming home from some other performance and Paula stopped at the side of the road to give an interview to this guy. He was asking her all these questions.

He asked really strange questions like "I understand women should be more free sexually," and Paula would say, "Well, what do you mean by that question?" And he said, "Well, be more free sexually." And Paula said, "I would think that you would hope so too." It bantered back and forth but what he really wanted to talk about was the fact that she was lesbian. So, they finally—I don't know the exact words—but they finally got down to it and Paula said that she was a lesbian. She also gave him the spiel about it being his responsibility not to sensationalize this information. So he said, "Oh, yes, fine, fine." She got back in the van and she said, "Boy, I hope that this guy is good with the material that I've just given him." She had a bad feeling about the interview. I never thought twice about it. Then all of a sudden, a couple of days later it dawned on me that this guy might write an incredible article that goes into the newspaper and I was absolutely terrified because every morning there is a teacher on staff who brings that paper into the staff room. So, anyway, the day that the article was supposed to appear (he gave us the date), I got to school super early and I paced the halls waiting for this guy to come in. He was sick that day, he had a sub [substitute teacher]. So the paper wasn't in the staff room and everything relaxed and I was fine. The next thing I know is that at noon hour, the guy that I coach with, Jeff (not his real name), goes home for lunch and what does he do, he reads the paper. He was insensed. He came back to school and I saw him coming. I was sitting beside the principal in the staff room. I saw his face. I just knew it. I saw the paper under his arm. He threw it down on the table, he pounded his fist on the article and said to the man phys. ed. teacher: "Take a look at this," and then he just shot me a look—well, it would have killed me. So I just got up from the table, I said to the principal "Excuse me," and I ran all the way down the hall to the librarian. My first instinct was that I've got to tell somebody on staff immediately, somebody whom I think will support me. Everybody on staff knew Paula and she had been at all staff functions, so they knew her really well and liked her. So anyway, I went to the librarian and said, "Jenny (not real name), sit down. Jeff is going to come down here with an article about Paula and it says that she is a lesbian." She just blanched. And I said, "And Jenny, I'm going to ask you for some support here." And she said, "What has that got to do with you?" And I said, "Jenny, I live with that woman,

I'm her partner." She said, "Are you a lesbian?" And I said, "Yes, that's what I'm telling you and will you support me?" She hemmed and hawed, and I just said again, "Jenny, please support me." And she said "OK, I'll support you." So anyway, Jeff came around the corner in the next two seconds and went and talked to Jenny, then he came up to talk to me and there was sweat all over his forehead. He was just white and he was shaking. I thought he was going to hit me. He just looked at me and said "I am"—I can't remember the word he used—it was something like *disgusted*. "I am disgusted as a parent and the teacher." So, I just looked at him. This is the guy that I worked with for two years and very closely because we'd coached together all the time. I just looked at him and said, "Jeff, I'm just really sorry that you had to find out this way. It is something that I don't broadcast, it is something that does not influence my work. I'm really sorry that you felt that you had to bring that article to the school." I just looked at him and I said, "Now we'll just have to deal with it." Well, I had nothing else to do. He had just backed me into a corner. I had expected the principal to call me in right away. He didn't. I was a basket case. I spent the afternoon of that day—well, just in a fog. I can't even remember what I did. I went home and I phoned my Dad right away. We were all relieved actually that it was finally out, because we were sort of expecting it, because Paula is very out and people write articles about her all the time. And she's on TV and she does talk shows and radio shows. So, in a manner speaking, it was almost a relief. I waited the next day and the principal had not called me in and nobody at work was speaking to me. The reason they were not speaking to me is that my trusty librarian friend had gone to the custodians and said that "Boy, did you know that Sandy was a lesbian?" And what had happened was that the custodians told every single staff member as they came into the school, "Hey, did you hear about the gym teacher, she's gay." So no one was talking to me except a couple of people who said, "You walk around here as if nothing happened, you just hold your head up." I just really appreciated that kind of support. Support from people that I would not have thought—but anyway. I thought, this was all over, and I was cleaning out my office. Then my principal called me in. I had seen him talking to Jeff and I could see that Jeff was shaking and was really angry. I knew that this was going to be it. The principal called me in. I sat down in a chair, he gave me a box of kleenex and I cried. I must have cried for about ten or

fifteen minutes, and he said, "Boy, you've been carrying a lot
with you for the last couple of days." And I said "yes." He said
that his concern was that the parents didn't find out and that
I made sure Paula wasn't around the school for a while and
that I was really careful in what I said and did for a little bit,
and that he realized that it was very unfair, that it would
make me angry but, you know, he didn't want it made more of
an issue than it already was. We talked about Jeff and my
principal said that the big thing with Jeff was that he was really hurt that I hadn't told him before and that he had to find
out in that way. I don't believe that. No, I believe that he
doesn't—didn't know anything about homosexuality and it
freaked him out, and he was extremely angry with me for—
for—even being in contact with the kids. He thought that in
some way it was damaging to them. It is funny because Jeff
and I—he's probably my closest friend on staff right now. I
make Paula go and visit Jeff and his wife. Like when we are at
track meets coaching together, if Paula comes in to see me,
Paula and I both go over and see Jeff and his wife. And I make
sure Paula and I—well, I always send them a Christmas
present, but now I make sure that Paula and I both send it.
We're just the same as we've always been with them. I tell Jeff
that I'm going to see Paula, or I tell Jeff when Paula had a car
accident, or I tell Jeff that Paula and I are going for a holiday
here, same as he always tells me about his wife. He is very
supportive; in fact, just this last week he did so much coaching
for me and he's been covering a lot for me lately—I've had a lot
of bad things happen in the last couple of weeks—a friend of
mine tried to commit suicide—really heavy. So anyway, he's
been covering my classes and taking my classes, just doing a
million favors for me. So I wanted to do something for him. I
offered to give him a gift certificate for a restaurant to take his
wife out for dinner, and he refused it. I had sent a note, so he
took it home and his wife wrote a letter back saying that "the
reason Jeff does this is because we're friends, and that you
would do the same thing and cover for Jeff." So we've gotten to
that point.

Sandy believed that none of the parents connected her with the
newspaper incident—or, if they did, they chose not to make an issue
of it. Nevertheless, at that time, she checked with her federation
and found that it would have supported her had there been a
problem.

Like Gwen, Sandy doubled her efforts to excel at her job. Like Gwen, if the board were to fire her, she wanted them to have no excuse other than her sexual orientation. It stands to reason that, since both women had brilliant teaching records, if either had been released from her position, she would have wanted to be able to appeal on the basis of discrimination alone.

Sandy's account ended on a very positive note:

[When this incident occurred] the whole world was focusing on what was going to happen with me. Most of the teachers said, "No, no, no, don't tell your principal for sure, keep him guessing, don't admit anything." And I just thought, the game is up, it's time to go. But I did tell him. The other thing is that he has since left the school, so we have a new principal. God knows if he knows. I don't know if he knows. I've always thought about going in to him and sitting him down one day and having a little chat with him, but my whole philosophy is that it doesn't influence my teaching, it shouldn't have any bearing on my work, so why would I want to bring it up? The only reason I would want to bring it up would be more to protect him than me. You know what I mean. But he's a big boy. I think he can handle things. And it's not as if the rest of the staff does not know. So if all a sudden it comes up and he is forced to deal with it and he turns to the staff and says, "Oh wow! here is a potentially dangerous issue," they can say, "Oh, we've known for years."

Both Gwen and Sandy experienced the actualization of every lesbian teacher's nightmare: an occurrence they await with apprehension, if not with outright dread. As Gwen's account demonstrates, coming out in the school system, like other occasions of self-disclosure, is a process. It is not sufficient to reveal one's sexual orientation once—even if the entire school is made privy to the information. It could require coming out every year to each class and new staff members. Gwen survived the horror of harassment, the goading, the antagonism, and even the apprehension of being fired, yet five years later, a whole new generation of high school students did not know of the struggle. She could potentially have resumed her place in the closet—an easier life, although one filled with the stress of hiding a part of oneself, but evidently one that is chosen by most women who are teachers as well as lesbians.

Finally, Sandy insisted that I include one final note that, although it applies to both women, may or may not always be true. In Sandy's words, "In terms of my experience, I think that one of the important differences is the big city/small city thing—that I'm giving you an experience which can only happen in a larger city."

# Consequences of Being
# a Lesbian at School

The school, in the Canadian context, is an institution based on hierarchy. The lowest rung in the educational ranking is occupied by classroom teachers. They are the ones responsible for impressing upon students' minds the various aspects of the Ministry of Education's programs, as well as for assessing, grading, and promoting each of their students according to set expectations. In the fulfillment of their job responsibilities, teachers have at their disposal several formal teaching aids, such as books, audiovisual equipment, and copying machines. They also receive tacit support from the structure of the school itself, which gives them legitimacy and validates their responsibilities. The task of teaching in an educational institution carries with it an inherent authority (above that which a teacher earns or achieves on her or his own) to handle and deal with students appropriately according to specified policies spelled out in each school as well as by board and ministry regulations. In the practice of their work, teachers often adopt idiosyncratic ways of relating to students, measures chosen from a repertoire of learned survival tactics. These include one or a combination of fear, charm, jokes, entertainment, sarcasm, coercion, goading, bribing, and persuasion. Connell et al. report that, from the point of view of the individual teacher, "authority is not something given them by virtue of their position, but must be achieved."[1] This "authority" is what allows a teacher to keep control of the class, to deliver the lesson and to grade the student. However, from my own experience, I would argue that authority is bestowed upon teachers by virtue of their position. Whether an individual teacher maintains or loses this authority is, fundamentally, what distinguishes a competent from a less competent teacher.

"Authority" in the classroom consists of more than just knowledge of the subject taught. It is also the "discipline" sustained—and

by "discipline" I mean the creation of an atmosphere of learning
rather than the mere control of noise level. As Paul Willis writes, a
"teacher's authority must be won and maintained on moral not co-
ercive grounds. There must be consent from the taught."[2] Moreover,
important but implicit in the term *authority* are the race, gender,
and personality of the teacher, students' enjoyment of or indif-
ference to the topic, and (unfortunately) the legitimacy tacitly accorded to a particular subject. In other words, often more "value"
is given mathematics and science in high school than to home economics or history; and, by extension, the teachers who offer these
courses are correspondingly esteemed. However, there are a few
more elements missing from what constitutes the "authority" of a
teacher. These include a combination of self-confidence, professional
respect, reputation, and credibility. Used within the educational
context, self-confidence results from the sum total of accumulated
teaching experience over the years. However, professional respect
and reputation, although mostly intangible qualities, can be described as a process. This process is partly embedded in the social
relations that are constituted in and are composed of the mutuality,
the interdependence, and the connections between the teacher and
her working environment. At the same time, the process also hinges
on the personality of the teacher herself (or himself). In other words,
how she is treated by her colleagues, students, the administration,
and so forth is contingent on how she is perceived by them. And how
she is perceived by them depends on a combination of and dynamics
between her race, gender, age, ethnic/religious/social background,
ability, qualifications, character, and private/public associations
with them. Indeed, it could even be said that the entire history of
women in teaching has a bearing on how each individual female
teacher is accepted. Finally, her credibility is built on the combination of both self-confidence and her professional respect or reputation. Credibility is another factor present in the term *authority*. It is
her "right" to speak as an "expert," it is her knowledge of the topic,
it is her position in the classroom or school, it is how she is acknowledged or perceived, it is how she sees or feels the tensions between
all these factors, and how she acts or reacts within them.

Notwithstanding the above, teachers in general are hired in
conformity with an assumed standard. They are expected to reflect
a conventionality that corresponds to the state's ideologically sanctioned model of behavior. This model of behavior is inextricably
linked with normative behavior. "Normalcy" intimates legitimacy,
which, in turn, lends credibility. "Normalcy" confers the confidence

of belonging to a majority (hegemonic) position, as well as the assurance of appropriate behavior. Schutz elaborates:

> The subjective meaning the group has for its members consists in their knowledge of a common situation, and with it of a common system of typifications and relevances. This situation has its history in which the individual members' biographies participate; and the system of typification and relevances determining the situation forms a common relative natural conception of the world.[3]

A teacher's private life is ostensibly invisible in the classroom, and yet there is an ease with which many heterosexual teachers are able to include personal details into a discussion or give information about their mate and/or child(ren). This is frequently absent with homosexual teachers. Heterosexuality is normative. It is hegemonic. It is also institutionally sanctioned, ideologically affirmed, and socially encouraged and expected. It is not surprising that the majority of heterosexual people presume that theirs is the "natural conception of the world." Conversely, homosexuals in general realize that their sexuality or lives or politics do not conform with the norm. Specifically, most lesbian teachers are aware that if their sexual preference were to be made public it would not be without some negative consequences—such as loss of legitimacy and authority. The respect they may have acquired previously would vanish in the light of their lesbianism. The appreciation of this reality is what leads many teachers to be particularly conscious of their behavior and how they are perceived. One teacher explained:

> I was nervous as could be if I went on any demonstrations, whereas before [as a heterosexual] I had no problem. I did gay demonstrations. That did not bother me because I wasn't gay, so if anybody challenged me, it was easy to say "I'm not gay, it doesn't bother me." But once I was [lesbian], it made me very nervous.

Given that the research for this project was completed before the Human Rights Code of Ontario was changed to include sexual orientation as one of the factors where individuals are protected from discrimination in employment, housing, and services, the reader must bear in mind that the following information is still relevant today but for different reasons.[4] All interviews had been completed prior to 1986 (Bill 7), although I seemed to have anticipated the possibility of a change in the law. At least one board of education in Ontario had a specific written policy protecting lesbian and gay teachers, and although teachers' federations (unions) often had policies protecting their teachers, for the most part, lesbians and gay men who were out publicly had no official protection regarding their jobs, their housing, or access to services.

Teachers I interviewed felt (as will be shown later) that even if boards of education officially condemned discrimination against gay men and lesbians,[5] coming out in the classroom (or even amongst peers) would complicate their lives as teachers. A number of women expressed their reluctance based on their understanding that the official directives and policies were more likely to give credit to the board than protection to the teacher. They stood to jeopardize more than their job. They could forfeit their "authority" in the classroom, their credibility with their peers, their "appropriateness" with the parents, and their legitimacy with the administration. For instance, a young teacher who worked for a small southern Ontario board explained:

> The thing is that when you teach elementary school the parents feel really close to you if you are the kind of person they can talk to. Especially the mothers, they come in and they can talk about their kids. It's really nice for them to have someone to talk to. And I would think about how those women would open up to me. And I would think, "if they only knew that I'm a lesbian and that their child—a six-year-old little thing is with me." They would just be shocked. They would be pulling their kids out. And yet here they are saying that "that's the best thing that's ever happened to Suzie, and it's really great, and I'm so glad I could talk to you, you really understand."

Questioned about how a sexual orientation protection clause in her collective agreement would potentially affect her life, another teacher was wary, not to mention cynical:

> I'm not sure that a protection clause would be much use in the face of a public outcry, because a contract, you know, as I have discovered, can be overruled by the Education Act. There is an overall clause that gives the board ultimate power in terms of the good of the child or something.[6]

Another teacher was even more succinct: "I would be protected from firing. I would not be protected from ostracism, or harassment, or from students, or from colleagues."

Although a sexual orientation protection clause in the collective agreement (more so when it became law) would offer some security against firing on the basis of one's sexual orientation, it would not guarantee the attitude of people who are made privy to that knowledge. It would not shelter one from their prejudices, from their antagonism, from their unwillingness to cooperate with a teacher who would declare herself publicly as lesbian. Most of the interviewees addressed this issue, pointing to the very limited protection such a clause could present, and yet not discounting it as totally useless. Its very inclusion in an agreement would implicitly acknowledge our existence, would give us some legal and institutional legitimacy, however restricted in its scope:

> It [a clause] would make me feel more secure, I suppose, in my choices, but in the long run, isn't it the way we are relating to the people around us that is important? A protection clause is actually probably going to polarize people more—I don't know. I'm not at all sure about political action as a means to sensitivity and understanding. But I would suggest that it would be a good thing from the point of view if there—and there is sure to be one rising up from the ashes soon with all the fundamentalist stuff coming up—there is sure to be someone who goes on a witch-hunt soon for the sake of the witch-hunt and his or her own viciousness, and a protection clause would be absolutely necessary in that case because people would lose their jobs left, right, and center. But I think in terms of just living, just in the classroom, your best bet is to be comfortable yourself, and that's a purely psychological thing. The more comfortable you are, the more you are relating directly and honestly— I use the term advisedly—then, that's your success. And I'm not saying that the next day if most of these kids heard that you were a lesbian that the day after they wouldn't be out with placards creating a "we want you fired" thing. Kids being what they are, they can love you one day and the next can be swayed completely. . . . A law never gets to people's hearts, and that's where your greatest liberalizing force comes from, and if their hearts are tight and narrow and restricted, no law is going to change that. I think that most people's hearts are tight and

narrow and restricted right now. I mean, you can't even get people to change to metric!

Most lesbian teachers agreed that a protection clause in the collective agreement or a law in the Human Rights Code was ultimately necessary. When the law became a reality in 1986 and I posed the same question to a number of these interviewees, they seemed to be of the same opinion as they were in this study: the law would protect a lesbian or gay teacher insofar as a conservative parent or board member or administrator went on a witch-hunt, but, as one teacher recently said to me, "I would want to fight my dismissal only if I had the support of my colleagues, or that of the students. Otherwise, I wouldn't stand a chance—law or no law." All would want to see teachers, ideally, evaluated on the basis of their teaching abilities rather than their sexuality or their gender (race, age, or ethnicity), but several women felt that legal protection is not enough:

> I think I could survive my job [with a protection clause], because I think it would be very difficult to prove that anything that I had ever done was in any way harmful to students that I have taught. On the other hand, I think that the feeling of distrust or feeling someone was always there waiting for me to make some kind of move which would validate their concerns might be a little bit too much for me. I don't know. It is difficult to tell when one gets one's back up how much one is willing to put up with. I'm not sure that I'd want to work in an environment like that. But on the other hand I might get my back up enough to say: Tough! I'm doing my job!

One teacher, who had been active on the affirmative action committee in her board and who was known as a feminist at her school, was adverse to the notion of coming out publicly, even with legal or contractual protection:

> I knew that what little legitimacy I had as a feminist, what little clout I had, would be completely gone if I was known as a lesbian. "What would you expect from a dyke!" *That's* the sort of thing I'd hear. I had worked up a fair bit of credibility in the administration and with certain members of the staff, and I just knew in some respect that that would be gone. That there was no way that anything that I said from then on about

feminism would be given any credence—because, "Why would you want to deal with a lesbian for?"—and that bothered me. Also, the possible reaction of the students. I see as important that a radical feminist influence be there, and be more or less taken seriously. And they do. At least the younger kids take it seriously enough to want to know more, and the older kids take it seriously enough to be heartily offended. So I do have some influence. That would be gone. Like, I remember when Billie Jean King, as someone put it recently, "was yanked out of her bisexual closet," one of the girls in my home class came to me the next day and said, "Did you read the news about Billie Jean King?" I said "Yes." And she said, "She used to be my favorite tennis player but not anymore!" I thought, well, that would be the reaction of a lot of people: I really liked her before but now she's gross.

A young teacher who worked for a rural board felt that lesbianism did not really interfere with her career, but then qualified the statement with "since I'm not an ambitious person and since I'm not looking beyond my own classroom. . . ." This young woman was convinced that the mere suspicion of her sexual preference could potentially ruin her chances for promotions. Another teacher worked for a large urban board. She had just recently come out to herself. She was and had been a feminist for a number of years, active politically in the community and in the school. She had made a point of including lesbian writers (she had seen to it that black and working-class women were represented as well) on her list of readings for her senior students. She recognized clearly how her new sexual identity affected her attitude in the classroom. She saw that, previously, she had spoken out quite frequently and openly in favor of lesbians, confident and secure in her heterosexuality. "Now," she said, "if we are doing a book that is written by a lesbian, I probably say statements that separate me from the book." As a heterosexual feminist, this woman had encountered endless harassment on the basis of her feminist beliefs and activities. She chose to teach courses related to women and was very outspoken regarding sexism and other issues. "What people thought was that if I'm saying all this about women, then I must obviously hate men, and if I hate men, I must be a lesbian." But since she was not, at the time, she continued her struggle undeterred. Later, as a lesbian, although she maintained her vigilance, she was aware that she had toned down her forcefulness. She remembers her previous innocence with wonder:

I think I was naive. I did not understand the extent of being called lesbian. Because I knew I was straight, I knew that I could always argue anyway, that even if people did go and say I was a lesbian to whomever, that I knew I could prove that I was straight. I felt that that offered me some safety. I think that was a bit naive. I don't know how I could have proved it. But I felt that. And I felt that it was important for me to stand up and support lesbians.

The next woman was more concerned for those lesbian teachers who held positions of responsibility. She felt that if the sexual preference of a classroom teacher were to become known in the school, she might lose her credibility with the staff, her authority with the students. However, for those women who held positions of responsibility, it could mean their job: "They could be destroyed, [they] are the ones who—with or without a sexual orientation clause—there's no way you'd get to be a principal if you're a dyke—'them perverts in the front office!' "

At a workshop of the International Gay Teachers' Association[7] many of the teachers present voiced the opinion that even a contractual clause could not protect a lesbian or gay teacher. She or he would be released on the basis of other pretenses. In the meantime, the teacher would have to endure taunts, harassment, and insults. There is no denying that some people would be supportive, but many teachers prefer not to take chances to find out. In short, loss of authority in the classroom and opportunities for promotion would be partial consequences. Teachers also worried about their isolation, their credibility, their legitimacy—indeed, they felt that their job would become a daily struggle rather than a fulfilling profession.

Evidently, none of the teachers who anticipated all these disastrous consequences had experienced coming out. Most took great pains not to reveal their sexual preference. There are many ways of avoiding being suspected of lesbianism, the most obvious of which is "passing" as heterosexual. Mary Meigs writes: "The need to pass is born of every form of discrimination, for the victim of it adopts the protective coloring that will allow him/her to pass, to live invisibly with the enemy."[8]

When I undertook this project, my focus was to discover how women passed as heterosexual in order to maintain their jobs. I never questioned that they all did. I was aware that I did, and that I did it well. I was conscious of how I dressed, how I walked and talked, what behavior was expected of my gender, in short, how to convey the message I intended. I know that I was successful (particularly in the beginning) because I was regularly courted by men, teased about my inability to settle for one man (I dated often), and advised that I should "settle down" soon. People would frequently invite me to parties in order for me to meet eligible bachelors, they would matchmake, they would speak glowingly of a man I was seeing. What they did not realize was that I saw a number of men because I was not interested in any, that I never intended to "get serious," nor was I likely ever to "settle down" unless it was with a woman.

As the years went by people ceased to be curious about my private life as they slowly understood that I was not particularly concerned with men and as I began to avoid studiously any situations that put me in contact with potentially sexual male partners. The way I passed in my mid thirties served only to deflect immediate suspicion, to conceal or reveal enough that there could be no certainties, merely speculations. By then I had lost my inclination to pass as heterosexual. Given my age, my avoidance of men, I chose to present myself as asexual, with just the occasional friendly encounter with a "sensitive" man. Because, for me, my methods had been successful, I assumed that the women I would interview would relate similar experiences. I was wrong. The eighteen teachers with whom I spoke had eighteen different stories, eighteen variations of the ways they could not afford to disclose their sexual preference, and eighteen ways in which they achieved their intended persona. I was so convinced that lesbian teachers all attempted to pass as heterosexual in the same way I did that when the first three interviewees denied any conscious attempts to portray themselves as other than what they were I assumed (a) I did not question them enough; (b) I did not question them well; and (c) they were just not aware of their own behavior.

Finally I heard what they were saying. Consequently, rather than try to mold them to fit my preconceived ideas of their behavior, I attempted to comprehend their perspectives. What I learned were the various ways lesbian teachers coped in the school system, in their homes, with their families, with friends who knew and those who did not. Each of their methods fit their own personality and their own specific situation. I also understood that the way they adapted to their peculiar circumstances could not be categorized simply as "passing" because "passing" characterized more how I conceptualized their actions (as a result of my familiarity with the social science discourse), how I described their success at concealing various aspects of themselves. Using Smith's suggestion to begin from the standpoint of women made visible the means each teacher chose to present herself to the world, whether in the public or in the private sphere. It revealed how they themselves perceived their world, how they explicated it, and how they functioned within it. I passed. I fit Meigs's description. I "adopted a protective coloring." But, concretely speaking, it did not make sense to generalize on the basis of my life or my knowledge exclusively. What is presented in the following pages are the experiences of the teachers interviewed. It is their perceptions of the ways they coped in a potentially hostile environment. It is how and why they learned to disclose only enough of their lives as they felt could be tolerated. It is their own words.

Choosing not to reveal one's sexual identity may take different forms. One may (as I did) adjust one's bearing and one's way of dressing to fit a particular self-concept (which one thinks corresponds with normative "feminine" behavior), one may neglect to conform to traditional gender-specific dress and behavior codes on the basis of "dressing for comfort," or one may simply choose to emphasize one's adherence to a nonconforming political group that may be seen to provide a "safer cover" for one's sexual preference.

Some women I interviewed preferred to be mistaken for a heterosexual, although they may not have actively attempted to portray themselves as such. Others did not care what people thought as long as there were no confrontational remarks about their looks. Given that, in this culture (as in most), heterosexuality is closely linked with gender identification, it stands to reason that men would want to be recognized as men and women as women. The easiest way to do so is by emphasizing gender-specific dress and behavior. As Frye suggests succinctly, "Queerly enough, one appears heterosexual by informing people of one's sex *very* emphatically and *very* unambiguously, and one does this by heaping into one's behavior and upon one's body ever more and more conclusive sex-indicators."[9]

When Susan Brownmiller discusses the concept of "femininity" in her book by the same name,[10] she makes the connection between how women are expected (by society) to dress in order to "prove" their sexuality. I would argue, as well, that in this patriarchal culture, women (and men) socially have to validate their femaleness (and maleness) in addition to their gender. In other words, to emphasize gender identity, you have to dress, to behave, to think, to react, to emote, to fear, to love, to nurture, and to look "like a woman" in order to *be* a woman. Furthermore, until very recently the concept of strength as a positive attribute for women was almost nonexistent, since men equated strength with "manliness," and consequently women who were strong were "mannish."

For lesbian teachers who do not want to broadcast their sexual preference it is important that they not appear masculine. They may choose to avoid traditional "feminine" attire, but they cannot afford to act like, dress like, or behave like men. Conventional wisdom, based on the turn-of-the-century sexologists' notion of "sexual inversion," perceives women who look like men as undoubtedly lesbian. It is the current stereotype of the lesbian. It is the image that often comes to mind when an individual is not familiar with lesbians. It is the construct that has been promoted ideologically by fiction writers, movie directors, medical doctors, and sociological and psychological theses—by the ruling apparatus that potentially benefits from women's conformity to a prescribed gender model of inferiority and dependency. Even as we acknowledge that the "masculine" lesbian is more of a stereotype than a reality, it is a picture that is prevalent enough that most lesbians in career or personal situations where they cannot afford to come out heed the prescriptions. A news item that appeared in early 1985, although not Canadian, confirms and elaborates this point:

> There's no need to prove that a teacher is a lesbian to fire her in West Virginia—rumor is good enough reason.
>
> Kindergarten teacher Linda Conway discovered that she needed only to refuse to act traditionally feminine to lose her job in the Hampshire County School system.[11]

Conway was forced to resign her job because of the reputation in the community that she was a lesbian. It stemmed mostly from the way she looked. Because she taught in a cafeteria where she had to lean over tables to teach, she preferred not to wear dresses. She explains in the article, "I'm not feminine to begin with. I'm heavy-set, and I wouldn't look good in some of the things those petite women wear."[12] Her clothes were perceived as offensive, her new haircut inappropriate. Finally, when she allowed a recently separated woman to move in with her, school officials and parents insisted that she had to be released. The school superintendent tried in vain to have her transferred. In the end, petitions from the community led him to impose on Conway a dress code that called for her to " 'wear a dress at least twice a week, no boots or manly clothes.' "[13]

Looking "like a woman" may not, essentially, mean dressing in a "feminine" fashion, having one's hair styled in a particular way, or necessarily talking, walking, and sitting in what has been perceived in this culture (Western, North American) as "feminine." Although it is very difficult to define what is meant by "feminine appearance," there seems to be a general consensus that one can "look" like a lesbian. However, even those who claim a sense of what a "lesbian looks like" have much trouble describing it. For instance, Brownmiller favors wearing her hair long because, she says, "I know what some people think about short hair—they say short hair is mannish, dyky."[14] Brownmiller may prefer to wear her hair long, but she persists in not wearing skirts or dresses. Although she realizes that in wearing trousers (and/or not caring about "feminine fashion") she risks "looking eccentric and peculiar, or sloppy and uncared for, or mannish, or man hating, or all of the above,"[15] she chances it in the name of comfort, warmth, and practicality. (It is interesting that despite her defiance and her lengthy defense of her preference for slacks, Brownmiller saw fit to pose in a dress for the book-jacket picture!)

The fear of being mistaken for a lesbian, or, conversely, of being recognized as one when a woman feels it necessary to conceal her sexual preference, may lead to a certain social conformity in dress and looks. But what is the look that is being avoided? What does it mean when someone exclaims, "She looks like a dyke!"? Is there really a lesbian fashion, a specific and recognizable appearance shared by enough lesbians that we/they can recognize one another? First of all, it is important to distinguish between politicized (involved in feminist and/or left politics) and nonpoliticized lesbians. Many of the former group (in general) conceive of their sexuality as an extension of, almost an espousal of, maybe even an articulation of, their politics. The latter frequently perceive their lesbianism as an isolated phenomenon, a sense that, given unknown circumstances in their personal lives, they prefer to express themselves sexually with women instead of with men. On the one hand, for the nonpolitical or the non–politicized lesbian, loving women is a private concern. It is an aspect to be compartmentalized, left at home, kept concealed. For this reason, many of these women often dress and look differently professionally and when they are relaxing. However, this is also true of women who, despite their politics, experience the need, for whatever reasons, not to reveal their sexual preference at work. On the other hand, politicized lesbians who are able and willing to carry over their radical political convictions into their workplace are more likely to approximate their appearance in both places. Thus, in very general terms, politicized lesbians may share a similarity of attire based on avoiding many patriarchal prescriptions of how a woman should look, that is, some combination of shaved legs, long hair, heavy makeup, frilly and/or revealing clothes, high heels, and so on. For a nonpoliticized lesbian, the need is to achieve a balance between comfort and traditionally "feminine" clothes. It usually means a dressed-up, possibly expensive, probably plain pattern of dressing. In the final analysis, how a lesbian dresses is more than just her politics. It is a combination of her situation, her race, her class, her possibilities, and her natural looks.

For a woman to "look like a dyke" may mean she is recognizably "butch." It must be clear that in this context the word *butch* refers to a particular appearance and not to lesbian role playing (butch and femme); therefore, the term covers all those women whose appearance, by choice or by default, "look" like a "butch." One young teacher I interviewed attempted to capture the image but had great difficulty when asked to specify what about the woman she was describing made her use the word *butch:*

> I mean manly, of course. I mean manly in dress code and also looking tough—in mannerisms as well—sitting like this [legs apart, elbows leaning on knees, hands dangling between legs], like a man. This woman has long hair. I'm trying to think how she looks like a man. I don't know. Maybe it is in the way you are. You are forward. I know for me, a real butch is a woman who dresses and wants to be like a man and I don't like it at all. It's like the men who dress completely feminine. It's an exaggeration of both sexes. . . . [In short], this woman was not the feminine type.

"Butch" is a notion that is difficult to describe but one that many would agree conveys the image of a strong, short-haired, low-voiced lesbian, a woman who would wear no makeup, who would choose to don shirts and trousers rather than pants and blouses. In short, it is the most prevalent mainstream lesbian stereotype, although not necessarily a description of the lesbian who eroticizes and adopts the dominant role in a butch/femme relationship.

In addition to "butch," a woman may also "look like a dyke" if she prefers athletic sportswear (although, obviously, physical education teachers are likely to teach in this type of attire but not all physical education teachers who wear sportswear are lesbians!).

Finally, a woman "looks like a dyke" if she seems unconcerned with her appearance, if she does not dress for male-directed "sex appeal," of if she dresses to attract other women. This description is not by any means complete because there are innumerable stated and tacit clues that may potentially signal lesbian sexuality. For instance, I may or may not "look like a dyke," but when my biography is added to my looks (over forty, never married, often in the company of women), it informs the way I may be perceived. However, there is no denying that there exists "a type," "a look," "a way of being" that, taking into consideration current fashions, combines dress, voice, hair style, mannerisms—in short, "the way a woman distributes air" that often indicates that she is a lesbian. Denise Kulp has written a semiserious article, "Dyke Aesthetics: Dressed to Cool," in which she maintains that her "proof" that "a dyke aesthetic really exists is the simple and frequently used phrase 'She looks like a Dyke.' Everybody uses it at some point or another—to try to support guesses about another woman's sexuality."[16] Kulp proceeds to describe the preferred attire/look of many lesbians but also admits to its nebulous quality and to the changing fashions or preferences.

Notwithstanding this attempt to understand what a dyke or lesbian looks like, there is a social stereotype, a mainstream model of the "typical" lesbian. She is often described as "mannish," "severe," "man-hating," and so forth. It is this homophobic image that lesbian teachers attempt to avoid. Whether they perceived themselves as "passing as heterosexual" or merely "dressing for comfort," most (if not all) the women I interviewed were careful not to be seen as "mannish," yet also not to be mistaken necessarily as actively interested in appealing to men. Although dress is only a partial factor in the total "look," Susan Brownmiller is compelled to point out that "homosexual men and straight women dress to enhance their sexual attraction while lesbian women and heterosexual men dress more carelessly or to conceal their bodies, having no urgent need to attract the judgmental male eye."[17] Evidently, Brownmiller's consistently heterosexist assumptions fail to distinguish between lesbian-preference not to appeal to the "judgmental male eye" and our inclination to dress to attract the appreciative female eye.

How one dresses is also a function of age and current mainstream fashions. It is easier to wear trousers when pants are popular than to stand out as the only woman not in a skirt or dress. Moreover, some nonconforming styles are more appropriate for youth (for instance, the sixties "hippy" or the eighties "punk") than for middle-aged women. Yet age itself affords an excuse for "comfortable clothes" since our culture is age conscious, and as such, dismissive of the attractiveness of older women. "Older" women are assumed to be "past their prime," meaning unappealing to men of their age. Given presumed male disinterest, women "of a certain age" are perceived as "too old to care," "too prim or prude to wear . . . ," "too late to dare." Indeed, age itself may provide a means of "passing."

Finally, when all is said and done, how one presents oneself to the world depends on the individual style, the circumstances, the economic and political situation, and the race or color of the person. It also depends on the context. A woman is seen as a total picture. Her age, looks, dress, jewelry, and accessories are all considered, as is whether she is or has been a mother, whether she is seen as seeking or avoiding males in her life, and whether she herself is appreciated, well-liked, or respected.

The words of the women I interviewed lend credence to the suggestion that lesbians are usually conscious of how they are perceived, and often how they want or expect to be seen. Moreover, most of the respondents had some notion of mainstream stereotypes, of what is considered "feminine," of what they potentially could do to conform. Whether they chose to ignore or take into account these images in the presentation of their everyday selves in the school environment, certainly every teacher voiced concerns about how she was perceived—and what, if anything, she did to avoid confrontation regarding her sexual preference. One older teacher summarized her feelings:

> I struggled the first half of my life to be a woman. I used to try to get my hair done and dress properly. By the time I was in my late thirties I gave it up . . . , since then, I dress the way I please. . . . I was scared, but I took precautions.

Some of the women actively attempted to convey a certain impression (of being straight, asexual, past their prime, dedicated teachers, single women, and so on), and others felt that they were aware of how they were perceived (as possibly lesbian), but as long as they were not confronted directly, they anticipated being tolerated for the time being. One teacher commented on how badly she dressed as long as she insisted on wearing what she felt was expected of her (dress, skirts, frilly blouses) rather than what clothes made her feel

at ease. She wanted to come across as "feminine," to conform to a
dress code that she assumed would make her more acceptable:

> So much so that I dressed really badly. It just is an embarrass-
> ment to me. I did [worry about wearing skirts] excessively
> until I finally decided trousers were the thing I was most com-
> fortable in and now I wear blouses and crew-neck sweaters
> and trousers and turtle-neck sweaters and blazers and loafers.
> And much to my surprise, now that I don't care and I'm not
> trying, except in my own way, I've had more kids say that they
> like the way I dressed than not. . . . But I have been challenged
> on that subject [dress] by—you'll be interested to know—a gay
> man who comes to school dressed in t-shirts and khaki trou-
> sers and desert boots—he's a head of department. He looks at
> me and says, "When are you going to wear a dress?" I suppose
> a couple of years ago, that really would have upset me, made
> me angry, you know. And although I'm irritated by the ob-
> vious nonsense involved in his saying something like that—he
> mustn't be far out of the closet either. I don't care.

It may take a lesbian teacher a while before she finds the
clothes that convey the message she intends. It is often is a process
of trial and error, of small steps that defy the expected, maybe even
anticipating tolerance as one becomes known and respected. A
young teacher described her own process vividly:

> I think the first year I was a bit more conscious of it [clothes]
> although it is contradictory because the first year I taught in a
> bigger center where almost anything goes. . . . So, initially, I
> wore dress pants and that kind of thing. But by the end of my
> first year I wore cowboy boots and corduroy pants and didn't
> think anything of it. When I got my job in the small town [the
> next year], at first, again, I always wore dress pants. I seldom
> wore dresses because I didn't really like to wear dresses. But
> again, by the end of my first year—I sort of started once a
> week, maybe I'd wear my cords and see what happened. And
> then nothing happened. Nobody would say anything. So then,
> twice a week. And then in my second year I basically only wore
> corduroy pants except maybe for class pictures or parents'
> night, things like that. Actually, I usually wore a dress the first
> day of school, and I usually wore a dress for the first parents'
> night. And then that was it. Then I didn't after that. I didn't

bother. So that I wore my corduroy pants tucked in my cowboy boots. I usually wore a brassier. I did try to make an effort. So I would do that. Like they wouldn't have thought that I was a lesbian because I didn't wear a brassier, but it would have drawn attention to my body and I didn't want to do that. Like I didn't want to do anything provocative, but I certainly didn't want to pass as anything really "femmy" in terms of my clothes.

For this young woman, to dress in "cords" and cowboy boots was comfortable. She is petite and wears her hair long, which made the overall effect more "informal" than "mannish." She succeeded in pushing the limits of the unstated but definitely present dress code, while at the same time she avoided drawing attention to herself.

Not all women can get away with wearing the kind of clothes just described. This next young teacher was taller and wore her hair very short. Although she taught in a large city school, when she donned her casual "cords" the school administration saw fit to intervene:

I was brought into the office by the principal and we talked about the way I dressed. Now, the way I dressed at the time—I wore, like cords and, usually a shirt and a vest and a jacket. Generally, I wore Wallabies [sport shoes with laces]. Well, they give you courses on how to get hired and how to dress, and that sort of thing, and he didn't think I was dressing particularly appropriately. So I gave him a very good argument about how my dress was appropriate and he was convinced. At least he said, "Well, you sound as if you've thought about it." Which is just a nice way of saying, "alright, you can do what you want." As the year wore on, I discarded the jacket, and in the summer, of course, I don't wear a woollen vest. Last year, I began to discard the Wallabies and turn up in Nikes [running shoes]. Last year, what you see me in now: cords, vest, shirt and sneakers is how I taught. The kids kind of liked it. The staff tolerated it. And the principal didn't say anything.

It is interesting that most of the women I interviewed mentioned the topic of dress and appearance even when, in some cases, I did not question them on the subject. This demonstrated a concern for how each presented herself that extends beyond the limits of mere variety because many women voiced an interest in not being noticed, or, in some instances, stated plainly that they did not care. One young woman explained:

> I am not a person who devotes a great deal of time, energy or money to dress. I found myself going through periods where I tended to dress more casually and would wear plaid skirts quite comfortably, but I find now that there's been a shift from that and a tendency to dress in what is for me comfortable but at the same time, somewhere acknowledges current style. I'm definitely more comfortable in trousers. I've not worn a skirt for years. I wear high heels quite comfortably, but they're definitely shoes that I feel comfortable with as opposed to what happens to be the current rage. I dress simply and without any deliberate attempt to present a "feminine" image.

This young woman worked for several years in the same school. She was well liked and respected. She noted that she found it curious that it was when she deviated from the mode of dress she had established that she received the most comments. If, for graduation or other social occasions, she appeared in a more formal attire, she was noticed: "I find myself amused at the response that I get. There's a definite surprise that I should dress that way."

Age and the achievement of a certain self-image may be a factor in the way a woman chooses to present herself. Whereas a very young teacher I interviewed found herself changing her style when she began teaching ("I never wear high heels and never makeup, but that summer [her first teaching job] I wore skirts and looked feminine—well, to a certain degree"). An older, more experienced woman suggested that she dressed to suit herself ("I think that I dress in a style which is more indicative of my personality rather than to hide or display something. It's just part of me"). But this particular teacher added, "I am sometimes conscious of an appearance that is butchy, and I would go out of my way to avoid that."

Another woman of almost the same age (forties) felt that she definitely had come to adopt a style of dressing that was more practical and comfortable than it was fashionable. She claimed not to make any effort to conform with school expectations and even less with community ideas of current styles:

> Given that I wear my hair short and straight, have done so for years, I have a tendency 99 percent of the time to wear slacks—I find them more comfortable—I detest nylons. I will

not wear or buy another pair of high-heeled shoes if I can help it (I cannot see why I should not). I wear woolly socks. I wear heavy sweaters, jackets. Very often, if I go to blouses, I will wear a neck scarf or even a tie arrangement. No, I don't think I am being subtle when it comes to clothes. I'd much rather be comfortable than cute. So I don't see it as: I'm putting on my nametag today—I'm just wearing what I'm comfortable in.

She did admit that when she had started to teach there had been a dress code and women teachers could not appear at work in slacks. However, since the dress codes had been relaxed, she claimed she did not even own a decent skirt: "It may be taken as an identification—it's *my* identification. I'm me. Again, I'm not *one of,* I'm me. One of the facets happens to be my own particular sexuality. It's mine."

Still another teacher of more or less the same age remembered when she *had* to wear dresses but took pride in the fact that at least she never succumbed to wearing makeup—"never, never, never." In addition, two other teachers mentioned not owning skirts and insisting on wearing slacks, even at the risk of being recognized. Both felt they dressed for comfort, and one, a physical education teacher, conceded that it had much to do with practical reasons: "Well, it's hard," she said, "everyday when I go to school, there is no time between periods to change my clothes, so that even if I'm in the classroom constantly I wear sweatsuits or rugby pants and a shirt."

Evidently, although these women seemed to be aware of how they presented themselves in the public sphere, not all cared in quite the same way about the image they conveyed. However, whether they acknowledged that they adopted a look to deflect suspicion regarding their sexuality or whether they claimed they dressed solely for comfort, most of the women (if not all) demonstrated an awareness of the institutional relations that dictated dress codes, that often expected men and women to conform to their respective gender, and that could, at any time demand that they observe gender-based conventions with regard to behavior and attire.

Conversely, if style of dress reflects a certain integration within the mainstream, rejection of current fashions or a refusal to conform to sexually prescribed gender distinctions in dress or looks creates a distance between those who comply and those who resist. It defines the limits of unstated decorum, since a lesbian teacher finds that she must learn to gage a community's level of tolerance if she wants to avoid undue provocation.

But dress and general demeanor are not in themselves enough to produce a desired image. Just as answers to the quintessential question "Why aren't you married, Miss?" has to change to suit the age and circumstances of a teacher, so must an adopted persona reflect the personality and reality of the woman. A fifty-year-old woman can attempt to "look cool" but runs the risk of affecting a disguise rather than assuming a plausible image. Evidently, it is necessary to present oneself in a manner that is congruent with one's age, race, looks, character, circumstances, and context as well as with the current social expectations.

Although almost all of the women I interviewed mentioned the subject of looks and dress, most claimed that they did little to appear heterosexual or more conventionally "feminine." And yet, at one point or another during the interview, a woman would disclose the ways in which she concealed her sexual preference. For instance, from a middle-aged respondent:

> I never went about trying to portray something that would make me appear to be a normal heterosexual-type person. I didn't worry too much about my feminine appearance. Again, in the phys. ed. field, I was usually in the tunic or sweatsuit— much more comfortable in slacks or jeans than in a skirt or dress. That, to me, was a pattern in my life and I didn't change that pattern in any way. I was perhaps a bit uncomfortable when people would discuss the topic of homosexuality in any form, and I didn't join in the conversation because of my own feelings of, perhaps, discomfort, but I certainly didn't go about portraying a pattern or a behavior that would make people think I was heterosexual.

This is the same woman who was quoted in another chapter as saying, "I told the woman that I met in 1968, we will be living together, I am the stereotype, I am butch, etc. For the safety of our profession I expect you to socialize with men and basically not give people an opportunity to talk about us."

Another women, slightly younger, recognized her own process clearly:

> The hiding comes to me in areas where I want to be more open, to be more open with my family, I want to be more open with my friends. I don't care one iota whether people where I work collectively understand my lifestyle. It is important to me be-

cause these people are not important to me. Individually, there might be a few, but if they're important, then I would inform them—and if they don't understand, then that's their hangup. But then, maybe I'm more concerned than I'm conscious of.

One woman went to great lengths to describe how little she cared about what people thought of her, that she dressed, looked and conducted her life exactly as she pleased even though she taught in a small community where she was known to most parents. Later, in the interview, she was describing one of her relationships and admitted:

> I had a relationship with a woman [who] was such a blatant lesbian, she used to frighten me because she walked down the middle of the street and declared what she was. And yes, it annoyed me that she would play this kind of game with my livelihood. It didn't matter to her, but it did to me.

Again, another teacher spent most of the interview time asserting her nonconforming lifestyle, insisting that she always presented herself exactly as she was both at school and in the community, and yet, when she began to account for the reasons why she enjoyed the company of other lesbians, she said, "because I can relax more." When questioned further, she conceded that with lesbians she was more at ease, "not necessarily having to guard every word, every gesture on every occasion."

There are other small clues that could potentially reveal a teacher's sexuality inadvertently, ones that cause some women anxiety. For instance, one teacher who lived in a small one-bedroom apartment with her lover was hesitant to invite any of her colleagues over for fear of probable questions. Another teacher observed that the one area in her life where she felt she actively conveyed a picture different from the actual situation was when she and her lover bought a two-bedroom house: "Maybe that's hiding. We have two bedrooms and I call one mine and one my lover's. . . . I wouldn't have somebody from work and have one bedroom." Another woman in more or less the same predicament dubbed the extra bedroom "the BB—the Bogus Bedroom!"

Essentially, for many of the women with whom I spoke, concealing their lesbian identity involved less of an active production of a certain image and more of an avoidance of any overt or blatant statements. One young woman who was a single mother was sure she did not "look like a lesbian" but also realized that her being a mother provided her with some protection.

> That's both good and frustrating at the same time. Certainly people assumed that if I have kids that I couldn't be a lesbian. When I was pregnant, if my lover and I walked arm in arm on the street, it was very confusing to people.

Another teacher appreciated that because she had a husband and children suspicion would be minimal. Even though she did not live with her husband, she understood that "the fact that he came to visit every once in a while would be a form of protection." This teacher admitted that despite her almost perfect cover, she "played the game in most towns [she] worked in," and, in addition, she said, "I went out of those towns for my recreation as much as possible."

Having a man in her life is obviously the best means a lesbian teacher has of deflecting suspicion. Several women remembered using this tactic at some point in their lives. Said one, "I probably did at one stage drop the name of the man I'd been seeing or had done something with. I think I am less likely to do that now." Moreover, a teacher I interviewed had more than her job to lose if her lesbianism were to become public. She was recently separated and feared the loss of her children if her husband were to discover her sexual orientation. At the time of the interview, she had been seeing a man regularly and was simultaneously involved with a woman. She observed:

> It's occurred to me, I'm in a relationship with this man for a year and a half. He's a very easygoing person and he's intelligent and he's fun to be with. He's not someone I'd like to spend my life with. . . . I've been questioning why I'm in this relationship because if I were looking for something permanent with a man, I would probably be out looking, or ending this relationship because it isn't going in the kind of way that one might hope for—isn't as intense, and I don't see it long range. And yet it is comfortable. I wonder if I'm using it in a kind of way so that—well, there's a couple of ways that I feel that I might be using it: one is that I have a relationship and so I'm not alone, and since I don't see myself or I don't know how to see myself in a primary relationship with a woman—at least now, possibly always—it's an unlikely thing to happen. The other thing is that it validates my heterosexuality to the outside.

Each of the women I interviewed found her own specific way to avoid drawing attention to her private life. Whether she dressed to conform or dressed for comfort, whether she chose to shield her sexuality behind the screen of a "safer" political label or whether her lesbianism was made invisible because the circumstances in her life produced a convenient image, each woman struggled to retain a certain honesty, an integrity balanced with a commonsense, practical need to protect her career and her way of life. In the final analysis, many women found that the easiest way to conceal their lesbianism, particularly in the workplace, was, as one teacher concluded,

I suppose the most obvious way: I don't brag about the situation. I don't admit it. I don't broadcast it. I just carry on being—well, maybe my defense is being surface friendly and basically more or less uninvolved with my colleagues, my students, etc., so there never comes a need or a time in which any kind of personal—and I consider this capital P, personal—discussion becomes relevant. I don't keep it in an area in which I am open in any way to personal attack—as far as I can help it.

Another woman concurred: "In an attempt to keep one's life a secret, I think one way would be that you don't tell people what you're doing, where you're going, the people that you're seeing." One teacher felt that she really never had to lie outright about her sexuality: "You don't have to lie about it. It just doesn't come up. People do not question you. I mean, what are they going to say to you? 'Are you a lesbian?' "

It may be true that few, if any, would confront a lesbian teacher with their suspicions or conclusions; however, malicious gossip and destructive behavior does not need final proof. It is for this reason that most of the women I interviewed spoke of active measures they could take to avoid "provocation." As one teacher summed it up:

There is certain circumspect behavior that you have to follow. For instance, the fact that I have been living with my lover—openly, in a sense for over ten years, same house, same everything—people always say "How's [lover]?" "Where's [lover]?" and so on. And in the last five or so years I have stopped trying to cover up her existence in my life. I used to never mention her name, right. And grabbing at any male name I could think of—brothers-in-law—you name it, and throwing them into the conversation and stuff like that—as ways of covering and showing there were men and women in my life. It didn't matter if it was the garbage man. But then, about five years or so ago I thought: this is so stupid. I mean, this isn't the way it is and I am not going to try and manufacture a life that is a blatant lie. I am simply going to live it here. But the circumspect behavior is: you can do *that* much, don't take it any further. Within the context of the straight school society you don't talk your lesbian position, you just talk about your friend. If people would put that together correctly—good. More is the better inasmuch as the available men on staff don't bug you, so you don't have to go through all that. In a big sense, your life becomes honest without coming out in a direct "I am" declarative way.

9

# Lesbian Teachers: Dilemma, Difference, and Devotion

There are at least two factors that influence the way a lesbian lives her life as a teacher. The first is the degree to which she is involved in feminist politics, how this helps her understand her choices, in what way her feminist vision informs her teaching, how she may be perceived within the context of her work community, and whether her feminist politics affect the course of her career. These questions have been woven throughout all chapters as each aspect has been discussed. Because a woman's feminism cannot be separated from the woman herself, this facet of her person surfaced in her talk, was evident in her choices, and was clearly manifested in her actions.

The second notable factor is the size of the city and/or board where the teacher is employed. As previously mentioned, on the one hand, women who live in small rural villages cannot count on the luxury of having a private as well as a public life. Both intermingle, both are significantly visible and can only rarely be separated. On the other hand, a woman who lives in a large urban center (or dwells near one), even if she works for a small board outside the city, is likely to be able to lead a double life with greater ease. An urban lesbian can abandon her teacher persona at the end of a teaching day and resume her private life, relatively safe in the knowledge that the size and anonymity of the city permits her to find other women with similar interests and concerns. A lesbian who lives in the city can afford to have distinct sets of friends and be somewhat confident that they will rarely mix. She will not have to acknowledge socially any of her colleagues unless she chooses to do so. Moreover, a large urban center can accommodate fundamentally divergent groups, beliefs, political stands, and ideological contradictions without necessarily polarizing the city or splitting loyalties.

There is evidently less need to take precautions as seriously as if a woman is living in a small village where the community is aware of exactly how much she spends on cars, clothes, alcohol, food, who and when she entertains, where she goes for holidays, or what she does for fun.

These two factors, a lesbian teacher's involvement in the politics of the women's movement and her physical location (where she lives), may be interrelated. The women's and gay movements have both created a counter-hegemonic process that is instrumental in producing a transvaluation of lesbian (and gay male) choices. In other words, both movements have induced a shift in the way lesbians and gay men think of themselves. This was accomplished after a long history of condemnation (see Chapter 1) that characterized homosexuality as sick and perverted. The prevailing negative stereotypes were generally internalized by lesbians and gay men alike until the beginning of the gay liberation movement (marked by the Stonewall riots in New York in 1969) and the second wave of the women's movement, both of which generated self-affirmation, promoted positive images of women and gays, and instigated revisions in the social science discourses dealing with homosexuality: in short, began the process of creating a supportive and visible culture, coupled with a strong political movement that could maintain and encourage these new changes. The effect of these historical and ideological shifts in the everyday life of lesbians and gay men in general, and of teachers in my study specifically, is that the more they were involved with or active in feminist and/or gay politics, the greater the transvaluation. Likewise, it is more likely that the closer a lesbian (teacher) is to a metropolitan center (where gay and feminist culture has a material existence in bookstores, events, bars, and so on) the more likely she is to be "politicized," and the more probable that she feels positively about her sexuality. These links are not always applicable: they are generally and reasonably possible when there is access to, support of, and contact with an established community.

For instance, the following statements are from women who lived in small rural settings where other lesbians were not within easy reach. One woman who lived in a small village explained that she and her lover (also a teacher) had very few friends in the community with whom they could be totally at ease. "We have very few people that we would drop in on, say, from school. Professional relationships at the school are no problem. Personal relationships outside the school are very limited." This woman mentioned that she and her lover had a few lesbian friends whom they saw occasionally.

Unfortunately, they are not from the immediate area. So, it's not a case of "Oh, four o'clock! the day has been deadly, drop in for a drink on your way home," or, "Let's stop by a restaurant and go for supper." There's no way after the staff meeting that I can say, "Why don't we all go to . . . ," so in that sense, it [friendship] is very limited.

Another woman, who lived with her lover in a remote village and taught for a small board, remembered that she was established in that community for more than fifteen years before she dared to make contact with another couple (whom she had known twelve of those fifteen years) who lived in a nearby town.

It's only in the last two years that I have met people who say, "Guess what, I'm a lesbian; we are living together, we are loving together." No matter how many suspicions or thoughts you may have had, it's not anything that one pursues without taking a considerable risk or leap in the presumed. It's been very, very pleasant to be able to relax amongst friends, so to speak. And, I think, maybe, for the first time that any lengthy conversations could have gone on. Now, we've known each other in terms of friendship for a very long time, but last summer was probably by far the most interesting conversations that we've ever had. Just in the sense that it's OK, that is stated now, this is out in the open, this is something we can add in terms of a dimension to school, teaching, etc.

Conversely, the following woman lived in a large city and was aware that there were many lesbians outside the school she may have chosen to visit. She felt that it was necessary to do so because it was important "just to be able to be oneself without pretending or without having to have any façade of any kind." Despite her appreciation of her ability to relax with lesbian friends, she was hesitant:

I'm not into the political lesbian world in the sense of the world where you have to be totally lesbian or not at all. I found in my own life that divisions of any kind are destructive and I don't think we help each other as women if we divide the world into all these lesbians and all those who are not lesbian.

For this woman, the divisions were more likely to occur in her own life "in the sense that if I talk about my life I leave out a part of it." However, she asserted positively that her home life was entirely her own choosing, that she maintained exactly the number of close companions she wanted, that she preferred few but interesting connections, and that she was unequivocally out with those people she finally accepted as friends. In her case, accessibility was not the issue. It was more her own personal choice of whether or not to become involved politically.

Location also affects the number of potential partners a woman can have, the books, lectures, conferences, bars, records, and entertainment to which a woman is exposed, and finally, but more significantly, the support one obtains from the mere knowledge that one is not alone in the world. The rural-based lesbian teachers I interviewed almost all mentioned that they often traveled to urban centers specifically in search of this type of sustenance. However, they spoke of the advantages one experiences as one is accepted into a small community, how people eventually become more indulgent of you because they know you, how much less suspicious neighbors become of your quirks once they've accepted you. That is not to say that they would tolerate a lesbian teacher—any more than an urban community would—as one teacher remarked succinctly: "I think any community is small when it comes to my particular preference." However, a teacher who lives and works in a small town is recognized by parents, remembered by past students, and often allowed to exist as long as she is seen to lead an outwardly conventional life, is preferably white, of a normative religion, and of course, does not "flaunt" her sexual preference. Although the word *flaunt* varies in meaning according to context (so that a teacher may be "flaunting" her lesbianism by the clothes she wears, whereas another in a different situation would be "flaunting" if she so much as mentioned homosexuality in the classroom), the word essentially refers to a teacher who "rocks the boat," who defies the norm, who is active politically (for feminist/gay/left issues), or who might be perceived as taking a stand or advocating other than mainstream, conservative values. Finally, *flaunting* may be an accusation used against a teacher whose behavior does not correspond with the expected female norm, in short, whose behavior is visibly lesbian (or gay).

Few teachers can afford the charge of "flaunting" their sexuality. Indeed, most attempt to downplay, if not conceal, that particular aspect of their lives. However, despite the hard work that goes into not arousing undue suspicion, many continue to feel threatened in varying degrees by the potential of being discovered. As one teacher wryly remarked, "There is always a little fear of somebody busting the balloon!" However, another teacher is of the opinion that lesbians who go into teaching have to be prepared to lose their jobs, if only so that they can stop worrying that they will.

I think people make their own hell in our profession by think-ing, by being afraid that somebody will get them, because you can't live like that. In our profession, it's worse maybe because we do deal with children. But I guess in our own conscience, if you know that you are not going to have anything to do with children, I think you're OK. I think you should not be scared. And if you are going to be, I don't think you should be teaching. You should get out of it and make yourself a new life where you can stand yourself. I just don't understand how you can work thirty-five years of your life and feel scared and at the same time live thirty-five years of your personal life and be scared too.

Nevertheless, the reality of women's everyday life is that they are concerned with how they are perceived, that they accommodate those anxieties by taking precautions that their nonlesbian sisters need not consider, and that they often live with their qualms about how honest they need or can afford to be about their life. Some women are even conscious of how they phrase statements for fear of being misconstrued or for fear that if it were known that they were lesbian, the focus would shift from "what you are saying to who you are, what you are," as one teacher put it. Another commented:

There's no doubt that I am conscious of how my relationship with a student will be perceived by other people, staff mem-bers, or other students. I would not choose to spend time with a student alone in a place that was not public. I would not put a student's reputation in jeopardy, in that sense.

Protecting others seems to run as a theme through a number of the interviews. Some women were aware how the mere knowledge about their lesbianism could affect those with whom they were in-timate or those to whom they had come out. Being seen with a les-bian, living with one, defending gay causes, or supporting gay issues is likely to brand a person homosexual regardless of her or his sex-ual orientation, a sort of "tainting" by association. Given prevailing attitudes, respondents mentioned warning heterosexual friends about the potential consequences.

One of my best friends at work is high on the hierarchical ladder, in a position to fire me. She is one of my closest friends and I could not be close to her and not let her know. So I told her and it's fine. She comes to our house, is good friends with us, but I've always said to her—if it ever comes that her job is on the line because of me, she should not take that risk, because I'm the one who wanted to tell her.

Despite claims from many of the women that they had nothing to hide, that most people had guessed but tolerated them, that the general public, in this day and age, understands and sympathizes, or that their lesbianism did not significantly alter their teaching life, a great majority of the women with whom I spoke anticipated very negative reactions if their sexual preference were to become public. This feeling superseded all previous suggestions of support, knowledge of successful coming out stories, of feelings of tolerance from staff, students, administration, or the community at large, or of confidence that their established reputation could carry them through such a crisis. Below are the women's own words. In some cases, they are in answer to the one or two questions I put to them on the subject; in others, mention of the subject sprang spontaneously from their own anxieties.

One woman, who had taught at least twenty years in the same rural area, articulated her feelings:

I probably would not lose my job, but I wouldn't think that I could function as a teacher—as an effective teacher. I still think that I'm a good teacher—at whatever I teach and I can relate to kids. If this happens, I'd fight for my job, but then I wouldn't be able to teach anymore. I mean, I could teach. I could go through the motions, but I would have lost my credibility. Like, they [students] will accept me, strange as I am. I can make them buy this because I explained it—you don't have to be like Tom, Dick and Harry; I don't have to wear the same little dresses Mrs. So and So is wearing, the same little six-inch heels, I explain this—they always have sore feet and they're always frozen. The kids think I'm a bit funny, but not queer—just odd. But if it came out, no way. No way. I couldn't. I'd be shot—as a teacher. At least, that's my opinion.

Another woman from a different but equally small village in rural Ontario felt certain that, although she might be able to keep her job, her life as a teacher would become worrisome:

I hope [the board] would be willing to back up the issue and say, "Well, your professional standing will keep you alive and well." I don't see it as a situation that would leave me at all in a very tenable position, probably from the point of view of the parents. Like it would be: "It's all right for you to teach some other class, but "get my kid out," may be the reaction. I don't know and I sure as hell wouldn't want to push the theory to find out.

One woman, who lived in a large city but taught for a small board in an elementary school, fantasized about the consequences of her lesbianism becoming public knowledge and whether it would inform everything anyone knew about her from then on:

I think it would color everything that they knew about me. That was my fantasy. I don't know if that's true. And I would think: Every little thing that they ever thought about me— like why I always wore corduroy pants—would become a real sign, like, "We always thought she was funny, I felt that anyway, wore cowboy boots, that's pretty funny," then worse, you know. "She was pretty tough" or . . .

One respondent, the youngest and the one with the least experience teaching, spent most of the interview time vascillating between her determination to come out to the school board once she succeeded in obtaining her permanent certificate and/or prevailed in convincing them of her superior abilities, and the anxiety that such a proposition produced in her when she thought of the consequences. Unfortunately, toward the end of our talk she had almost convinced herself that coming out at work would not be such a wise decision, given that people, in general, were intolerant of homosexuals working with children because of the prevalent mistaken belief that gay men and lesbians tend to seduce youngsters. With this thought, she reached the following conclusion: "If it was ever found out that I was gay, I would immediately be fired. There is no question in my mind that the parents would get together and would not accept a lesbian teaching their children." Another interviewee, a middle-aged woman who worked for a middle-sized board, discussed the fine balance a lesbian teacher must achieve between revealing enough to maintain her integrity and concealing just enough about herself not to provoke the mainstream community. Her argument is convincing, her misgivings apparent:

People know. People suspect and are often pretty certain of what they suspect, but it's not until the knowledge becomes actual fact that they really are concerned. Kind of contradictory in a way. It's OK to suspect, but it's not OK to know. But, had they known, it would have had a great bearing on my relationship with the people I saw socially (most of whom are teachers). It would have had a bearing on the way they viewed me, and I'm certain it would have had a bearing on my teaching career. Exactly what it would be, I can't say, but one is always afraid that that's going to happen.

A different woman of approximately the same age was clearer about what she felt the consequences of her coming out publicly would mean in terms of her keeping her job. She had had a long and successful career teaching, mostly for the same board, yet she felt there would be no hesitation to end this mutually beneficial relationship once her lesbianism was known:

I'd be out of teaching if it could be proven. Wouldn't I? Well, it would be a long process. You can't be a good teacher if you're hitting the paper with that. The kids aren't ready yet for that. For all this, a good percentage of them are into it, but they're not going to admit it either.

However, not all teachers expressed the same degree of pessimism. Several women felt that boards, in general, tended to give most teachers the benefit of the doubt.

I feel that my school board is not out to act on rumor. I feel that they are not about to go on a witch-hunt. I think that there's a feeling that because I do nothing to draw attention to myself or my sexual orientation, that they are satisfied with the way things are.

One teacher who taught very young children had composed a scenario in her head of how the knowledge of her lesbianism might be used against her, what she would do about it, whether she would be released, and what she expected her options to be:

I think if the kids found out they would have found out through their parents. So they would already know "it's a terrible thing." I mean, I did think about this. I was involved with one of the teachers on staff, so you think about it on that level as well because you are taking a pretty big risk to do that. So we did think about whether we would get out. In terms of the kids, I did think about trying to explain that to them, and getting caught between the fact that they could probably relate to it or understand it or you could say, "Look, you and Johnny, you and Bill are really good friends, and this is just an extension of that . . ." I think you could explain it to kids, but I think that the parents would have made every effort to get rid of me. In my first two years I was probationary because I had a two-year probation, so I was pretty conscious of being on probation and of not wanting to get caught. But I would fantasize what it would be like being called in and being asked to resign. That's what I always thought would happen: They would call me in and ask me to resign. Then I'd say why. Then they'd say "mumble, mumble," and then I'd say, why. And then they'd say, "because, mumble, mumble, you're homosexual." And then I'd be in that position, and I would refuse to resign and I would refuse to deny it. I mean, that was the point I got to deciding about it. Because if they know, they know. There's not a lot of point in denying it. But I would not resign. I would not resign.

Finally, an older teacher did take into consideration the length of time she had worked for a particular board, the amount of time she had lived in the same small town, and the reputation she had established for herself throughout these years. Nevertheless, she also voiced concerns about the rising conservative mood of the country and wondered whether the previous record could, indeed, serve her in good stead if her lesbianism were to become an issue.

I've been in the system for a long while. I have known or got to know a few of the people in town. I've taught their children. My reputation as a teacher had been maintained throughout. I get comments still from parents who fill me in on what their children are doing in the postsecondary world. I'm middle-aged (that's another label!). I can't see anyone being interested anymore. However, I'm not ready to make any declarations—I'm not pushing my luck, I can't see why anyone would care, outside of the fact that the Moral Majority is making its move these days, and books are being banned. I suppose teachers can be banned, too, even if they are over the hill.

Since most of the women I interviewed had strong misgivings about ever being accepted as lesbian if their sexual preference were to become known, I often raised the issue with the respondents of whether they felt their sexuality had an effect on their work, if their needing to conceal an integral part of their lives influenced how they functioned as teachers. With a number of lesbian teachers, the answer was readily supplied when they were describing their self-image as teachers. I seldom had to ask a direct question in this regard.

There were at least two ways of dealing with the question. One was to see one's sexuality as a potential interference, but one kept it at bay because it simply had no business in the classroom. The other was to perceive being a lesbian as a life that offers a unique and rich addition, one that lends itself to produce exceptional teachers with increasingly heightened sensitivity to other oppressions and minority viewpoints (of course, this is not always true). Some women even suggested that a lesbian teacher potentially has more time and energy to devote to teaching because she is not distracted by family and male demands on her time. However, I shall let the women, once more, speak for themselves, especially since their opinions are not as polarized as I present them.

The first woman definitely separated her private from her public life:

As far as being a lesbian at work. I never think about it. Work is work, pleasure is pleasure. People know I live with a woman, but I've never been asked or questioned or anything. I don't think it's a big conflict in my life. I don't see a need to shout it out or to tell people that I'm a lesbian. I don't see where it would help anybody.

This woman held a high-ranking administrative position with her board. Because she worked with other teachers rather than with children, she did not feel her lesbianism was a relevant factor in her career, at least insofar as interfering with her work.

The next woman was younger. She excelled in her field and knew that if her sexuality was ever considered it would be held against her. For this reason, she chose to shine as a teacher so that she would have to be fired entirely on the basis of her lesbianism. She felt it gave her better grounds to prove discrimination if she was ever released.

When I was hired, there was no mention of my sexual preference or anything. It was a straight-ahead interview. I was in a very good position to get a job simply because I had won awards in university . . . and as soon as I was hired, I began to think of the implications of me being a lesbian and teaching. I know that it does not influence my work in any way—or my teaching. So, to me, it was quite irrelevant. But it became more obvious to me as I began teaching that people were really concerned because I was quite out and someone could find out. I didn't really worry about it a great deal, but I took extra precautions to protect myself in terms of doing a good job at work, and in terms of building up my resume, and professional development, and just making sure that professionally I was just untouchable.

One young teacher had taken very stringent precautions not to arouse suspicion about her private life. She had begun to avoid going to demonstrations that supported lesbian or gay causes, and she was extra careful with whom she was seen and how she spent her leisure time. But then she was laid off because of declining enrollment. It changed her views:

All that year [her first after coming out] I had been very, very, very clean, because I was serious. I was going to be a teacher and get my act together and get a job and be stable and pass my probation. And when I was laid off because they had over-hired and there was declining enrollment, it was as if everything snapped for me, because I realized I could be the best teacher in the whole school and the most serious and the cleanest and the most upstanding citizen and I could still be laid off. It had nothing to do with anything. It made a lot less sense being worried about being found out as a lesbian.

An older teacher, a woman very close to retirement who had devoted her whole life and energy to the profession, was quite adamant about how little her lesbianism entered her work:

Teaching is teaching. It's a profession. Personal, private life, although it can affect your mood when you're teaching—if you're disturbed at home because of something that's happened, you're not going to wipe the disturbance out as soon as you walk into the classroom—but my private or personal behavior had no carryover into the classroom, other than perhaps the mood I was in, but certainly not my behavior.

The same opinion, but argued much more strongly, came from this next teacher. She was younger, held a higher position in the teaching hierarchy, and felt very strongly about the role a teacher should play in a student's life.

I don't think your sexual life should interfere with your professional life. I could see where we have a difficult life—like sometimes I wish they can see why I didn't do this or didn't do that—but I see my professional life as so different from my personal life. My professional life stimulates and satisfies one part of me, and my personal life stimulates and satisfies another part of me. If they were ever to come into real conflict so that I couldn't live with myself, I would stop being a teacher and develop another career. For many reasons, the first one being that when I went into teaching—I guess it's my sense of what I believe and what I don't—I personally don't believe that you should take your sexual orientation, whatever you are, whether you are straight or anything, into your professional life. I think as a teacher and in our type of jobs we deal directly with people who are growing up. Some people say that we need role models, but I'd rather they had them when they were older. I'd rather not be a role model—I don't think telling the world who we are is going to change anything. If it did, maybe I would, but I haven't seen any changes. If a teacher had said to me when I was young that she was gay, I don't think it would influence me. I wouldn't have known what it was then.

I might add that role models are not necessarily a literal ideal figure in place for children to emulate, but are rather a means of legitimizing a particular way of life and normalizing the potential "choices." If children grew up with the notion that their favorite teacher (doctor, actor, parent, corner store owner) was straight or gay and that each or either was equally valid as a way of living, their choices in life would potentially be less limited.

Being a lesbian gave some teachers strength and independence, for some it had a neutral effect on their school life, and for still others it may have worked to discourage them from accepting positions of responsibility that could have put their lives in the lime-light or simply invalidated some aspects of their teaching because they did not represent normative female behavior. Nevertheless, all the women agreed that their lives as lesbian teachers, at worst, had no effect on students (any more than other teachers) and, at best, distinguished them as devoted, dedicated, dauntless teachers. For instance, asked how she would describe herself as a teacher, one woman said it in one word: "Superstar!"

The statement of the one ex-student I interviewed substan-tiates the opinions affirming that lesbian teachers' contributions in the field of education are not only valued by some in terms of competency, uniqueness of perspective, or dedication with respect to time spent at their job: they are also frequently perceived as necessary:

> I'd like to mention that although I never took the chance to talk to with Miss [lesbian teacher], knowing about her was im-portant to me. Seeing her as a lesbian and also as a fairly well put together, successful person helped me to see that the ste-reotype of the lesbian dyke was not true. I saw that it might be possible for me to be a lesbian and still live the type of life I wanted.

In sum, a teacher who is a lesbian lives a life filled with di-lemma. On the basis of personal experience and after talking with so many women (in and out of this study) who are lesbians and teachers, I suggest it is not simply a question of the more obvious inconsistencies with which one has to deal on a day-to-day basis— for instance, knowing that almost everyone around assumes that you are heterosexual, that you enjoy the attention of men, that your weekends are spent searching, finding, being with, talking to, or talking about males, that the day will come when you too will want to "settle down," or, conversely, regret not doing so. No. The issue is more the small ways in which a lesbian teacher is silent. It is the invisibility of her life. It is the denials she articulates, the deflec-tions she manages, the defenses she feels compelled to put up. It is often the "faggot" jokes and name-calling she has to endure, the knowledge that she is the one they are unknowingly ridiculing or insulting. It is the pride she takes in being the best teacher coupled with the shame of having to lie to keep her job. It is the colleagues and students with whom she cannot discuss her life, her good mo-ments, her triumphs, her pain. It is the friends she makes at work but whom she suspects might reject her if they "knew." It is having to talk about gays and lesbians as "they," having to describe a way of life, a political perspective, a sexual preference, and not be able to claim it as hers. It is watching her colleagues berate a young student's struggle with her or his sexuality and not being able to do more than simply "defend" a choice, not being able to stand up and say, "I am a lesbian and proud of it." It is seeing the soulful eyes of a young girl who has a crush on her (the teacher) and not be able to give comfort and reassurance without giving herself away.

It is all of this. And more importantly, it is the fundamental inability to identify herself as a lesbian, publicly, generally, continually—not to have to justify her existence, not to have to defend her preference, or to have to explain her life to anyone, and yet to be accepted completely and totally, legitimately and with dignity.

# Conclusion

The methodology developed by Dorothy Smith (discussed in Chapter 4), compelled me, the researcher, to begin from the standpoint of women in order to gain some understanding of a particular problematic, to embed their experiences in the social organization that informs those experiences and gives them meaning and from which those experiences arise. The problematic that interested me was how lesbian teachers managed their sexual identity (or the label that could be attached to them) within the context of the school, the classroom, and the community that provided them with their teaching job.

The eighteen women who were involved in this study give us a very detailed and yet incomplete picture of their lives. However, they were bound by my questions, by the context of how I organized my framework, and by the narrowness of my interest in their lives. Since I caught them, for the most part, on one specific day in one particular mood, what has been captured is this moment, bracketed and analyzed, a moment in their lives as well as in my own. Missing are their relationships with their families, the people with whom they chose to associate when not at work, their opinions, beliefs, politics, how they came to be teachers, and what constitutes their ambitions and their hopes. In addition, missing are the processes, the contradictions, the developments, and the changes that occur by the mere fact that each of us is alive in an ever-changing historical context.

In the intervening years since this project was completed, I have continued to be interested in the lives and work of lesbian teachers. I came into contact with more women through my work when I was invited to address some women who have organized a lesbian teachers' group in a large urban center, or at conferences, or through other related research that I have undertaken since, or even in my everyday life. Furthermore, several historical and political events have occurred that have made lesbians and gays more visible to more people, individuals who, a few years ago, would have cared little and known even less about our existence. A combination of the AIDS crisis and more demands for equality and recognition (such as representation on police forces, or in the army, same-sex spouse coverage for health insurances, "out" politicians, and so on) have forced the media to take note of our existence. Gay Pride is celebrated in many Canadian and American cities with the participation of huge crowds, multitudes that are powerful, political, and pleasureful. Our concerns, our dances, and our events are often announced in daily papers or on the radio in some cities. Certainly, we have made our appearance on prime time television and in several films, and have been talked about by celebrities and stars. Lesbian and gay-related courses are being taught in universities and colleges in North America, and workshops on every aspect of gay and lesbian lives seem to be abundant. Mainstream bookstores carry books about us, and straight women read lesbian mysteries and science fiction, not to mention scholarly journal articles. But although the concept of homosexuality has entered more commonly into the daily currency of language, and although many of us believe that it is both safer and easier to come out now, the decision is still difficult. The reality of our lives is still one of wariness, and the more visible lesbians and gay men become generally, the more difficult it becomes for them to hide. However, if lesbian teachers cannot come out outright in their jobs, there is a prevailing "tolerance" if they do not rock the boat. Lesbian teachers with whom I have spoken recently, for the most part, are happier with changes that allow us more protection, and yet, as one pointed out to me not long ago, "Look at what happened in England with their Clause 28."[1]

In addition, some of my thinking is developing in areas not covered by this research, possibly ideas for later projects. For instance, I failed to question in more detail the lesbian teachers I interviewed, who, by their very choices of an alternative sexuality (to heterosexuality), can be described as rebels or, at the very least, subversive in some ways to the systems and institutions in which they live and work, on whether they question more, less, or conform to the curriculum for which they have, in general, only guidelines. Secondly, whatever gave strength to these teachers (and others) or permission to rebel against the norm sexually, does this strength carry over into the rest of their lives? And how do they feel it is manifested? Do they feel more creative, more diligent, more sensitive to students than their heterosexual colleagues?

Finally, the words of these women as teachers always must be seen in the context of where they live: the state-controlled institutions in which they work, the prevailing ideologies, the capitalist exigencies that promote and encourage a systematic control over, and the continued, if more subtle, appropriation of, female labor and sexuality. Their words cannot and should not be separated from the historical connections that inform and give meaning to the present possibilities. In other words, both as a woman and as a lesbian, a female teacher embodies the past and present struggles of women to be accepted as equal in salaries and opportunities in the profession, as well as the recent gains made by feminist and gay movements and the discourses that accompanied them and were later informed by them, especially with regard to analyzing and making visible the prevailing and hegemonic effects of a capitalist patriarchal social and economic structure. Finally, the words of these women are theirs. They are unique to each one of them as she lives her life, teaches her classes, has her fun. They are exclusive to her, yet are historically, culturally, and geographically specific.

The life of each woman who granted me an interview, as we have seen throughout the book, is not without its risks, the danger of losing her job, of invalidating her credibility, of harassment if her lesbianism were to become public. Many of the women affirmed that as long as they conformed to normative standards, as long as they did not stand out as different, as long as their identity as lesbians was not made an issue, the "public" tolerated them. Some pointed out that they were safe as long as they were not recognized as an alternative, and as long as they did not present their lives as valid. This analysis is accurate, supported by historical evidence that demonstrates that as long as lesbians are hidden, are "integrated," are silent, are invisible, they are allowed to exist. When the love between women is experienced only within the confines of "legitimate" heterosexual marriages, when it can be safely explained and therefore sanctioned by men as nothing more than "passionate friendships," then it can be accepted by the patriarchal ruling apparatus. It becomes a threat when women begin to understand that they can live independently of men, that being called a lesbian is not an insult, that loving women is natural, and good, and healthy, and wonderful, and, in Faderman's terms, can surpass the love of men!

The danger lies, not in the knowledge of a lesbian's (teacher's) sexuality itself, but in the implications such a life has on normative, patriarchally prescribed female lives. The danger lies in women universally, but in different ways, becoming conscious of our strengths outside of men and regardless of our sexual preferences. The danger lies, finally, in all these invisible options becoming visible, and therefore possible, therefore potent.[2]

# Notes

## Introduction

1. D. D. Taylor, "Tobie," *RFR/DRF* 12, No. 1 (March 1983): 8–9.

2. The term *lesbian* in the title of the book and its application to women who do not identify as such will be taken up in Chapter 3.

3. I have chosen what can be considered a minute but representative sample of the type of article to which I am referring: *Medical:* A. L. Becker, "A Third Sex? Some Speculations on Sexuality Spectrum," *Medical Proceedings* 13, No. 4 (1967): 67–74; Desmond Curren and Denis Parr, "Homosexuality: An Analysis of 100 Male Cases Seen in Private Practice," *British Medical Journal* 5022 (1957): 797–789; Edmund Bergler, *Counterfeit Sex: Homosexuality, Impotence, Frigidity,* 2nd ed. (New York: Grune and Stratton, 1958). *Psychiatric:* Rene Bozarth and Alfred A. Gross, "Homosexuality: Sin or Sickness? A Dialogue," *Pastoral Psychology* 13, No. 129 (1962): 35–42; Gustave Bychowski, "The Ego and the Object of the Homosexual," *International Journal of Psycho-Analysis* 42, No. 3 (1961): 255–259; Thomas R. Clark, "Homosexuality and Psychopathology in Non-Patient Males," *American Journal of Psychoanalysis* 35 (1975): 163–168. *Sociological:* John Gagnon and William Simon, "Sexual Deviance in Contemporary America," *Annals of the American Academy of Political and Social Science* 376 (1968): 106–122; Jay Corzine and Richard Cole, "Cruising the Truckers: Sexual Encounters in a Highway Rest Area," *Urban Life* 6, No. 2 (1977): 171–192. For a more comprehensive list, see Lillian Faderman, *Odd Girls and Twilight Lovers* (New York: Columbia University Press, 1991).

4. For the best sampling of historical works, see Vern Bullough et al., *An Annotated Bibliography of Homosexuality and Other Stigmatized Behavior* (New York: Garland, 1976). In addition, the bibliographies of such books as the following can prove very valuable: David Greenberg, *The Construction of Homosexuality* (Chicago: University of Chicago Press, 1988); and John D'Emilio and Estelle B. Freedman, *Intimate Matters: A History of Sexuality in America* (New York: Harper and Row, 1988). A Canadian source is Gary Kinsman, *The Regulation of Desire: Sexuality in Canada* (Montreal: Black Rose, 1987).

5. For sources in anthropology, see the *Human Relations Area Files* (formerly, The Yale Cross-Cultural Survey) and relevant documents in

Jonathan Katz, *Gay American History* (New York: Avon, 1976). More recently, gays and lesbians writing about their own cultures have been recorded in such anthologies as Julia Penelope and Sarah Valentine, eds., *Finding the Lesbians: Personal Accounts from Around the World* (Freedom, Calif.: Crossing Press, 1990); and the gay American Anthology compiled by gay American Indians, *Living the Spirit A Gay American Indian Anthology.* (New York: St. Martin's Press, 1988) which gives hints of the extent and universality of "lesbian" and "gay" experiences.

6. Religious references include Derrick Sherwin Bailey, *Homosexuality and the Western Christian Tradition* (London: Longman's Green, 1955); or, for a more sympathetic treatment, John Boswell, *Christianity, Social Tolerance and Homosexuality* (Chicago: University of Chicago Press, 1980).

7. Adrienne Rich, "Compulsory Heterosexuality and Lesbian Existence," *Signs* 5, No. 4 (Summer 1980): 631–660. See also any number of feminist works beginning with the late 1960s: for example, Dolores Klaich, *Woman + Woman* (New York: Morrow Quill Paperbacks, 1979); and works by Anne Koedt, Julia Penelope, Abbott and Love, Evelyn Torton Beck, Margaret Cruickshank, Lillian Faderman, Audre Lorde, Cheri Moraga and Gloria Anzaldua, Barbara Smith, and others.

8. Exceptions are two excellent issues: *Fireweed,* Issue 13, 1982, and *Resources for Feminist Research* 12, No. 1 (March 1983). See also various articles over the years published in *Broadside, The Body Politic, Pink Ink,* and *Rites;* articles in anthologies such as Maureen Fitzgerald, Connie Guberman, and Margie Wolfe, eds., *Still Ain't Satisfied* (Toronto: The Women's Press, 1982); and the very practical *Stepping Out of Line, A Workbook on Lesbianism and Feminism,* ed. Nym Hughes, Yvonne Johnson, and Yvette Perrault (Vancouver: Press Gang Publishers, 1984). More recently, many books and articles have been published: see additional issues from *RFR/DRF* and *Fireweed* and books by such authors as Gary Kinsman and Mariana Valverde, as well as an anthology by Sharon Stone.

9. For further information regarding the rights of lesbians and gays in Canada, see Laurie Bell, *On Our Own Terms: A Practical Guide for Lesbian and Gay Relationships* (Toronto: Coalition for Lesbian and Gay Rights in Ontario, 1991). According to Laurie Bell, only Quebec, Ontario, Manitoba, and the Yukon Territory include sexual orientation in their Human Rights Code. For the United States, consult *Sexual Orientation and the Law,* prepared by the editors of the *Harvard Law Review* (Cambridge: Harvard University Press, 1989).

10. Didi Khayatt, "Legalized Invisibility: The Effects of Bill 7 on Lesbian Teachers," *Women's Studies International Forum* 13, No. 3 (1990): 185–193.

11. See *Sexual Offences Against Children,* Vols. 1 and 2, Report of the Committee on Sexual Offences Against Children and Youths (The Badgley Reports), Ministry of Supply and Services, Canada, 1984.

12. Ibid.

13. See, for example, Vern Bullough, *Sexual Variance in Society and History* (Chicago: University of Chicago Press, 1976); specific to North America, see Martin Bauml Duberman, Martha Vicinus, and Gearge Chauncey, Jr., eds., *Hidden from History: Reclaiming the Gay and Lesbian Past* (New York: New American Library, 1989); or D'Emilio and Freedman, *Intimate Matters.*

## Chapter 1. Homosexuality in Perspective: The Discourse

1. I am focusing on Western capitalist societies specifically because I presume they share much of the same recent social historical trends. I am not excluding other cultures or political systems from my remarks. However, since the context of this book is Canadian specifically and North American generally, I shall refer to and be concerned with primarily Western capitalist societies.

2. For greater detail regarding the treatment of homosexuality in ancient civilizations, see Vern Bullough, *Sexual Variance,* pp. 31–158. For an analytic overview of the ancient world, see Duberman, Vicinus, and Chauncey, *Hidden from History,* especially the following articles: John Boswell, "Revolutions, Universals, and Sexual Categories," pp. 17–36; David M. Halperin, "Sex Before Sexuality: Pederasty, Politics, and Power in Classical Athens," pp. 37–53; and Robert Padgug, "Sexual Matters: Rethinking Sexuality in History," pp. 54–66.

3. Bullough, *Sexual Variance,* p. 74. The biblical injunction can be found in Genesis 1:28.

4. Leviticus 18:6–20 in the Old Testament; Corinthians 6:9–10 in the New Testament.

5. For more information about biblical laws, see Bullough, *Sexual Variance,* pp. 74–89; Louis M. Epstein, *Sex Laws and Customs in Judaism* (New York: Bloch Publishing Co, 1948); and John Boswell, *Christianity, Social Tolerance and Homosexuality: Gay People in Western Europe from the Beginning of the Christian Era to the Fourteen Century* (Chicago: University of Chicago Press, 1980), pp. 91–117.

6. Judith Plaskow, *Standing Again at Sinai: Judaism from a Feminist Perspective* (San Francisco: Harper San Francisco, 1991), p. 182.

7. Bullough, *Sexual Variance,* p. 79.

8. Ibid., p. 180.

9. Louis Crompton, "The Myth of Lesbian Impunity: Capital Laws from 1270 to 1791," *Journal of Homosexuality* 6, Nos. 1/2 (Fall/Winter 1980/81): 11.

10. Susan Hanley, Benjamin Schlesinger, and Paul Steinberg, "Lesbianism: Knowns and Unknowns," in *Sexual Behavior in Canada: Patterns and Problems,* ed. Benjamin Schlesinger (Toronto: University of Toronto Press, 1977), p. 126.

11. J. D. Steakley presents a good case that lesbians were arrested, incarcerated, and placed in concentration camps. They were classified as "asocial" rather than homosexual because their crime against the state was perceived as a rejection of their "natural" roles of wives and mothers. As such, they wore the black triangles and were often not counted in the number of homosexuals who died under Nazi German rule. See James Steakley's "Gays under Fascism," a slide presentation given in Toronto in July 1985 at the conference "Sex and the State. Their Laws, Our Lives." See also Steakley's book *The Homosexual Emancipation Movement in Germany* (New York: Arno Press, 1983). Another mention of this information is documented by Terrie A. Couch, "An American in West Germany or 'Did Lesbians Wear Pink Triangles?' " *Off Our Backs* 21, No. 3 (March 1991): 23.

12. Marilyn Frye, "To Be and Be Seen: The Politics of Reality," in her *The Politics of Reality: Essays in Feminist Theory* (Trumansberg, N.Y.: Crossing Press, 1983), p. 159.

13. See Blanche Weisen Cook, "The Historical Denial of Lesbianism," *Radical History Review* 20 (Spring/Summer 1979): 60–65. See also David Reuben, *Everything You Wanted to Know about Sex—But Were Afraid to Ask* (New York: W. H. Allen, 1970), p. 125.

14. Crompton, "The Myth of Lesbian Impunity," p. 13.

15. Ibid., p. 17.

16. Cross-dressing was specifically condemned in the Bible; see Deuteronomy 22:5.

17. See Crompton, "The Myth of Lesbian Impunity," pp. 16–18; and "A Lesbian Execution in Germany: The Trial Records," trans. from transcripts from the Prussian State Archives of the trial of two lesbians that took place in Halberstadt in 1721, by Brigitte Ericson, *Journal of Homosexuality* 6 (Nos. 1/2): 27–40; also, Judith C. Brown, "Lesbian Sexuality in Renaissance Italy: The Case of Sister Benedetta Carlini," *Signs* 9, No. 4 (Summer 1984): 751–758. This article has since become a book: *Immodest Acts: The Life of a Lesbian Nun in Renaissance Italy* (Oxford: Oxford University Press, 1986). Also see Julie Wheelwrite, *Amazons and Military*

*Maids: Women Who Dressed as Men in Pursuit of Life, Liberty and Happiness* (London: Pandora, 1989).

18. Mary Daly, *Gyn/Ecology: The MetaEthics of Radical Feminism* (Boston: Beacon Press, 1978): 183–185. Daly's account of European witch burning is dealt with in the chapter entitled "European Witchburnings: Purifying the Body of Christ." Her interpretations strongly suggest that women were punished for being powerful and/or independent of male control rather than for actual sexual license.

19. Ibid., p. 189.

20. Crompton, "The Myth of Lesbian Impunity," pp. 17–19.

21. Ibid., p. 19.

22. Hanley et al., "Lesbianism," p. 129.

23. D'Emilio and Freedman, *Intimate Matters*, p. 122.

24. Ibid., p. 123. Also see Faderman, *Odd Girls*, pp. 37–61.

25. Sheila M. Rothman, *Woman's Proper Place: A History of Changing Ideals and Practices 1870 to the Present* (New York: Basic Books, 1978), pp. 14, 21–26.

26. Jonathan Katz, *Gay/Lesbian Almanac: A New Documentary* (New York: Harper and Row, 1983), p. 140.

27. George Chauncey, Jr., "From Sexual Inversion to Homosexuality: Medicine and the Changing Conceptualization of Female Deviance," in *Homosexuality: Sacrilege, Vision, Politics* (Salmagundi: Skidmore College, 1982/83), p. 118.

28. Ibid.

29. Katz, *Gay/Lesbian Almanac*, p. 140.

30. Lillian Faderman, *Surpassing the Love of Men* (New York: William Morrow, 1981), p. 156.

31. George M. Beard, *Sexual Neurasthenia*, ed. A. D. Rockwell (New York: E. B. Trent, 1884), p. 106. Quoted in Chauncey, "From Sexual Inversion to Homosexuality," p. 119.

32. Chauncey, "From Sexual Inversion to Homosexuality," p. 119.

33. Havelock Ellis, *Sexual Inversion: Studies in the Psychology of Sex*, Vol. 2 (1897: rpt. Philadelphia: F. A. Davis, 1927), p. 250. For an excellent analysis of Ellis's work on lesbianism, see Sheila Jeffreys, *The Spinster and Her Enemies: Feminism and Sexuality 1800–1930* (London: Pandora Press, 1985), pp. 107–138.

34. Chauncey, "From Sexual Inversion to Homosexuality," p. 125.

35. Katz, *Gay/Lesbian Almanac*, p. 144.

36. Jonathan Katz, in his chapter "Passing Women" documents cases of women who cross-dressed, worked and lived like men, and often took "wives." See Katz, *Gay American History*, pp. 322–422. Also see Carroll Smith-Rosenberg, "The Female World of Love and Ritual," in *A Heritage of Her Own*, ed. Nancy Cott and Elizabeth H. Pleck (New York: Simon and Schuster, 1979), pp. 311–342; and Nancy Sahli, "Smashing: Women's Relationships before the Fall," *Chrysalis* 17, No. 18 (Summer 1979): 18–27; as well as Faderman, *Odd Girls* and *Surpassing the Love of Men*, for evidence of romantic friendships and their role in women's lives from the middle of the nineteenth century to the 1920s.

37. Bullough observes that two of the twelve articles against Joan of Arc dealt with her impersonating a male, as did two of the six admonitions against her: *Sexual Variance*, p. 394.

38. Ibid., p. 395.

39. Alan Berube, "Lesbian Masquerade," *Gay Community News*, November 17, 1979.

40. Smith-Rosenberg, "The Female World," p. 316.

41. Sahli, "Smashing," p. 27.

42. Chauncey, "From Sexual Inversion to Homosexuality," p. 115.

43. Jeffrey Weeks, "Movements of Affirmation: Sexual Meanings and Homosexual Identities," *Radical History Review* 20 (Spring/Summer 1979): 168.

44. See Katz, *Gay/Lesbian Almanac*, pp. 153–154, for a history of the word *homosexuality*. Also see Wayne Dynes, *Homolexis: A Historical and Cultural Lexicon of Homosexuality* (New York: Gai Saber, Monograph No. 4, 1985), pp. 67–68.

45. Weeks, "Movements of Affirmation," p. 168.

46. Christina Simmons, "Companionate Marriage and the Lesbian Threat," *Frontiers* 4, No. 3 (1979): 55.

47. Ibid.

48. Ibid.

49. Jeffrey Weeks, *Sex, Politics and Society: The Regulation of Sexuality since 1800* (London: Longman, 1981), p. 206.

50. "In 1895 just as education for women was really coming into its own, there was a great public outcry when a survey revealed that more

than half the graduates of women's colleges remained spinsters." Faderman, *Surpassing the Love of Men,* p. 227.

51. Jeffreys, *The Spinster,* p. 112.

52. Simmons, "Companionate Marriage," p. 55.

53. Ibid., p. 56.

54. Katz, *Gay/Lesbian Almanac,* p. 141.

55. Klaich, *Woman + Woman,* p. 133.

56. See Smith-Rosenberg's chapter "The New Woman as Androgyne: Social Disorder and Gender Crisis, 1870–1936" in *Disorderly Conduct: Vision of Gender in Victorian America* (New York: Knopf, 1985), pp. 245–296. Also check Faderman, *Odd Girls,* pp. 62–117.

57. See Esther Newton, "The Mythic Mannish Lesbian: Radcliffe, Hall and the New Woman," *Signs* 9, No. 4 (Summer 1984): 557–575; Faderman, *Surpassing the Love of Men,* pp. 361–363; Louise de Salvo and Mitchell A. Leaska, eds., *The Letters of Vita Sackville-West to Virginia Woolf* (New York: William Morrow, 1985); Janice Robinson, *H. D.: The Life and Work of an American Poet* (Boston: Houghton Mifflin, 1982); Weeks, *Sex, Politics and Society,* pp. 108–121; E. M. Forster, *The Life to Come and Other Stories* (Harmondsworth: Penguin, 1975), where he claims he wants "to love a strong, young man of the lower classes and be loved by him" (p. 16); Barbara Fassler, "Theories of Homosexuality as Sources of Bloomsbury's Androgyny" *Signs* 5, No. 2 (1979): 237–251; and Lesbian History Group, *Not a Passing Phase: Reclaiming Lesbians in History 1840–1985* (London: The Women's Press, 1989). These are a few references of the period; the list is by no means exhaustive.

58. Simmons, "Companionate Marriage," p. 58. For an excellent and concise bibliography of the cautionary literature between 1910 and 1930, see Simmons's endnotes in the same article.

59. Weeks, *Sex, Politics and Society,* p. 124.

60. Ruth Roach Pierson, *"They're Still Women After All": The Second World War and Canadian Womanhood* (Toronto: McClelland and Stewart, 1986), p. 219. Pierson's interpretation is based on Allan Berube, "Coming Out under Fire: The Untold Story of the World War II Soldiers Who Fought on the Front Lines of Gay and Lesbian Liberation," *Mother Jones* 7, No. 2 (February/March 1983): 23–29, 45. See also Allan Berube, *Coming Out under Fire: The History of Gay Men and Women in World War Two* (New York: The Free Press, 1990).

61. Weeks, *Sex, Politics and Society,* pp. 222–223.

62. John Newson in 1948 as quoted in ibid., p. 237.

63. Frank S. Caprio, *Female Homosexuality: A Psychoanalytic Study of Lesbianism* (London: Icon Books, 1955; rpt. 1963), p. 157.

64. Ibid., p. 176.

65. D. J. West, *Homosexuality* (Harmondsworth: Pelican, 1955; rpt. 1963), p. 139.

66. Ibid.

67. Jack H. Hedblom, "The Female Homosexual: Social and Attitudinal Dimensions," in *The Homosexual Dialectic,* ed. Joseph A. McCaffrey (Englewood Cliffs, N.J.: Prentice-Hall, 1972), p. 26.

68. Ibid., p. 37.

69. For further information regarding Evelyn Hooker's study, see her articles listed in footnote 12, p. 112, in John D'Emilio, *Sexual Politics, Sexual Communities: The Making of a Homosexual Minority in the United States 1940–1970* (Chicago: University of Chicago Press, 1983). Also in the same book, see pp. 144–145 for information on the Wolfenden Report. For another viewpoint on the Wolfenden Report, see Jeffrey Weeks, *Sex, Politics and Society,* especially pp. 239–244; also Hedblom, "The Female Homosexual," pp. 101–107.

70. Hedblom, "The Female Homosexual," pp. 42–43.

71. For a firsthand account of this organization, see its founders' book: Del Martin and Phyllis Lyon, *Lesbian/Woman* (New York: Bantam Books, 1972, rpt. 1980). See also D'Emilio, *Sexual Politics,* pp. 101–107.

72. First published by "Daughters of Bilitis" in October 1956, it then became the quintessential lesbian newsmagazine and survived until 1970. See D'Emilio, *Sexual Politics,* pp. 229–230.

73. Mary McIntosh, "The Homosexual Role," *Social Problems* 16, No. 2 (Fall 1968); rpt. in Kenneth Plummer, ed., *The Making of the Modern Homosexual* (London: Huchinson, 1981), pp. 30–44 (with a postscript interview of Mary McIntosh by Jeffrey Weeks and Kenneth Plummer).

74. Ibid., p. 33.

75. Robert Padgug, "Sexual Matters: On Conceptualizing Sexuality in History," *Radical History Review* 20 (Spring/Summer 1979): 14.

76. McIntosh in Plummer, *The Making of the Modern Homosexual,* p. 46.

77. Weeks, "Movements of Affirmation," p. 164.

78. Kenneth Plummer, *Sexual Stigma: An Interactionist Account* (London: Routledge and Kegan Paul, 1975), p. 94.

79. Weeks, "Movements of Affirmation," p. 171.

80. Ibid.

81. John Gagnon and William Simon, *Sexual Conduct: The Sources of Human Sexuality* (Chicago: Adline Publishing, 1973), p. 178.

82. Anabel Faraday, "Liberating Lesbian Research," in Plummer, *The Making of the Modern Homosexual,* p. 124.

83. Quoting Jeffrey Weeks, "Discourse, Desire and Sexual Deviance: Some Problems in a History of Homosexuality," in Plummer, *The Making of the Modern Homosexual,* p. 96.

84. Michel, Foucault, *The History of Sexuality,* Vol. 1: *An Introduction,* trans. Robert Hurley (New York: Vintage Books, 1980), p. 11.

85. Gary Kinsman, "The Social Construction of Homosexual Cultures: Heterosexual Hegemony and Homosexual Resistance," Diss. Toronto: University of Toronto, 1983, p. 50.

86. Foucault, *History of Sexuality,* Vol. 1, p. 43.

87. Catharine MacKinnon, "Feminism, Marxism, Method and the State: An Agenda for Theory," *Signs* 7, No. 3 (1982): 526, footnote 22. However, since I cannot do justice to Foucault's brilliant though controversial theories, I refer the reader to his own books, particularly the *The History of Sexuality* series. For excellent reviews of Foucault's work, see Jeffrey Weeks, "Foucault for Historians," *History Workshop,* Issue 14 (Autumn 1982): 106–119; Kinsman, "Social Construction," particularly pp. 51–54; and finally, for feminist perspectives, Irene Diamond and Lee Quinby, eds., *Feminism and Foucault: Reflections on Resistance* (Boston: Northeastern University Press, 1988).

88. Robin Morgan, "Feminist Diplomacy" (Editorial), *MS* 1, No. 6 (May/June 1991): 1.

89. Gay Left Collective, "Why Marxism?" in *Pink Triangles: Radical Perspectives on Gay Liberation,* ed. Pam Mitchell (Boston: Alyson Publications, 1980), p. 102.

90. Margaret Coulson, "The Struggle for Femininity," in *Homosexuality: Power and Politics,* ed. Gay Left Collective (London: Allyson and Busby, 1980), p. 25.

91. Faraday, "Liberating Lesbian Research," p. 113.

92. MacKinnon, "Feminism, Marxism," p. 531.

93. Radicalesbians, "The Woman Identified Woman," in *Radical Feminism,* ed. Ann Koedt, Ellen Levine, and Anita Rapone (New York: Quadrangle Books, 1973), p. 242.

94. Adrienne Rich, "Compulsory Heterosexuality and Lesbian Existence," *Signs* 5, No. 4 (Summer 1980): 650.

95. A homosexual association founded in Los Angeles in 1951 whose membership and concerns were primarily male.

96. One of the two founders of Daughters of Bilitis. The other is Phyllis Lyon.

97. Interview with DOB member Helen Sanders; Del Martin in *The Ladder,* October 1959, p. 19. For other instances of DOB members defending an autonomous women's organization, see *The Ladder,* June 1957, p. 8; December 1957, p. 19; and October 1958; p. 5. Quoted in D'Emilio, *Sexual Politics,* p. 105, and footnote 28.

98. For United States laws that affect lesbians and gay men, see Editors of the *Harvard Law Review, Sexual Orientation and the Law,* particularly pp. 9–43.

99. John A. Yogis, QC. *Canadian Law Dictionary* (Toronto: Barron's Educational Series, 1983), p. 56.

100. Laurie Bell, *On Our Own Terms: A Practical Guide for Lesbian and Gay Relationships* (Toronto: Coalition for Lesbian and Gay Rights in Ontario, 1991), p. 12.

## Chapter 2. Women in Teaching: A Short History

1. Sections of this chapter have been modified and used in my article, "Lesbian Teachers: An Invisible Presence," in *Feminism and Education: A Canadian Perspective,* ed. Frieda Forman, Mary O'Brien, Jane Haddad, Dianne Hallman, and Philinda Masters (Toronto: Centre for Women's Studies in Education, The Ontario Institute for Studies in Education, 1990), pp. 191–218.

2. Alison Prentice, "The Feminization of Teaching," in *The Neglected Majority* ed. Susan Mann Trofimenkoff and Alison Prentice (Toronto: McClelland and Stewart, 1977), pp. 50–51. For an equivalent article reviewing the feminization of teaching in the United States, see Geraldine J. Clifford, " 'Daughters into Teachers': Educational and Demographic Influences on the Transformation of Teaching into 'Women's Work' in America," in *Women Who Taught: Perspectives on the History of Women and Teaching,* ed. Alison Prentice and Marjorie R. Theobald (Toronto: University of Toronto Press, 1991), pp. 115–135. This article was reprinted from *History of Education Review* 12, No. 1 (1983): 15–28.

3. Prentice, "The Feminization of Teaching," p. 49.

4. Ibid., pp. 51–52.

5. Rothman, *Woman's Proper Place*, p. 14.

6. *Centennial Story: The Board of Education for the City of Toronto 1850–1950*, dir. E. A. Hardy, ed. Honora M. Cochrane (Toronto: Thomas Nelson and Sons, 1950), p. 170.

7. Ibid.

8. Private conversation with Norma Higgs, a now retired teacher and a friend, March 1984.

9. Nancy Hoffman, *Woman's "True" Profession* (Old Westbury, N.Y.: The Feminist Press, 1981), p. 10.

10. Catharine Beecher to Mary Dutton, 1830. Quoted in ibid.

11. Egerton Ryerson, quoted in Prentice, "The Feminization of Teaching," p. 54.

12. Quoted in *The Shortest Shadow*, a descriptive study of the Federation of Women Teachers' Associations of Ontario. The study was conducted between 1967 and 1969. Research committee: Margaret Beckingham, Marie Harvie, and Isabel Ward; n.d., p. 40.

13. Alison Prentice, *The School Promoters* (Toronto: McClellan and Stewart, 1977), p. 167.

14. Myra Strober and David Tyack, "Why Do Women Teach and Men Manage? A Report on Research on Schools," *Signs* 5, No. 3 (Summer 1980): 497.

15. Elizabeth Graham, "Schoolmistresses and Early Teaching in Ontario," in *Women at Work 1850–1930*, ed. Janice Acton, Penny Goldsmith, and Bonnie Shepard (Toronto: Canadian Women's Educational Press, 1974), p. 181.

16. Prentice, "The Feminization of Teaching," p. 64.

17. Martha Vicinus, *Independent Women: Work and Community for Single Women, 1850–1920* (Chicago: University of Chicago Press, 1985), p. 209.

18. Prentice, "The Feminization of Teaching," pp. 60–61.

19. Marta Danylewicz, Beth Light, and Alison Prentice, "The Evolution of the Sexual Division of Labour in Teaching: A Nineteenth Century Ontario and Quebec Case Study," *Histoire social/Social History* 16, No. 3, (mai/May 1983): 99.

20. Ibid., p. 82.

21. Faderman, *Surpassing the Love of Men*, p. 227.

22. Ramsay Cook and Wendy Mitchison, eds., *The Proper Sphere. Women's Place in Canadian Society* (Toronto: Oxford University Press, 1976), p. 136.

23. Beth Light and Alison Prentice, eds. *Pioneer and Gentlewomen of British North America, 1713–1867* (Toronto: New Hogtown Press, 1980), p. 46.

24. The word *spinster* once referred to unmarried women who were required to earn their keep in the home by spinning. See Patricia O'Brien, *Women Alone* (New York: Quadrangle, 1973), p. 74; Daly, *Gyn/Ecology* pp. 386–424; or Jeffreys, *The Spinster*.

25. Ontario contract, circa 1923.

26. For a collection of these accounts, see Hoffman, *Woman's "True" Profession*.

27. Frances Widdowson, *Going up into the Next Class: Women and Elementary Teacher Training 180–1914* (London: Hutchinson, 1983), p. 66.

28. See, for example, "Minutes of the Toronto Board of Education," May 16, 1946. I thank Cecelia Reynolds for calling attention to this reference.

29. Widdowson, *Going up into the Next Class,* p. 65; and Judith Arbus, "Historical Bases of a Sex-Segregated Labour Force: Women Teachers' Experience during the Great Depression." Diss. Toronto: University of Toronto 1984, pp. 83–85.

30. Widdowson, *Going up into the Next Class,* p. 65.

31. Mary V. Holman, *How It Feels to Be a Teacher* (New York: Bureau of Publications, Teachers College, Columbia University, 1950), p. 59.

32. See ibid., p. 158, for examples of U.S. contracts forbidding teachers to dance, drink, accompany men, ride automobiles, and so forth.

33. O'Brien, *Women Alone,* p. 33.

34. Ibid.

35. Alison Oram, " 'Embittered, Sexless, or Homosexual': Attacks on Spinster Teachers 1918–1939," in Lesbian History Group, *Not a Passing Phase,* pp. 101–102.

36. Holman, *How It Feels,* p. 17.

37. Ibid.

38. Sybil Shack, *Women in Canadian Education: The Two-Thirds Minority* (Toronto: University of Toronto Press, 1973), p. 5.

39. Oram, "'Embittered, Sexless, or Homosexual,'" p. 114. This whole article is wonderful in making the link between spinster teachers and lesbian teachers, and how the former were stigmatized because they implicitly represented the latter.

40. Symptomatic of the issue of "Johnny" as the model student, see Rudolf F. Flesch, *Why Johnny Can't Read: What You Can Do about It* (New York: Harper and Row, 1955, rpt. 1966); and its sequel by the same author, *Why Johnny Still Can't Read: A New Look at the Scandal of Our Schools* (New York: Harper and Row, 1981). Although these books do not deal with why the model student is always a male "Johnny," the unproblematic use of a male model speaks for itself. I remember in my Teachers College days (North Bay, 1969–70) referring to the model "Johnny." Other, more recent, books continue the tradition: for instance, Morris Kline, *Why Johnny Can't Add: The Failure of the New Math* (New York: St. Martin's Press, 1973); Opel Moore, *Why Johnny Can't Learn* (Milford, Mich.: Mott Media, 1975).

41. Arbus, "Historical Bases," p. 88.

42. *Centennial Story*, p. 172.

43. Danylewycz and Prentice, "Teachers' Work: Changing Patterns and Perceptions in the Emerging School Systems of Nineteenth and Early Twentieth-Century Central Canada," in *Women Who Taught*, ed. Alison Prentice and Marjorie R. Theobold. (Toronto: University of Toronto Press, 1991), p. 153.

44. Ibid., p. 154.

45. *We the Teachers of Ontario*, OTF/FEO, the fourteenth revised edition authorized by the Board of Governors of OTF (Toronto: Ontario Teachers' Federation, 1990), p. 4.

46. Sara Delamont, "The Contradictions in Ladies' Education," in *The Nineteenth Century Woman* ed. Sara Delamont and Lorna Duffin (London: Croom Helm, 1978), p. 145.

47. Cited in Doris French, *High Button Boot Straps: Federation of Women Teachers Association of Ontario 1918–1968* (Toronto: Ryerson Press, 1968), pp. 156–157.

48. Ibid., pp. 159–169.

49. *The Shortest Shadow*, pp. 56–57.

50. Ibid.

51. Judith Arbus, "Grateful to Be Working: Women Teachers During the Great Depression," in *Feminism and Education: A Canadian Perspective* ed. Frieda Forman et al., (Toronto: Centre for Women's Studies in Education, OISE, 1990), p. 182.

52. Dorothy E. Smith, Marilee Reimer, Connie Taylor, and Yoko Ueda, "Working Paper on the Implications of Declining Enrollment for Women Teachers in Public Elementary and Secondary Schools in Ontario," paper commissioned and prepared for the Commission on Declining Enrollments in Ontario, July 1978, p. 2.

53. Ontario Secondary School Teachers' Federation (OSSTF), *Forum,* April 1981, p. 59.

54. Laura S. Weintraub, "Equitable Conceptions and Resistance to Delivery: Employment Equity in the Education Sector," in Forman et al., *Feminism and Education,* p. 69.

55. Part-time teachers, most often women, were, until recently, often not granted fringe benefits. However, most collective agreements have currently negotiated equitable salaries and conditions of work for part-time teachers. Previously, the seniority of part-time teachers suffered because they needed two years for every one counted on both the salary grid and the seniority list. Also, although a number of collective agreements had specified what constituted a "part-time timetable," some principals were known to spread the specified number of teaching periods across a full teaching day. This unfair teaching practice was rectified in collective agreements with mention of "consecutive teaching periods." Other principals were known to demand full coaching loads (coaching is not remunerated in Ontario but is considered extracurricular and voluntary, although pressure is put on certain teachers to coach, such as, for instance, physical education teachers), and still others neglected to grant part-time teachers preparation periods, as is custumary for full-time teachers.

56. I personally remember being warned of this rule as a young teacher. The reason for it was never officially explained. The rule is mentioned in *The Shortest Shadow,* p. 60.

57. See Weintraub, "Equitable Conceptions," p. 67–121.

58. Smith et al., "Working Paper," pp. 13–14.

59. Ibid., p. 16.

60. Dale Spender, "Education: The Patriarchal Paradigm and the Response to Feminism," in *Men's Studies Modified: The Impact of Feminism on the Academic Disciplines,* ed. Dale Spender (Oxford: Pergamon Press, 1981), p. 164.

61. Smith et al., "Working Paper," p. 16.

62. Ibid., p. 17.

63. *The Shortest Shadow,* p. 45.

64. Smith et al., "Working Paper," p. 9.

65. Ibid., p. 18.

66. Shelagh Luka, "The Status of Women in the Teaching Profession," *Forum* (OSSTF) 7, No. 2 (April 1981): 57.

67. Smith et al., "Working Paper," p. 19.

68. Luka, "The Status of Women," p. 59.

69. Weintraub, "Equitable Conceptions," p. 70.

70. Ibid., pp. 70–76, especially p. 76.

71. John Melady, "Attitudes," *Forum* (OSSTF) 7, No. 2 (April 1981): 60.

72. See, for instance Rosemary Deem, ed., *Schooling for Women's Work* (London: Routledge and Kegan Paul, 1980). See articles included. See also Dale Spender and Elizabeth Sarah, eds., *Learning to Lose: Sexism in Education* (London: The Women's Press, 1980); Dale Spender, *Invisible Women: The Schooling Scandal* (London: Writers and Readers Publishing Cooperative, 1982); R. W. Connell, D. J. Ashenden, S. Kessler, and G. W. Dowsett, *Making the Difference* (Sydney: George Allen and Unwin, 1982); Charlotte Bunch and Sandra Pollack, *Learning Our Way: Essays in Feminist Education* (Trumansberg, N.Y.: Crossing Press, 1983); Joyce Antler and Sari Knopp Bilken, eds., *Changing Education: Women as Radicals and Conservators* (Albany, N.Y.: State University of New York Press, 1990); Valerie Walkerdine, *Schoolgirl Fictions* (London: Verso, 1990); Susan L. Gabriel and Isaiah Smithson, eds., *Gender in the Classroom: Power and Pedagogy* (Urbana: University of Illinois Press, 1990); Madeleine R. Grumet, *Bitter Milk: Women and Teaching* (Amherst: University of Massachusetts Press, 1988); Kathleen Weiler, *Women Teaching for Change: Gender, Class and Power* (South Hadley: Bergin and Garvey, 1988); Lois Weis, ed., *Class, Race, and Gender in American Education* (Albany, N.Y.: State University of New York Press, 1988); and Madeleine Arnot, ed., *Race and Gender: Equal Opportunities Policies in Education* (Oxford: Pergamon Press, in association with The Open University, 1985, rpt. 1988). These are just a few titles that deal with gender, race and class in education.

73. Some of the titles that could provide increased understanding of the issues of race and class as these intersect with gender, particularly in the area of women and education , are as follows: Dionne Brand, *No Burden to Carry: 1920–1950* (Toronto: The Women's Press, 1991); Afua Cooper, "The Search for Mary Bibb, Black Woman Teacher in 19th Century Canada West," *Ontario History* 83, No. 1 (March 1991): 39–54; Mary Crnkovich, ed., *"Gossip": A Spoken History of Women in the North* (Ottawa: Canadian Arctic Resources Committee, 1990); Jean Barman, "Separate and Unequal: Indian and White Girls at All Hallows School, 1884–1920," in *Indian Education in Canada,* ed. Jean Barman, Yvonne Hebèrt, and Don McCaskill

(Vancouver: University of British Columbia Press, 1986), pp. 110–131; The
Clio Collective, eds., *Quebec Women: A History* (Toronto: The Women's
Press, 1987); *Enough is Enough: Aboriginal Women Speak Out,* as told to
Janet Silman (Toronto: The Women' Press, 1987); Beth Brant, ed., "A Gath-
ering of the Spirit," *Sinister Wisdom* 22/23, 1983 (a special issue on North
American Indian Women); Paula Giddings, *When and Where I Enter: The
Impact of Black Women on Race and Sex in America* (New York: Bantam,
1985); bell hooks, *Talking Back, Thinking Feminist, Thinking Black* (Bos-
ton: South End Press, 1989); and Evelyn Torton Beck, ed., *Nice Jewish
Girls: A Lesbian Anthology* (Watertown, Mass.: Persephone Press, 1982).

## Chapter 3. Theoretical Framework

1. Virginia Woolf, *Three Guineas* (London: Hogarth, 1938, rpt. Harmondsworth: Penguin, 1982), p. 155.

2. Kate Millett, *Sexual Politics* (1969, rpt. New York: Ballantine
Books, 1978); p. 34.

3. Veronica Beechey, "On Patriarchy," *Feminist Review* 3 (1979): 66.

4. Roisin McDonough and Rachel Harrison, "Patriarchy and Relations of Production," in *Feminism and Materialism*, ed. Annette Kuhn and
AnnMarie Wolpe (London: Routledge and Kegan Paul, 1978), p. 12.

5. See for instance, Mary O'Brien, *The Politics of Reproduction* (London: Routledge and Kegan Paul, 1981); Annette Kuhn and AnnMarie
Wolpe, eds., *Feminism and Materialism* (London: Routledge and Kegan
Paul, 1978) (most articles are relevant); Dorothy Smith and Varda Burstyn,
*Women, Class, Family and the State* (Toronto: Garamond Press, 1985); sub-
missions by Michele Barrett and/or Mary McIntosh in *Feminism, Culture
and Politics*, ed. Rosalind Brunt and Carolyn Rowan (London: Lawrence
and Wishart, 1982); Rosalind Coward, *Patriarchal Precedents: Sexuality
and Social Relations* (London: Routledge and Kegan Paul, 1983); and Dorothy E. Smith, *The Everyday World as Problematic: A Feminist Sociology*
(Boston: Northeastern University Press, 1987).

6. Millett, *Sexual Politics,* p. 35.

7. Ibid., p. 81.

8. Stephen Walker and Len Barton, "Gender, Class and Education:
A Personal View," in *Gender, Class and Education,* ed. Stephen Walker and
Len Barton (Sussex: Falmer Press, 1983), p. 4.

9. See Michele Barrett and Mary McIntosh, "The 'Family Wage,' " in
*The Changing Experience of Women,* ed. Elizabeth Whitelegg et al. (Oxford:
Martin Robertson, in association with The Open University, 1982), p. 71–87.

10. Dorothy E. Smith, "Women, Class and Family," in *Women, Class, Family and the State*, p. 27. This long article presents a concise analysis of women's dependence on and subordination to men in contemporary capitalist Western societies, particularly within the context of the family. Smith gives a historical account of the different structures and means of subsistence of family units, the changing relationship of the family and the state, and the consequent situation of women in a capitalist mode of production.

11. McDonough and Harrison, "Patriarchy," p. 38.

12. Varda Burstyn, "Masculine Dominance and the State," in Smith and Burstyn, *Women, Class*, p. 64.

13. MacKinnon, "Feminism, Marxism," p. 533.

14. Burstyn, "Masculine Dominance."

15. According to Laurie Bell (*On Our Own Terms*), "there is nothing in federal or provincial legislation permitting or prohibiting gays and lesbians to marry. However, in 1974 a gay couple tried to have their marriage legally recognized in the province of Manitoba (*North vs. Matheson, 1974*). The Judge relied on dictionary definitions and the encyclopedia. He ruled that marriage was understood to be between members of the opposite sex" (p. 11). Likewise, in the United States, marriage of same-sex partners is prohibited, according to the editors of the *Harvard Law Review*, (pp. 96–101) and, despite social and legal evolution, "courts and legislatures continually have refused to grant gay and lesbian couples family status" (p. 94 of *Sexual Orientation and the Law*, 1990; see also pp. 96–101). By extension, many of the benefits granted heterosexual couples do not apply to same-sex couples: for instance, government benefits (Canada Pension Plan, War Veteran's Allowance, and so forth), old age security, provincial family and disability benefits, welfare allowance, workers' compensation, injury and death benefits, and inheritance rights (Bell, *On Our Own Terms*, pp. 8–9). Although homosexuality has been legal in Canada for almost two decades, it has not been socially, culturally, politically validated. For instance, it is still difficult to find public funding for lesbian or gay research or cultural and artistic events. Although in Ontario, since 1986, lesbians and gays are officially protected from discrimination in the areas of employment, housing, and services, only heterosexuality is validated by the state. For example, a woman cohabitating with a male lover stands to lose her welfare benefits, whereas if she were living with her lesbian lover, her benefits would not be affected. This renders the lesbian option invisible. The improvements that have occurred recently include a number of provincially sponsored government employments that recognize same-sex lovers as legitimate for the purposes of benefits (medical, insurance, pension, and so forth).

16. Frye, "To Be and Be Seen," p. 157.

17. Dynes, *Homolexis*, p. 65.

18. I am grateful to Line Chamberland for forcing me to elaborate on the meaning of *heterosexuality*.

19. Jonathan Katz, *Gay/Lesbian Almanac*, p. 147.

20. I am grateful, once more, to Line Chamberland for focusing my attention on the issue of multiple and hierarchicalized sexualities. Scholars who treat these concerns include Michel Foucault, *History of Sexuality*, Vol. 1; Jeffrey Weeks, *Sexuality and Its Discontent: Meanings, Myths, and Modern Sexualities* (London: Routledge, and Kegan Paul, 1985); Guy Hocquenghem, *Homosexual Desire* (London: Allison and Busby, 1978); and Gayle Rubin, "Thinking Sex: Notes for a Radical Theory of the Politics of Sexuality," in *Pleasure and Danger: Exploring Female Sexuality*, ed. Carol Vance (London: Routledge and Kegan Paul, 1984), pp. 257–319. These are but a few of many who treat the subject of multiple sexualities.

21. Dorothy E. Smith, "The Ideological Practice of Sociology," *Catalyst* 8 (Winter 1974): 45.

22. Michele Barrett, *Women's Oppression Today* (London: Verso, 1980), p. 67.

23. See Rich, "Compulsory Heterosexuality." Although this piece is problematic in some of its assumptions, Rich makes a case to demonstrate how women (and men) are induced through cultural, social, legal, and other policies into expressing their sexuality in particular, dominant, and socially acceptable ways.

24. Chantal Mouffe, "Hegemony and Ideology in Gramsci," in *Gramsci and Marxist Theory*, ed. Chantal Mouffe (London: Routledge and Kegan Paul, 1979), p. 181.

25. Ibid., p. 187.

26. Ibid., p. 196.

27. Millett, *Sexual Politics*, p. 35.

28. Christine Buci-Gluckmann, "Hegemony and Consent: A Political Strategy," in *Approaches to Gramsci*, ed. Anne Shortstack Sassoon (London: Writers and Readers Publishing Cooperative Society, Ltd., 1982), p. 119.

29. See, for instance, Dale Spender's books *Invisible Women* and *Learning to Lose;* or Katherine Claricoates, "The Importance of Being Ernest . . . Emma . . . Tom . . . Jane . . . The Perception and Categorization of Gender Conformity and Gender Deviation in Primary Schools," in Deem, *Schooling for Women's Work*, pp. 26–41; and Grumet, *Bitter Milk*.

30. See Smith and Burstyn, *Women, Class;* O'Brien, *The Politics of Reproduction;* Barrett, *Women's Oppression Today;* Barrett and McIntosh, "The 'Family Wage' ";* Dorothy Smith, *Everyday World;* Kuhn and Wolpe,

*Feminism and Materialism;* Barbara Smith, ed., *Home Girls: A Black Feminist Anthology* (New York: Kitchen Table, Women of Color Press, 1983); Gloria T. Hull, Patricia Bell Scott, and Barbara Smith, eds., *All the Women Are White, All the Blacks are Men, But Some of Us Are Brave* (Old Wesbury, N.Y.: The Feminist Press, 1982): these are just a few who deal with analyses of women's oppression in Western capitalist societies.

31. Heterosexuality, like homosexuality, must be perceived as existing in its pluralities. There is not one heterosexuality any more than there is one homosexuality. However, for the purpose of the arguments of this chapter, and since I am elaborating a *state defined* "heterosexuality," I will therefore continue to use the term in the singular.

32. Marilyn Frye refutes the notion that lesbianism is a crime against nature by using a philosophical argument. In her words, "The fact that these [lesbian] relations are characterized as unnatural is revealing. For what is unnatural is contrary to the laws of nature, or contrary to the nature of the substance of entity in question. But what is contrary to the laws of nature cannot happen: that is what it means to call these laws the laws of nature. And I cannot do what is contrary to my nature, for if I could do it, it would be my nature to do it." Quoted from "To Be and Be Seen," pp. 158–159.

33. Rich, "Compulsory Heterosexuality," p. 645.

34. Coulson, "The Struggle for Feminity," p. 25.

35. This thought was inspired by Dorothy Smith's analysis. "Women, Class and Family," p. 10.

36. Louis Althusser, *Lenin and Philosophy and Other Essays,* trans. Ben Brewster (London: Monthly Review Press, 1971), p. 175.

37. Ibid., p. 157.

38. Samuel Bowles and Herbert Gintis, *Schooling in Capitalist America* (New York: Basic Books, 1976), p. 265.

39. Madeleine MacDonald, "Socio-Cultural Reproduction and Women's Education," in Deem, *Schooling for Women's Work,* p. 15.

40. See, for example, Dorothy E. Smith, "A Peculiar Eclipsing: Women's Exclusion from Man's Culture," *Women's Studies International Quarterly* 1 (1978): 281–295; and MacDonald, "Socio-Cultural Reproduction." Also check all other contributions in Deem's book, as well as Michele Stanworth, *Gender and Schooling* (London: Hutchinson, 1983); and the work of Jean Anyon, Veronica Beechey, AnneMarie Wolpe, Jenny Shaw, Rosemary Deem, Madeleine Grumet, Kathleen Weiler, Miriam David, Valerie Walkerdine, Dale Spender, and others.

41. Madeleine MacDonald, "Schooling and the Reproduction of Class and Gender Relations," in *Schooling, Ideology and the Curriculum,* ed. Len Barton, Roland Meighan and Stephen Walker (Sussex: Falmer Press, 1980), p. 35.

42. See, for instance, Madeleine Arnot's (formerly MacDonald) more recent anthology, *Race and Gender,* which incorporates issues of class as well as gender.

43. Education is compulsory between the ages of six and sixteen years. See Section 20(1)(a,b) of the *Education Act.* Revised Statutes of Ontario, 1980, Chapter 129, September 1990.

44. Ibid., Section 236(j,k,l,m).

45. Ibid., Section 150(1)(11).

46. Ibid., Section 22 (1,2,3).

47. Ibid., Section 235(1)(c).

48. Ibid., Section 29(1), which reads: "A parent or guardian of a child of compulsory school age who neglects or refuses to cause the child to attend school is . . . guilty of an offense and on conviction is liable to a fine of not more than $100."

49. Jenny Shaw, *"In Loco Parentis:* A Relationship Between Parent, State and Child," in *Politics, Patriarchy, and Practice,* Vol. 2, ed. Roger Dale et al. (Sussex: Falmer Press, 1981), p. 259.

50. Ibid., p. 264.

51. Bob Davies, "Sifted, Sorted, Slotted and Streamed," *Mudpie* 4, No. 2 (February 1983): 8.

52. Willard Waller, *The Sociology of Teaching* (New York: John Wiley, 1932, rpt. 1976), p. 147.

53. Michael Apple and Lois Weis, "Ideology and Practice in Schooling: A Political and Conceptual Introduction," in *Ideology and Practice in Schooling,* ed. Michael Apple and Lois Weis (Philadelphia: Temple University Press, 1983), pp. 6–7.

54. Editors of the *Harvard Law Review, Sexual Orientation and the Law,* p. 90.

55. Ibid., p. 91.

56. Ibid.

57. Andrew Gitlin, "School Structures and Teachers' Work," in Apple and Weis, *Ideology and Practice,* p. 209.

58. Rosemary Chessum, "Teacher Ideologies and Pupil Disaffection," in *Schooling, Ideology and the Curriculum,* ed. Len Barton et al. (Sussex: Falmer Press, 1980), p. 115.

59. Ibid., pp. 113–114.

60. R. W. Connell et al., *Making the Difference,* p. 103.

61. Erving Goffman, *Stigma: Notes on the Management of Spoiled Identity* (Englewood Cliffs, N.J.: Prentice-Hall, 1963), p. 3.

62. Ibid., p. 6.

63. Ibid., p. 74.

64. Ibid., p. 51.

65. *Selections from the "Prison Notebooks" of Antonio Gramsci,* ed. and trans. Quintin Hoare and Geoffrey Nowell Smith (New York: International Publishers, 1971; rpt. 1980), pp. 422–423.

66. Ibid., pp. 192–193.

67. Gramsci sees the state as "the entire complex of practical and theoretical activities through which the ruling class not only justifies and maintains its dominance, but manages to win the active consent of those over whom it rules," *"Prison Notebooks,"* p. 244.

68. See Chapter 1 ("Homosexuality in Perspective") for an examination of passionate friendships between women and the historical progression that documents how women's attachments to each other were condemned when they gained social and economic independence from men. For greater detail, see Lillian Faderman, *Odd Girls.*

69. Carl Boggs, *Gramsci's Marxism* (London: Pluto Press, 1976), p. 72.

70. See Kinsman, "Social Construction." This work is a very commendable attempt to adapt Gramsci's hegemony to the issue of sexuality.

71. D'Emilio, *Sexual Politics,* p. 247.

72. Edwin M. Schur, *Labelling Women Deviant: Gender, Stigma and Social Control* (Philadelphia: Temple University Press, 1984), p. 129.

73. Alfred Schutz, *On Phenomenology and Social Relations,* edited and introduced by Helmut R. Wagner (Chicago: University of Chicago Press, 1970), p. 274.

74. Ibid.

75. It would interesting to be able to make a distinction between *stigma* and *discrimination, stigma* referring to the blemish or disgrace felt, indeed, internalized (in some cases) by the stigmatized individual, and

*discrimination* meaning that the bias against the stigma becomes the responsibility of those who hold that prejudice. The distinction (if it were possible), would be interesting in cases where, for political or ideological or social reasons, a particular belief or position is stigmatized but where the individuals who adhere to that belief or position see themselves as part of counter-hegemonic movements. This would mean that a person in that position might choose to conceal her or his membership in the stigmatized group but would, at the same time, take pride in that membership. For instance, during the McCarthy era in the United States, Communists were stigmatized, although members of that movement felt that they were discriminated against (that society was biased against them). They kept their membership concealed but did not internalize the negative characteristics of which the McCarthyists were accusing them. Therefore, from the perspective of the members of the Communist Party, it was unsafe but OK to belong. It was not a stigma but rather discrimination that they had to bear. Similarly, post-Stonewall, we may say "Gay, OK" but that does not mean that "Gay is safe." However, from the perspective of those outside the group, a stigma is not OK, and neither is it (some of the time) safe.

76. "Lesbian Appeals," *Off Our Backs* vol. 14, (June 1984): 10.

77. Editors of the *Harvard Law Review, Sexual Orientation, and the Law,* pp. 86–87.

78. Harold Garfinkel, *Studies in Ethnomethodology* (Englewood Cliffs, N.J.: Prentice-Hall, 1967), p. 181.

79. That policy read: "Be it resolved that every teacher has the right to participate equally in, and have equal opportunity in the teaching profession, regardless of race, colour, creed, political beliefs, private and personal practices, marital status, age, sex, sexual orientation, national origin, ancestry, grade or subject taught." Toronto Teachers' Federation, adopted December 14, 1979. Cited in Coalition for Gay Rights in Ontario, *The Human Rights Omission,* n.d., p. 31.

80. *The Education Act,* Section 234, Revised Statutes of Ontario, 1980, Chapter 129, September 1990.

81. *OSSTF* Handbook, 1990/91, p. 64B: "General Duties of Members."

82. S. G. B. Robinson, *Do Not Erase: The Story of the First Fifty Years of OSSTF* (Toronto: Ontario Secondary School Teachers' Federation, 1971), pp. 167–168.

83. See the Badgley Reports, *Sexual Offences Against Children and Youth,* Vols. 1 and 2, report of the Committee on Sexual Offences Against Children and Youths, appointed by the Minister of Justice and Attorney General of Canada and the Ministry of Health and Welfare.

84. Private telephone conversation with Jim Whitehead, OSSTF, Toronto, April 25, 1985.

85. "Our Policy on Equal Opportunity," the Toronto Board of Education, Equal Opportunity Office, prepared by the Personnel Division of the Equal Opportunity Office of the Toronto Board of Education, February 1985.

86. "Board Report Recommendation," *Rites* 1, No. 7 (December/January 1984/85), p. 7.

87. "Growing Up Gay," CITY TV, July 20, 1985.

88. Didi Khayatt and George Smith, "An Investigation of the Barriers, on the Basis of Sexual Orientation, to the Provision of Quality Education for Gay and Lesbian Students." This research was funded by the block transfer grant from the Ontario Ministry of Education to the Ontario Institute for Studies in Education. My research involved lesbian students, and George Smith worked with the gay male students.

89. "Halton Code of Behaviour 'redundant' said Joe Harwood," *Federation Update 9, No. 15 (December 14, 1981): 2.*

## Chapter 4. Methodology

1. Dorothy E. Smith, "A Sociology for Women," in *The Prism of Sex: Essays in the Sociology of Knowledge,* ed. Julia A. Sherman and Evelyn Torton Beck (Madison: University of Wisconsin Press, 1979), p. 135. This article is reproduced in Smith's book: *Everyday World,* pp. 49–104. All citations in this chapter refer to the original article in Sherman and Beck's book.

2. See, for instance, Smith, "A Peculiar Eclipsing" reproduced in Smith's book: *Everyday World,* pp. 17–43; also, Tillie Olsen, *Silences* (New York: Delacort Press, 1965); Dale Spender, *Man-Made Language* (London: Routledge and Kegan Paul, 1980); Faderman, *Surpassing the Love of Men,* Sheila Rowbotham, *Women's Consciousness, Men's World* (Harmondsworth: Penguin, 1973); bell hooks, *Feminist Theory: From Margin to Center* (Boston: South End Press, 1984); or Cherrie Moraga and Gloria Anzaldúa, eds., *This Bridge Called My Back: Writings by Radical Women of Color* (Watertown: Mass.: Persephone Press, 1981). This is only a partial list.

3. Smith, "Sociology for Women," p. 137.

4. Rowbotham, *Women's Consciousness,* p. 31.

5. Smith, "Sociology for Women," p. 139.

6. Ibid., p. 140.

7. Ibid.

8. Ibid., p. 142.

9. Ibid., p. 143.

10. Ibid., 158.

11. Ann Oakley, cited in ibid., p. 147.

12. Ibid., p. 159.

13. Ibid., p. 160.

14. Ibid., pp. 160–161.

15. Karl Marx and Frederick Engels, *The German Ideology*, Part 1, edited and introduced by C. J. Arthur (New York: International Publishers, 1970, 1978, p. 64.

16. Smith, "Sociology for Women," p. 165.

17. Ibid.

18. Ibid., p. 173.

19. Ibid., p. 176.

20. Ibid., p. 183.

21. Dorothy Smith, "Ideological Practice," p. 47.

22. Marilyn Frye, "To Be and Be Seen," p. 159.

23. For innumerable variations of individual acceptance rejection of the label or identity *lesbian,* see Julia Penelope Stanley and Susan J. Wolfe, *The Coming Out Stories* (Watertown, Mass.: Persephone Press, 1980); Moraga and Anzaldúa, *This Bridge;* and Anita Cornwell, *Black Lesbian in White America* (Tallahassee, Fla.: Naiad Press, 1983). Finally, for a historical account of variations in labels and identities lesbians and others choose to signify women who love women, see Faderman, *Odd Girls.*

24. Smith, *Everyday World*, p. 111.

25. Ibid.

26. Ibid., p. 141.

27. Ibid.

28. Ibid.

29. I have traced my intellectual development toward feminism and my understanding of my sexual preference in "Sexual Politics and Sexuality," *Resources for Feminist Research* (RFR/DRF), Vol. 19, Nos. 3&4 (December 1990) pp. 8–12.

30. *Lesbian* was not a term used to describe the identity of a woman, but rather her sexual "tendencies." The relevant factor was whether a woman was interested sexually in women. Her "identity" as a lesbian was

virtually nonexistent. Very often these women were married or intended to marry. To live as a "lesbian" was unlikely, even if we were able to refer to several women we knew as "lesbian." By that we meant that they were open to sexual experience with women.

31. Faderman, *Odd Girls,* pp. 156–157.

32. The following is a copy of the guarantee that I read to each informant:

"I, Madiha Didi Khayatt, will ensure the confidentiality of this interview by observing the following precautions:

- I shall personally transcribe the interview following each tape-recording.
- I shall eliminate all identifying material contained in the interview. I shall use pseudonyms where appropriate, change the names of places, and remove any further details which may reveal the identity of the respondent.
- I shall transcribe this section I am reading as part of the interview. This will serve as the only record outlining the measures I have taken to ensure confidentiality.
- Immediately after transcription, I shall erase the tape-recording of the interview.
- I shall use sections of this interview in my research and future publications, but I guarantee there will be no identifying references in any quotations used.
- The above measures dissolve the relationship between you, the respondent, and the information you have given in this interview.
- A copy of the transcript of this interview will be sent to you for your records.
- I shall keep no records of names or addresses of any respondent. The only connection between the information given and the respondents will be in my head.
- No written consent form or signed document is possible so as not to implicate informants.
- Respondents' exact words will be quoted in my work. However, the respondents will not exist as continuous persons in the text, thus further avoiding possible recognition."

33. Smith, *Everyday World,* p. 157.

34. Here is the list of subjects: Location: Relation or distance from students; nonlegitimacy as a single woman or lesbian; gay or lesbian students; avoidance of the questions re: marriage; relationship with colleagues; single or lesbian on the job; self-image as a teacher; student crushes; fear of gossip or blackmail; lesbian self-identity; labels; coming out experiences; denial of lesbian experiences; first lesbian relationships; relationships with

family, relationships with lover; anticipated social reactions; passing; negative lesbian labels; social school functions; class discussion of homosexuality; recognition of other lesbians; "moral turpitude"; negative lesbian self-image; coming out to friends; coming out to colleagues; community standards; positive self-image; family background; gay bars; heterosexual marriage or involvement; pre–coming out incidents; effect on work; lesbian or feminist power; childhood sexuality; examples of Dorothy Smith's methodology; rural or urban; coming out at school; stereotypes; miscellaneous.

## Chapter 5. Discovering Lesbian Identity

1. Cherrie Moraga, "La Guera," in Moraga and Anzaldúa, *This Bridge*, pp. 32–33.

2. Meg Christian, "Ode to a Gym Teacher," Thumbelina Music, BMI, Olivia Records, 1974.

3. Adrienne Rich, "Taking Women Students Seriously," in *On Lies, Secrets and Silences: Selected Prose 1966–1973* (New York: W. W. Norton, 1979), p. 243.

4. See for instance, Blanche Weisen Cook, "The Historical Denial of Lesbianism," *Radical History Review* 20 (Spring/Summer 1979): 6–65; Faderman, *Surpassing the Love of Men;* Smith-Rosenberg, "The Female World"; and Kathy Peiss and Christina Simmons, eds., *Passion and Power: Sexuality in History* (Philadelphia: Temple University Press, 1989); to name a few.

5. For a detailed account of history of the ideological term *lesbian,* see Faderman, *Odd Girls.*

6. Ibid., p. 205.

7. Helena Feinstadt, "Towards Lesbianism as an Intentional Change," Paper, 1984/85.

8. Smith, "Sociology for Women," p. 135.

9. Eve Zaremba, "Shades of Lavender: Lesbian Sex and Sexuality," in *Still Ain't Satisfied,* ed. Maureen Fitzgerald, Connie Guberman, and Margie Wolfe (Toronto: The Women's Press, 1982), p. 89.

10. Rich, "Forward" to Stanley and Wolfe's *Coming Out Stories,* p. xiii.

11. It is interesting to note that in a recent conversation a retired teacher, informed me that between 1950 and 1952 "there was a spill-over [into Canada] from the McCarthy investigations from the United States." She remembered, as a young teacher living in a small town in southern On-

tario, that there was talk that all teachers should be forced to reswear an oath of allegiance to Canada because of the Communist witch-hunts. She remarked that many teachers were appalled. She added, "However, it died a quiet death—thank God."

12. Plummer, *Sexual Stigma*, p. 80.

13. WASP is an acronym for White Anglo Saxon Protestant.

14. See Jean Swallow, ed., *Out from Under: Sober Dykes and Our Friends* (San Francisco: Spinsters, Ink, 1983), for first-person accounts on the reasons for and the consequences of alcoholism on lesbians of all ages.

15. See Del Martin and Lyon, *Lesbian/Woman,* for examples of the lives of women in the United States prior to the women's and gay movements.

## Chapter 6. Lesbians in School

1. Apple and Weis, "Ideology and Practice," p. 28. The whole article is useful for understanding the cited statement.

2. MacDonald, "Socio-Cultural Reproduction," p. 24. See also Arnot, *Race and Gender* (by the same author).

3. In Ontario, such "extracurricular" activities as coaching, organizing trips or special interest clubs, and so on are not remunerated financially.

4. Khayatt, "Legalized Invisibility."

5. In honor of Gay Pride Week 1991, two Toronto daily newspapers, one of which is considered Canada's national paper, published articles about being lesbian or gay in the nineties. One was Warren Gerard, "Is Gay Bashing Out of Control?" *The Toronto Star,* Saturday, June 29, 1991, Section D: "Insight," p. D1; the other was a full two-page article by Alana Mitchell, "Gay in the Nineties," *The Globe and Mail,* Saturday, June 29, 1991, Section D: "Focus," pp. D1 and D4. This latter article has a subtitle: "Canada's 250,000 'out' gay men and lesbians, a diverse and diffuse community united solely by sexual orientation, finds cause for anger and joy as they press their case for equality."

6. *The Body Politic* was a national gay paper, now defunct.

7. Friend, who prefers to remain unnamed, in a private conversation, September, 1985.

8. See, for instance, Waller, *The Sociology of Teaching,* pp. 140–143; Caprio, *Female Homosexuality,* pp. 130–136; and Jess Stearn, *The Grapevine* (London: Frederick Muller Limited, 1965), pp. 54–63. The first is from

the field of sociology of education, the second is from psychology, and the third is a journalistic account of lesbianism. There are many more such traditional books. For a good bibliographic list, see M. T. Saghir and E. Robins, *Male and Female Homosexuality* (Baltimore: Williams-Wilkins, 1973). And for feminist historical accounts, see Nancy Sahli, "Smashing: Women's Relationship before the Fall," *Chrysalis* 17, No. 8 (Summer 1979), pp. 17–27; Martha Vicinus, "Distance and Desire: English Boarding-School Friendships," *Signs* 9, No. 4 (Summer 1984): 600–622; and Faderman, *Surpassing the Love of Men*.

9. Schools, even today, avoid dealing with the issue of youth homosexuality. In 1990–91, I was involved, along with a gay man, George Smith, in a project funded by a transfer grant from the Ministry of Education to the Ontario Institute for Studies in Education. We each interviewed gay and lesbian youths, respectively, and we both could safely say that the subject of homosexuality rarely, to this day, surfaces within the framework of school curricula. Students, both male and female, complained that even the library, the guidance office, or the health department either lacked information or was reluctant to provide information regarding the subject of homosexuality. Students of both sexes, but mostly the boys, related incidents of harassment and sometimes violence against them. However, some did provide very positive experiences with understanding and sensitive teachers and peers.

10. In the study undertook by George Smith and I in 1990–91, it was evident that *both* gay young men and young lesbians sought out *female* teachers, some of whom may have been lesbian.

11. This statement was borne out in the study George Smith and I undertook in 1990–91. Without exception, the gay and lesbian students we each interviewed protected the "privacy" of the teachers they suspected or about whom they were sure.

## Chapter 7. Implications of Coming Out in the Classroom

1. R. W. Connell, *Teachers' Work* (Sydney: George Allen and Unwin, 1985), p. 126.

2. Ibid., p. 116.

3. She mentioned several books, including Jill Johnston, *Lesbian Nation* (New York: Touchstone, 1973); Sally Miller Gearhart, *The Wanderground* (Watertown, Mass.: Persephone Press, 1979); Del Martin and Phyllis Lyon, *Lesbian/Woman* (Glide, 1972, rpt. New York: Bantam, 1980).

## Chapter 8. Consequences of Being a Lesbian at School

1. Connell et al., *Making the Difference*, p. 103.

2. Paul Willis, *Learning to Labor: How Workingclass Kids Get Workingclass Jobs* (New York: Columbia University Press, 1977; rpt. 1981), p. 64.

3. Schutz, *On Phenomenology*, p. 82.

4. See Khayatt, "Legalized Invisibility," pp. 185–193.

5. As did, for example, the Toronto Board of Education in a policy statement condemning discrimination on the basis of race, gender, ethnicity, sexual orientation, and so forth. This policy has since been revoked by the Toronto board, presumably because the Human Rights Code in Ontario provides enough protection from discrimination.

6. This teacher is referring to *Education Act,* Revised Statutes of Ontario, 1980, revised September 1990, Section 234, which reads:

> Notwithstanding the other provisions of this Part and notwithstanding anything in the contract between the board and the teacher, where a permanent or probationary teacher is employed by the board and a matter arises that in the opinion of the Minister adversely affects the welfare of the school in which the teacher is employed, (a) the board or teacher may, with the consent of the Minister, give the other party thirty days written notice of termination, and the contract is terminated at the expiration of thirty days from the date of notice given; . . .

7. International Gay Teachers' Association workshop at the International Gay Association Conference, Toronto, July 1985.

8. Mary Meigs, *The Medusa Head* (Vancouver: Talonbooks, 1983), p. 32.

9. Marilyn Frye, *The Politics of Reality: Essays in Feminist Theory* (Trumansburg, N.Y.: Crossing Press, 1983), p. 24.

10. Susan Brownmiller, *Femininity* (New York: Linden Press, Simon and Schuster, 1984).

11. Paula Krebs, "To Teach or Not to Teach?" *Off Our Backs* Vol. 14, No. 12 (January 1985): 5.

12. Ibid.

13. Quote of the superintendent's words, ibid.

14. Brownmiller, *Femininity*, p. 55.

15. Ibid., p. 81.

16. Denise Kulp, "Dyke Aesthetic: Dressed to Cool," *Off Our Backs*, 14, No. 7 (July 1984): 24.

17. Brownmiller, *Femininity*, p. 97.

## Conclusion

1. For a good account of what it is like being a lesbian or gay teacher in England after Clause 28 was introduced, see Gillian Squirrell, "In Passing . . . Teachers and Sexual Orientation," in *Teachers, Gender and Careers,* ed. Sandra Acker (Barcombe, Lewes, East Sussex: Falmer Press, 1989), pp. 87–106; or, by the same author, "Teachers and Issues of Sexual Orientation." *Gender and Education* 1, No. 1 (1989): 17–34.

2. Clearly, visibility does not always spell out potency, but it can be the basis on which discrimination is practiced, as in the case of race and color, or religion, or gender, in which cases political movements are necessary to provide possibilities of change. However, visibility, when passing is possible, is a political act.

# Selected Bibliography

The following is a short list of books pertaining to the subject of "lesbian teachers." It is by no means complete and includes only those books and articles I found useful and of which I am aware. It would be useful for the interested researcher to check the bibliographies of most of the following entries.

Bullough, Vern, and Bonnie Bullough. "Lesbianism in the 1920s and 1930s: A Newfound Study." *Signs* 2, No. 4 (1977): 895–904.

Burbridge, Michael and Jonathan Walters, eds. *Breaking the Silence: Gay Teenagers Speak for Themselves.* London: Printed by Community Press. Published by Joint Council for Gay Teenagers, 1981.

Clark, Don. *Loving Someone Gay.* New York: A Signet Book. New American Library, 1977, rpt. 1978.

Crew, Louis. "Thriving Decloseted in Rural Academe." In *After You're Out,* ed. Karla Jay and Allen Young. New York: Pyramid Books, 1975, rpt. 1977, pp. 96–102.

Crew, Louis, and Karen Keener. "Homophobia in the Academy: A Report of the Committee on Gay/Lesbian Concerns." *College English* 43, No. 7 (November 1981), pp. 682–689.

Cruikshank, Margaret. "Lesbians in the Academic World." In *Our Right to Love: A Lesbian Resource Book,* ed. Ginny Vida. Produced in cooperation with the women of the National Gay Task Force. Englewood Cliffs, N.J.: Prentice-Hall, 1978, pp. 164–167.

————, ed. *Lesbian Studies: Present and Future.* New York: The Feminist Press, 1982.

Daly, Mike. "At Work." in *Prejudice and Pride: Discrimination Against Gay People in Modern Britain,* ed. Bruce Galloway. London: Routledge and Kegan Paul, 1983, pp. 35–61.

DeVito, Joseph. "Educational Responsibilities to the Gay and Lesbian Student." Annual Meeting of the Speech Communication Association, 65th, San Antonio, Texas, November 10–13, 1979.

Dobson, Michael. "At School." In *Prejudice and Pride: Discrimination Against Gay People in Modern Britain,* ed. Bruce Galloway. London: Routledge and Kegan Paul, 1983, pp. 19–34.

Faderman, Lillian. *Odd Girls and Twilight Lovers: A History of Lesbian Life in Twentieth-Century America.* New York: Columbia University Press, 1991.

———. *Scotch Verdict\*: Miss Pirie and Miss Woods v. Dame Cumming Gordon.* New York: Quill, 1983.

Friedman, Meryl. "Lesbian as Teacher, Teacher as Lesbian." In *Our Right to Love: A Lesbian Resource Book,* ed. Ginny Vida. Produced in cooperation with women of the National Gay Task Force. Englewood Cliffs, N.J.: Prentice-Hall, 1978, pp. 157–162.

*Harvard Law Review* Editors. *Sexual Orientation and the Law.* Cambridge: Harvard University Press, 1990.

Hemmings, Susan. "Horrific Practices: How Lesbians Were Presented in the Newspapers of 1978." *Homosexuality: Power and Politics,* ed. Gay Left Collective. London: Allison and Busby, 1980, pp. 157–171.

Heron, Ann. ed. *One Teenager in 10.* Boston: Alyson Publications, 1983.

Hughes, Yvonne Johnson, and Yvette Perrault, eds. *Stepping Out of Line: A Workbook on Lesbianism and Feminism.* Vancouver: Press Gang Publishers, 1984, pp. 115–119.

Jackson, Stevi. *Childhood and Sexuality.* Oxford: Basil Blackwell, 1982.

Kehoe, Constance. "School Subcultures and Peer Group Pressures in Adolescent Deviance." Diss. Toronto: University of Toronto, 1971.

LaRiviere, Robert. "Bundles of Twigs in New Hampshire: A High School Teacher's Report." In *After You're Out,* ed. Karla Jay and Allen Young. New York: Pyramid Books, 1975, rpt. 1977, pp. 105–112.

Lesbian Rights Committee of TACWL. "The Law and Us. Lesbian and Gay Youth." *Pink Ink,* October 1983, p. 29.

Levine, Martine, and Robin Leonard. "Discrimination Against Lesbians in the Workforce." *Signs* 9, No. 4 (Summer 1984): 700–710.

Olsen, Myrna R. "A Study of Gay and Lesbian Teachers." *Journal of Homosexuality* 13, No. 4 (Summer 1987): 73–81.

*Ontario Department of Labour,* Toronto: Research Branch. "Homosexuality in Specific Fields: The Arts, the Military, the Ministry, Prisons, Sports, Teaching, and Transexuals. A Selected Bibliography." Number 13. Compiled by Alan V. Miller, October 1978.

*Open and Positive: An Account of How John Warburton Came Out at School and the Consequences.* London: Published by Gay Teachers' Group, and Printed by Women in Print, 1978.

Oram, Allison. " 'Embittered, Sexless or Homosexual': Attacks on Spinster Teachers 1918–1939." In *Not A Passing Phase: Reclaiming Lesbians in History 1840–1985,* ed. Lesbian History Group. London: The Women's Press, 1989.

Parmeter, Sara Hope, and Irene Reti, eds. *The Lesbian in Front of the Classroom.* Santa Cruz, Calif.: HerBooks, 1988.

Paterson, Ian. "High School Faggot." *The Body Politic,* May 1985, pp. 30–31.

*Radical Teacher* 24 (Gay and Lesbian Studies), 1980.

*Radical Teacher* 29 (Teaching Sexuality), September 1985.

Rofes, Eric E. *Socrates, Plato, and Guys like Me.* Boston: Alyson Publications, 1985.

Squirrell, Gillian. "In Passing . . . Teachers and Sexual Orientation." In *Teachers, Gender, and Careers,* ed. Sandra Acker. Barcombe, Lewes, East Sussex: Falmer Press, 1989, p. 87–106.

———. "Teachers and Issues of Sexual Orientation." *Gender and Education* 1, No. 1 (1989): 17–34.

Stanfield, Rebecca. "Confessions of a Lesbian Teacher." *Off Our Backs,* October 1988, p. 14.

Stoddard, Thomas B., et al. *The Rights of Gay People: An American Civil Liberties Handbook.* New York: Bantam Books, 1983, pp. 21–23.

*The Body Politic.* "Gay Teachers Organize." May 1977, p. 4.

The Gay Teachers' Group. *School's Out.* London: The Gay Teacher's Group, 1987.

Vicinus, Martha. "Distance and Desire: English Boarding School Friendships." *Signs* 2, No. 4 (Summer 1984): 600–622.

## Fiction

Dane, Clemence. *Regiment of Women.* London: William Heinemann, 1917.

Gilbert, Harriet. *The Riding Mistress.* London: Methuen, 1983.

Hellman, Lillian. "The Children's Hour." In *Plays* New York: Random House, 1942.

*Selected Bibliography*

Weis, Deborah. *Hodag Winter.* Racine, Wisc.: Mother Courage Press, 1991.

Winsloe, Christa. *The Child Manuela.* Trans. Agnes Neil Scott. New York: Farrar and Rinehart, 1933.

# Bibliography

Abbott, Sidney, and Barbara Love. *Sappho Was a Right-On Woman: A Liberated View of Lesbianism.* 1972. Rpt. New York: Day Books, 1978.

Abdul-Rauf, Mohammad. *The Islamic View of Women and the Family.* New York: Robert Spitter and Sons, 1977.

"Alberta School Trustees Panic." *Kinesis* 8, No. 1.

Althusser, Louis. *Lenin and Philosophy and Other Essays.* Trans. Ben Brewster. London: Monthly Review Press, 1971.

Antler, Joyce, and Sari Knopp Biklin, eds. *Changing Education: Women as Radicals and Conservatives.* Albany, N.Y.: University of New York Press, 1990.

Apple, Michael, and Lois Weis. "Ideology and Practice in Schooling: A Political and Conceptual Introduction." In *Ideology and Practice in Schooling,* ed. Michael Apple and Lois Weis. Philadelphia: Temple University Press, 1983, pp. 3–33.

Arbus, Judith. "Grateful to Be Working: Women Teachers During the Great Depression." In *Feminism in Education: A Canadian Perspective,* ed. Frieda Forman et al. Toronto: Centre for Women's Studies in Education, The Ontario Institute for Studies in Education, 1990, pp. 169–190.

———. "Historical Bases of a Sex-Segregated Labour Force: Women Teachers' Experience During the Great Depression." Diss. Toronto: University of Toronto, 1984.

Arnot, Madeleine. *Race and Gender: Equal Opportunity Policies in Education.* London: Pergamon, in association with The Open University, 1985, rpt. 1988.

Bailey, Derrick Sherwin. *Homosexuality and the Western Christian Tradition.* London: Longmans, Green and Company, 1955.

Barman, Jean. "Separate and Unequal: Indian and White Girls at All Hallows School, 1884–1920." In *Indian Education in Canada,* ed. Jean Barman, Yvonne Hébert and Don McCaskill. Vancouver: University of British Columbia Press, 1986, pp. 110–131.

Barrett, Michele. *Women's Oppression Today.* London: Verso, 1980.

Barrett, Michele, and Mary McIntosh. "The 'Family Wage'." In *The Changing Experience of Women,* ed. Elizabeth Whitelegg et al. Oxford: Martin Robertson and The Open University, 1982, pp. 71–87.

Beard, George M. *Sexual Neurasthenia.* Ed. A. D. Rockwell. New York: E. B. Trent and Company, 1984.

Beck, Evelyn Torton, ed. *Nice Jewish Girls: A Lesbian Anthology.* Watertown, Mass.: Persephone Press, 1982.

Becker, A. L. "A Third Sex? Some Speculations on a Sexuality Spectrum." *Medical Proceedings* 13, No. 4 (1967): 67–74.

Beechey, Veronica. "On Patriarchy." *Feminist Review* 3 (1979): 66–82.

Bell, Laurie. *On Our Own Terms: A Practical Guide for Lesbian and Gay Relationships.* Toronto: The Coalition for Lesbian and Gay Rights in Ontario, 1991.

Bergler, Edmund. *Counterfeit-Sex: Homosexuality, Impotence, Frigidity.* New York: Grune and Stratton, 1958.

Berube, Allan. *Coming Out under Fire: The History of Gay Men and Women in World War Two.* New York: The Free Press, 1990.

———. "Lesbian Masquerade." *Gay Community News* 17 (Nov. 1979): 8–9.

"Board Report Recommendation." *Rites* 1, No. 7 (December/January 1984/85): p. 7.

Boggs, Carl. *Gramsci's Marxism.* London: Pluto Press, 1976.

Boswell, John. *Christianity, Social Tolerance and Homosexuality.* Chicago: University of Chicago Press, 1980.

Bowles, Samuel, and Herbert Gintis. *Schooling in Capitalist America.* New York: Basic Books, 1976.

Bozarth, Rene, and Alfred Gross. "Homosexuality: Sin or Sickness? A Dialogue." *Pastoral Psychology* 13, No. 129 (1962): 35–42.

Brand, Dionne. *No Burden to Carry.* Toronto: The Women's Press, 1991.

Brant, Beth. *Sinister Women.* North American Indian Women's Issue Number 22/23, 1982.

Brown, Judith C. *Immodest Acts.* Oxford: Oxford University Press, 1986.

———. "Lesbian Sexuality in Renaissance Italy: The Case of Sister Benedetta Carlini." *Signs* 9, No. 4 (Summer 1984): 751–758.

Bibliography              281

Brownmiller, Susan. *Femininity.* New York: Linden Press, Simon and Schuster, 1984.

Brunt, Rosalind, and Carolyn Rowan, eds. *Feminism, Culture and Politics.* London: Lawrence and Wishart, 1982.

Buci-Gluckman, Christine. "Hegemony and Consent: A Political Strategy." In *Approaches to Gramsci,* ed. Anne Shortstack Sassoon. London: Writers and Readers, 1982, pp. 116–126.

Bullough, Vern. *Sexual Variance in Society and History.* Chicago: University of Chicago Press, 1976.

Bullough, Vern, and Bonnie Bullough. "Lesbianism in the 1920s and 1930s: A Newfound Study." *Signs* 2, No. 4 (1977): 895–904.

Bullough, Vern, Dorr Legg, Barry Elcano, et al. *An Annotated Bibliography of Homosexuality and Other Stigmatized Behavior.* New York: Garland, 1976.

Bunch, Charlotte, and Sandra Pollack. *Learning Our Way: Essays in Feminist Education.* Trumansburg, N.Y.: Crossing Press, 1983.

Burbridge, Michael, and Jonathan Walters, eds. *Breaking the Silence: Gay Teenagers Speak for Themselves.* London: Joint Council for Gay Teenagers, 1981.

Burstyn, Varda. "Masculine Dominance and the State." In *Women, Class, Family and the State,* ed. Dorothy E. Smith and Varda Burstyn. Toronto: Garamond Press, 1985, pp. 45–89.

Bychowski, Gustave. "The Ego and the Object of the Homosexual." *International Journal of Psycho-Analysis* 42, No. 3 (1961): 255–259.

Caprio, Frank S. *Female Homosexuality. A Psychoanalytic Study of Lesbianism.* London: Icon, 1955, rpt. 1963.

"A Case for 'Just Cause' Clauses." *Conditions of Work Bulletin.* (OSSTF) No. 22, 1981.

*Centennial Story: The Board of Education for the City of Toronto 1850–1950.* Dir. E. A. Hardy. Ed. Honora M. Cochrane. Toronto: Thomas Nelson and Sons, 1950.

Chamberland Line. "Le lesbianisme: Continuum féminin ou marronage? Réflexions féministes pour une théorization de l'experience lesbienne." *Recherches féministes* 2, numéro 2 (1989): 135–145.

Chauncey, George, Jr. "From Sexual Inverts to Homosexuality: Medicine and the Changing Conceptualization of Female Deviance." In *Homosexuality: Sacrilege, Vision, Politics.* Salmagundi: Skidmore College, 1982/83, pp. 114–146.

Chessum, Rosemary. "Teacher Ideologies and Pupil Disaffection." In *Schooling, Ideology and the Curriculum,* ed. Len Barton et al. Sussex: Falmer Press, 1980, pp. 113–130.

Christian, Meg. "Ode to a Gym Teacher." On *I Know You Know.* Thumbelina Music, BMI. Olivia Records, 1974.

Claricoates, Katherine. "The Importance of Being Ernest ... Emma ... Tom ... Jane. ... The Perception and Categorization of Gender Conformity and Gender Deviation in Primary Schools." In *Schooling for Women's Work,* ed. Rosemary Deem. London: Routledge and Kegan Paul, 1980, pp. 26–41.

Clark, Don. *Loving Someone Gay.* New York: Signet, 1977, rpt. 1978.

Clark, Thomas R. "Homosexuality and Psychopathology in Non-Patient Males." *American Journal of Psychoanalysis* 35 (1975): 163–168.

Clio Collective. *Quebec Women: A History.* Trans. Roger Gannon and Rosalind Gill. Toronto: The Women's Press, 1987.

Coalition for Gay Rights in Ontario. *The Ontario Human Rights Omission.* Brief to Members of the Ontario Legislature, Toronto, 1981 and 1986.

Connell, R. W., D. J. Ashenden, S. Kessler, and G. W. Dowsett. *Making the Difference.* Schools, Families and Social Division. Sydney: George Allen and Unwin, 1982.

Connell, R. W. *Teacher's Work.* Sydney: George Allen and Unwin, 1985.

*Consenting Adults.* Made for Television Movie, 1985.

Cook, Blanche Wiesen. "The Historical Denial of Lesbianism." *Radical History Review* 20 (Spring/Summer 1979): 60–65.

Cook, Ramsey, and Wendy Mitchison, eds. *The Proper Sphere: Women's Place in Canadian Society.* Toronto: Oxford University Press, 1976.

Cooper, Afua. "The Search for Mary Bibb, Black Woman Teacher in Nineteenth-Century Canada West." *Ontario History* 83, No 1. (March 1991): 39–54.

Cornwell, Anita. *Black Lesbian in White America.* Florida: Naiad, 1983.

Corzine, Jay, and Richard Cole. "Cruising the Truckers: Sexual Encounters in a Highway Rest Area." *Urban Life* 6, No. 2 (1977): 171–192.

Cosin, Ben, and Margaret Hales. *Education, Policy and Society.* London: Routledge and Kegan Paul, 1983.

Couch, Terrie. "An American in West Germany or 'Did Lesbians Wear Pink Triangles?' " *Off Our Backs* 21, No. 3 (March 1991): 23.

Coulson, Margaret. "The Struggle for Femininity." In *Homosexuality: Power and Politics,* ed. Gay Left Collective. London: Alyson and Busby, 1980, pp. 21–37.

Coward, Rosalind. *Patriarchal Precedents: Sexuality and Social Relations.* London: Routledge and Kegan Paul, 1983.

Crew, Louis. "Thriving Decloseted in Rural Academe." In *After You're Out,* ed. Karla Jay and Allen Young. Pyaramid Books, 1975, rpt. 1977. pp. 96–102.

Crew, Louis, and Karen Keener. "Homophobia in the Academy: A Report of the Committee on Gay/Lesbian Concerns." *College English* 43, No. 7 (November 1981): 682–689.

Crnkovick, Mary, ed. *"Gossip": A Spoken History of Women in the North.* Ottawa: Canadian Arctic Resources Committee, 1990.

Crompton, Louis. "The Myth of Lesbian Impunity: Capital Laws from 1270 to 1791." *Journal of Homosexuality* 6, Nos. 1/2 (Fall/Winter 1980/81): 11–25.

Cruikshank, Margaret. "Lesbians in the Academic World." In *Our Right to Love,* ed. Ginny Vida. Englewood Cliffs, N.J.: Prentice-Hall, 1978, pp. 164–167.

————, ed. *Lesbian Studies: Present and Future.* Old Westbury, N.Y.: The Feminist Press, 1982.

Curran, Desmond, and Denis Parr. "Homosexuality: An Analysis of 100 Male Cases Seen in Private Practice." *British Medical Journal* 5022 (1975): 797–801.

Dale, Roger, et al., eds. *Politics, Patriarchy and Practice.* Vols. 1 and 2. Sussex: The Falmer Press, 1981.

Daly, Mary. *The Church and the Second Sex.* 1968. Rpt. New York: Harper and Row, 1975.

————. *Gyn/Ecology: The MetaEthics of Radical Feminism.* Boston: Beacon Press, 1978.

Daly, Mike. "At Work." in *Prejudice and Pride: Discrimination Against Gay People in Modern Britain,* ed. Bruce Galloway. London: Routledge and Kegan Paul, 1983, pp. 35–61.

Dane, Clarence. *Regiment of Women.* London: William Heinemann, 1917.

Danylewecz, Martha, Beth Light, and Alison Prentice. "The Evolution of the Sexual Division of Labour in Teaching: A Nineteenth Century Ontario and Quebec Case Study." *Histoire sociale/Social History* 16, No. 3 (mai/May 1983): 81–109.

Davis, Bob. "Sifted, Sorted, Slotted and Streamed." *Mudpie* 4, No. 2 (February 1983): 8.

Deem, Rosemary, ed. *Schooling for Women's Work.* London: Routledge and Kegan Paul, 1980.

Delamont, Sara. "The Contradictions in Ladies' Education." In *The Nineteenth Century Woman,* ed. Sara Delamont and Lorna Duffin. London: Croom Helm, 1978, pp. 134–163.

D'Emilio, John. *Sexual Politics, Sexual Communities: The Making of a Homosexual Minority in the United States 1940–1970.* Chicago: University of Chicago Press, 1983.

D'Emilio, John, and Estelle B. Freedman. *A History of Sexuality in America.* New York: Harper and Row, 1988.

DeVito, Joseph. "Educational Responsibilities to the Gay and Lesbian Student." Paper presented at the Annual Meeting of the Speech Communication Association, 65th, San Antonio, Texas, November 10-13, 1979.

Diamond, Irene, and Lee Quimby, eds. *Feminism and Foucault: Reflections and Resistance.* Boston: Northeastern University Press, 1988.

Dobson, Michael. "At School." In *Prejudice, and Pride: Discrimination Against Gay and Lesbian People in Modern Britain,* ed. Bruce Galloway. London: Routledge and Kegan Paul, 1983, pp. 19–34.

"Does AIDS Spell the End of the Sexual Revolution?" *The Toronto Star,* September 14, 1985, pp. A1, A12.

Duberman, Martin Bauml, Martha Vicinus, and George Chauncey, Jr., eds. *Hidden from History: Reclaiming the Gay and Lesbian Past.* New York: New American Library, 1989.

Dynes, Wayne. *Homolexis: A Historical and Cultural Lexicon of Homosexuality.* New York: Gai Saber Monograph No. 4, 1985.

*Education Act.* Revised Statutes of Ontario, 1980, Chapter 129, September 1990.

Ehrenreich, Barbara, and Diedre English. *For Her Own Good: 150 Years of the Experts' Advice to Women.* New York: Anchor Books, 1979.

Ellis, Havelock. *Sexual Inversion: Studies in the Psychology of Sex.* Vol. 2. Philadelphia: F. A. Davis, 1927.

*Enough Is Enough: Aboriginal Women Speak Out.* As told to Janet Silman. Toronto: The Women's Press, 1987.

Epstein, Louis M. *Sex Laws and Customs in Judaism.* New York: Bloch, 1948.

Faderman, Lillian. *Odd Girls and Twilight Lovers: A History of Lesbian Life in Twentieth-Century America*. New York: Columbia University Press, 1991.

——. *Scotch Verdict\*: Miss Pirie and Miss Woods v. Dame Cumming Gordon*. New York: Quill, 1983.

——. *Surpassing the Love of Men: Romantic Friendship and Love Between Women from the Renaissance to the Present*. New York: William Morrow, 1981.

Faraday, Anabel. "Liberating Lesbian Research." In *The Making of the Modern Homosexual*, ed. Kenneth Plummer. London: Hutchinson, 1981, pp. 112–129.

Fassler, Barbara. "Theories of Homosexuality as Sources of Bloomsbury's Androgyny." *Signs* 5, No. 2 (1979): 237–251.

Feinstadt, Helena. "Towards Lesbianism as an International Change." Paper, 1984/85.

*Fireweed* (The Lesbian Issue). A Feminist Quarterly, Issue 13 (1982).

Fitzgerald, Maureen, Connie Guberman, and Margie Wolfe, eds. *Still Ain't Satisfied*. Toronto: The Women's Press, 1982.

Flesch, Rudolf F. *Why Johnny Can't Read: What You Can Do About It*. New York: Harper and Row, 1955, rpt. 1966.

——. *Why Johnny Still Can't Read: A New Look at the Scandal of Our Schools*. New York: Harper and Row, 1981.

Forman, Frieda, Mary O'Brien, Jane Haddad, Diane Hallman, and Philinda Masters, eds. *Feminism and Education: A Canadian Perspective*. Toronto: Centre for Women's Studies in Education, The Ontario Institute for Studies in Education, 1990.

Forster, E. M. *The Life to Come and Other Stories*. Harmondsworth: Penguin, 1975.

Foster, Jeannette H. *Sex Variant Women in Literature*. Jeannette Foster, 1956; rpt. 1975; Florida: Naiad, 1985.

Foucault, Michel. *The History of Sexuality. Vol. 1: An Introduction*. Trans. Robert Hurley. New York: Vintage, 1980.

——. *Power/Knowledge: Selected Interviews and Other Writings 1972–1977*. Trans. Colin Gordon, Leo Marshall, John Mepham, and Kate Soper. Ed. Colin Gordon. New York: Pantheon, 1980.

French, Doris. *High Button Boot Straps: FWTAO 1918–1968*. Toronto: Ryerson Press, 1968.

Friedman, Meryl. "Lesbian as Teacher, Teacher as Lesbian." In *Our Right to Love,* ed. Ginny Vida. Englewood Cliffs, N.J.: Prentice-Hall, 1978, pp. 157–162.

Frye, Marilyn. "To Be and Be Seen: The Politics of Reality." In her *The Politics of Reality: Essays in Feminist Theory.* New York: Crossing Press, 1983, pp. 152–174.

Gabriel, Susan L, and Isaiah Smithson, eds. *Gender in the Classroom.* Urbana: University of Illinois Press, 1990.

Gagnon, John, and William Simon. *Sexual Conduct: The Sources of Human Sexuality.* Chicago: Aldine, 1973.

―――. "Sexual Deviance in Contemporary America." *Annals of the American Academy of Political and Social Science* 376 (1968): 106–122.

Garfinkel, Harold. *Studies in Ethnomethodology.* Englewood Cliffs, N.J.: Prentice-Hall, 1967.

Gay Left Collective, "Why Marxism?" In *Pink Triangles: Radical Perspectives on Gay Liberation,* ed. Pam Mitchell. Boston: Alyson, 1980, pp. 98–106.

"Gay Teachers Organize." *The Body Politic,* (May 1977), p. 4.

Gearhart, Sally Miller. *The Wanderground.* Watertown, Mass.: Persephone Press, 1979.

Gerard, Warren. "Is Gay Bashing Out of Control?" *The Toronto Star,* Saturday, June 29, 1991, Section D, "Insight", p. D1.

"Getting Through Coming Out." *The Globe and Mail,* February 26, 1983, Section "Fanfare," p. 3.

Giddings, Paula. *When and Where I Enter: The Impact of Black Women on Race and Sex in America.* New York: Bantam, 1984.

Gilbert, Harriet. *The Riding Mistress.* London: Methuen, 1983.

Gitlin, Andrew. "School Structures and Teachers' Work." In *Ideology and Practice in Schooling,* ed. Michael Apple and Lois Weis. Philadelphia: Temple University Press, 1983, pp. 193–212.

Goffman, Erving. *Stigma: Notes on the Management of Spoiled Identity.* Englewood Cliffs, N.J.: Prentice-Hall, 1963.

Graham, Elizabeth. "Schoolmistresses and Early Teaching in Ontario." In *Women at Work 1850–1930,* ed. Janice Acton, Penny Goldsmith, and Bonnie Sheppard. Toronto: Canadian Women's Educational Press, 1974, pp. 165–209.

Greenberg, David F. *The Construction Of Homosexuality*. Chicago: University of Chicago Press, 1988.

Griffin, Susan. *Woman and Nature: The Roaring Inside Her*. New York: Harper Colophone Books, 1978.

"Growing Up Gay." CITY tv, July 20, 1985.

Grumet, Madeleine. *Bitter Milk: Women and Teaching*. Amherst: University of Massachusetts Press, 1988.

"Halton Code of Behavior 'Redundant', said Joe Harwood." *Federation Update* 9, No. 15 (December 1981): 2.

Hanley, Susan, Benjamin Schlesinger, and Paul Steinberg. "Lesbianism: Knowns and Unknowns." In *Sexual Behavior in Canada: Patterns and Problems,* ed. Benjamin Schlesinger. Toronto: University of Toronto Press, 1977, pp. 126–147.

Hedblom, Jack H. "The Female Homosexual: Social and Attitudinal Dimensions." In *The Homosexual Dialectic,* ed. Joseph A. McCaffrey. Englewood Cliffs, N.J.: Prentice-Hall, 1972.

Hellman, Lillian. "The Children's Hour." In *Plays*. New York: Random, 1942.

Hemmings, Susan. "Horrific Practices: How Lesbians Were Presented in the Newspapers of 1978." In *Homosexuality: Power and Politics,* ed. Gay Left Collective. London: Allison and Busby, 1980, pp. 157–171.

Heron, Ann, ed. *One Teenager in 10*. Boston: Alyson Publications, 1983.

Hoffman, Nancy. *Woman's "True" Profession*. Old Westbury, N.Y.: The Feminist Press, 1981.

Holman, Mary V. *How It Feels to Be a Teacher*. New York: Columbia University Press, 1950.

hooks, bell. *Feminist Theory: From Margin to Center*. Boston: South End Press, 1984.

———. *Talking Back. Thinking Feminist. Thinking Black*. Boston: South End Press, 1989.

Hughes, Nym, Yvonne Johnson, and Yvette Perrault, eds. *Stepping Out of Line*. Vancouver: Press Gang Publishers, 1984.

Jackson, Stevi. *Childhood and Sexuality*. Oxford: Basil Blackwell, 1982.

Jeffreys, Sheila. *Anticlimax: A Feminist Perspective on the Sexual Revolution*. London: The Women's Press, 1990.

———. *The Spinster and Her Enemies: Feminism and Sexuality 1800–1930*. London: Pandora, 1985.

Johnston, Jill. *Lesbian Nation*. New York: Touchstone, 1973.

Katz, Jonathan. *Gay American History*. New York: Avon, 1976, rpt. 1978.

———. *Gay/Lesbian Almanac. A New Documentary*. New York: Harper and Row, 1983.

Kehoe, Constance. "School Subcultures and Peer Group Pressures in Adolescent Deviance." Diss. Toronto: University of Toronto, 1971.

Khayatt, M. Didi. "Legalized Invisibility: The Effect of Bill 7 on Lesbian Teachers." *Women's Studies International Forum* 13, No. 3 (1990): 185–193.

———. "Lesbian Teachers: An Invisible Presence." In *Feminism in Education: A Canadian Perspective,* ed. Frieda Forman et al. Toronto: Centre For Women's Studies in Education, OISE, 1990.

Kinsman, Gary. *The Regulation of Desire: Sexuality in Canada*. Montreal: Black Rose, 1987.

———. "The Social Construction of Homosexual Culture: Heterosexual Hegemony and Homosexual Resistance." Diss. Toronto: University of Toronto, 1983.

Klaich, Dolores. *Woman + Woman*. New York: Morrow Quill Paperbacks, 1979.

Kline, Morris. *Why Johnny Can't Add: The Failure of the New Math*. New York: St. Martin's Press, 1973.

Koedt, Anne, Ellen Levine, and Anita Rapone, eds. *Radical Feminism*. New York: Quadrangle Books, 1973.

Krebs, Paula. "To Teach or Not to Teach?" *Off Our Backs* (January 1985): 5.

Kuhn, Annette, and AnnMarie Wolpe. *Feminism and Materialism*. London: Routledge and Kegan Paul, 1978.

Kulp, Denise. "Dyke Aesthetic. Dressed to Cool." *Off Our Backs* 14, No. 7 (July 1984): 24.

Lariviere, Robert. "Bundles of Twigs in New Hampshire: A High School Teacher's Report." In *After You're Out,* ed. Karla Jay and Allen Young. New York: Pyramid Books, 1975, rpt. 1977, pp. 105–112.

"Lesbian Appeals." *Off Our Backs* Vol. 14 (June 1984): 10.

Lesbian History Group. *Not a Passing Phase: Reclaiming Lesbians in History 1840–1985*. London: The Women's Press, 1989.

Lesbian Rights Committee of TACWL. "The Law and Us. Lesbian and Gay Youth." *Pink Ink,* October 1983, p. 29.

Levine, Martin, and Robin Leonard. "Discrimination Against Lesbians in the Workforce." *Signs* 9, No. 4 (Summer 1984): 700–710.

Light, Beth, and Alison Prentice, eds. *Pioneer and Gentlewomen of British North America, 1713–1867.* Toronto: New Hogtown Press, 1980.

Lorde, Audre. "Uses of the Erotic: The Erotic as Power." Fourth Berkshire Conference on the History of Women, Mount Holyoke College, August 25, 1978. Published as a pamphlet by Out and Out Books (available from The Crossing Press).

Luka, Shelagh. "The Status of Women in the Teaching Profession." *Forum* (OSSTF) 7, No. 2 (April 1981): 57–59.

MacDonald, Madeleine. "Schooling and the Reproduction of Class and Gender Relations." In *Schooling, Ideology and the Curriculum,* ed. Len Barton, Roland Meighan, and Stephen Walker. Sussex: Falmer Press, 1980, pp. 19–49.

———. "Socio-Cultural Reproduction and Women's Education." In *Schooling for Women's Work,* ed. Rosemary Deem. London: Routledge and Kegan Paul, 1980, pp. 13–25.

MacKinnon, Catharine. "Feminism, Marxism, Method and the State: An Agenda for Theory." *Signs* 7, No. 3 (1982): 515–544.

"Married Lesbians: Living with a Mistake." *The Toronto Star,* September 26, 1983, Section D, p. D1.

Martin, Del, and Phyllis Lyon. *Lesbian/Woman.* New York: Bantam, 1972, rpt. 1980.

Marx, Karl, and Frederick Engels. *The German Ideology.* Ed. C. J. Arthur. New York: International Publishers, 1978.

McDonough, Roisin, and Rachel Harrison. "Patriarchy and Relations of Production." In *Feminism and Materialism,* ed. Annette Kuhn and Ann-Marie Wolpe. London: Routledge and Kegan Paul, 1978, pp. 11–41.

McIntosh, Mary. "The Homosexual Role." *Social Problems* 16, No. 2 (Fall 1968); rpt. in *The Making of the Modern Homosexual,* ed. Kenneth Plummer. London: Hutchinson, 1980, pp. 30–44.

Meigs, Mary. *The Medusa Head.* Vancouver: Talonbooks, 1983.

Melady, John. "Attitudes." *Forum* (OSSTF)) 7, No. 2 (April 1981): 60.

Mernissi, Fatima. *Beyond the Veil.* New York: John Wiley and Sons, 1975.

Millett, Kate. *Sexual Politics.* 1969, rpt. New York: Ballantine Books, 1978.

Mitchell, Alana. "Gay in the Nineties." *The Globe and Mail,* Saturday, June 29, 1991, Section: "Focus," p. D1.

Moore, Opel. *Why Johnny Can't Learn.* Milford, Mich.: Mott Media, 1975.

Moraga, Cherie, and Gloria Anzaldúa, eds. *This Bridge Called My Back: Writings by Radical Women of Color.* Watertown, Mass.: Persephone Press, 1981.

Morgan, Robin. "Feminist Diplomacy." *MS* (Editorial) 1, No. 6 (May/June 1991): 1.

Mouffe, Chantal. "Hegemony and Ideology in Gramsci." In *Gramsci and Marxist Theory,* ed. Chantal Mouffe. London: Routledge and Kegan Paul, 1979, pp. 168–204.

*My Two Loves.* Wrts. Reginald Rose and Rita Mae Brown, ABC, April 7, 1986.

Newton, Esther. "The Mythic Mannish Lesbian: Radcliffe Hall and the New Woman." *Signs* 9, No. 4 (Summer 1984): 557–575.

O'Brien, Mary. *The Politics of Reproduction.* London: Routledge and Kegan Paul, 1981.

O'Brien, Patricia. *Women Alone.* New York: Quadrangle, 1973.

Olsen, Myrna R. "A Study of Gay and Lesbian Teachers." *Journal of Homosexuality* 13, No. 4 (Summer 1987): 73–81.

Olsen, Tillie. *Silences.* New York: Delacorte/Seymour Lawrence, 1965.

Ontario Department of Labour. Toronto: Research Branch, "Homosexuality in Specific Fields: The Arts, The Military, The Ministry, Prisons, Sports, Teaching, and Transexuals." A Selected Bibliography, No. 13. Compiled by Alan V. Miller, October 1978.

*Open and Positive: An Account of How John Warburton Came Out at School and the Consequences.* London: Gay Teachers' Group, 1978.

*OSSTF Handbook.* Toronto: OSSTF, 1990/91.

"Our Policy on Equal Opportunity." The Toronto Board of Education, Equal Opportunity Office. Personnel Division, 1985.

Padgug, Robert. "Sexual Matters: On Conceptualizing Sexuality in History." *Radical History Review* 20 (Spring/Summer 1979): 3–23.

Pagels, Elaine. *The Gnostic Gospels.* New York: Random House, 1979.

Paterson, Ian. "High School Faggot." *The Body Politic,* May 1985, pp. 30–31.

Peiss, Kathy, and Christina Simmons, eds. *Passion and Power: Sexuality in History.* Philadelphia: Temple University Press, 1989.

Pierson, Ruth Roach. *"They're Still Women After All": The Second World War and Canadian Womanhood.* Toronto: McClelland and Stewart, 1986.

Plaskow, Judith. *Standing Again at Sinai: Judiasm from a Feminist Perspective*. San Francisco: Harper San Francisco, 1990.

Plummer, Kenneth. *Sexual Stigma: An Interactionist Report*. London: Routledge and Kegan Paul, 1975.

Prentice, Alison. "The Feminization of Teaching." In *The Neglected Majority*, ed. Susan Mann Trofimenkoff and Alison Prentice. Toronto: McClelland and Stewart, 1977, pp. 49–65.

————. *The School Promoters*. Toronto: McClelland and Stewart, 1977.

Prentice, Alison, and Marjorie Theobald, eds. *Women Who Taught: Perspectives on the History of Women and Teaching*. Toronto: University of Toronto Press, 1991.

Radicalesbians. "The Woman Identified Woman." In *Radical Feminism*, ed. Ann Koedt, Ellen Levine, and Anita Rapone. New York: Quadrangle, 1973, pp. 240–245.

*Radical Teacher* 24 (Gay and Lesbian Studies), 1980.

*Radical Teacher* 29 (Teaching Sexuality), September 1985.

Reedy, Sara, and Martin Woodhead, eds. *Family, Work and Education*. London: Hodder and Stoughton, in association with The Open University, 1982.

*Resources for Feminist Research* (The Lesbian Issue) 12, No. 1 (March 1983).

Reuben, David. *Everything You Wanted to Know About Sex—But Were Afraid to Ask*. New York: W. H. Allen, 1970.

Rich, Adrienne. "Compulsory Heterosexuality and Lesbian Existence." *Signs* 5, No. 4 (Summer 1980): 631–660.

————. "Foreword" to *The Coming Out Stories*. Ed. Julia Penelope Stanley and Susan J. Wolfe. Watertown, Mass.: Persephone Press, 1980.

————. *Of Woman Born: Motherhood as Experience and Institution*. 1976, rpt. New York: Bantam, 1977.

————. "Taking Women Students Seriously." In *On Lies, Secrets and Silences: Selected Prose 1966–1973*. New York: W. W. Norton and Co., 1979, pp. 237–246.

Robinson, Janice. *H. D.: The Life and Work of an American Poet*. Boston: Houghton Mifflin, 1982.

Robinson, S. G. B. *Do Not Erase: The Story of the First Fifty Years of OSSTF*. Toronto: OSSTF, 1971.

Rofes, Eric E. *Socrates, Plato, and Guys Like Me*. Boston: Alyson Publications, 1985.

Rothman, Sheila. *Woman's Proper Place: A History of Changing Ideals and Practices 1870 to the Present*. New York: Basic Books, 1978.

Rowbotham, Sheila. *Women's Consciousness, Men's World*. Harmondsworth, England: Penguin, 1973.

Rubin, Gayle. "Thinking Sex: Notes for a Radical Theory of the Politics of Sexuality." In *Pleasure and Danger: Exploring Female Sexuality*, ed. Carol S. Vance. London: Routledge and Kegan Paul, 1984, pp. 267–319.

Rule, Jane. *Lesbian Images*. Trumansburg, N.Y.: Crossing Press, 1975.

Russ, Joanna. "The New Misandry." In *Amazon Expedition*, ed. Phyllis Birkey et al. New York: Times Change Press, 1973, pp. 27–32.

Saadawi, Nawal el. *The Hidden Face of Eve*. London: Zed Press, 1980.

Saghir, M. T., and E. Robins. *Male and Female Homosexuality*. Baltimore: Williams-Wilkins, 1973.

Sahli, Nancy. "Smashing: Women's Relations Before the Fall." *Chrysalis* 17, No. 8 (Summer 1979): pp. 17–27.

Salman, Madiga. "Arab Women." *Khasmin: Journal of Revolutionary Socialists of the Middle East* 6 (1978): 24–32.

Salvo, Louise de, and Mitchell A. Leaska, eds. *The Letters of Vita Sackville-West to Virginia Woolf*. New York: William Morrow, 1985.

Schur, Edwin M. *Labelling Women Deviant: Gender, Stigma and Social Control*. Philadelphia: Temple University Press, 1984.

Schutz, Alfred. *On Phenomenology and Social Relations*. Ed. Helmut R. Wagner. Chicago: University of Chicago Press, 1970.

*Selections from the "Prison Notebooks" of Antonio Gramsci*. Ed. and trans. Quentin Hoare and Geoffrey Nowell Smith. New York: International Publishers, 1971.

*Sexual Offences Against Children and Youth*. Vols. 1 and 2. Report of the Committee on Sexual Offences Against Children and Youths (The Badgley Reports). Ministry of Supplies and Services, Canada, 1984.

Shack, Sybil. *Women in Canadian Education: The Two-Thirds Minority*. Toronto: University of Toronto Press, 1973.

Shaw, Jenny. "*In Loco Parentis*: A Relationship Between Parent, State and Child." In *Politics, Patriarchy and Practice*, vol. 2, ed. Roger Dale et al. Sussex: Falmer Press, 1981, pp. 257–268.

*The Shortest Shadow*. A Descriptive Study of the Federation of Women Teachers' Associations of Ontario. Res. Comm. Margaret Buckingham, Marie Harvey, Isabel Ward. [Toronto]: n.p., n.d.

Simmons, Christina. "Companionate Marriage and the Lesbian Threat." *Frontiers* 4, No. 3 (1979): 54–59.

Smith, Barbara. "Doing Research on Black American Women or All the Women are White, All the Blacks Are Men, But Some of Us Are Brave." *The Radical Teacher* 3, 1976.

Smith, Dorothy E. *The Everyday World as Problematic: A Feminist Sociology*. Boston: Northeastern University Press, 1987.

——— . "The Ideological Practice of Sociology." *Catalyst* 8 (Winter 1974): 40–56.

——— . "Institutional Ethnography: A Feminist Method." Paper, n.d.

——— . "A Peculiar Eclipsing: Women's Exclusion from Man's Culture." *Women's Studies International Quarterly* 1 (1978): 281–295.

——— . "A Sociology for Women." In *The Prism of Sex: Essays in the Sociology of Knowledge,* ed. Julia Sherman and Evelyn Torton Beck. Madison: University of Wisconsin Press, 1979, pp. 135–187.

——— . "Women, Class and Family." In *Women, Class, Family and the State,* ed. Dorothy E. Smith and Varda Burstyn. Toronto: Garamond Press, 1985, pp. 1–44.

Smith, Dorothy, et al. *Working Paper on the Implications of Declining Enrollment for Women Teachers in Public Elementary and Secondary Schools in Ontario*. Toronto: Commission on Declining Enrollment in Ontario, 1978.

Smith-Rosenberg, Carroll. *Disorderly Conduct*. New York: Knopf, 1985.

——— . "The Female World of Love and Ritual: Relations Between Women in Nineteenth Century America." In *A Heritage of Her Own: Toward a New Social History of American Women,* Edited and introduced by Nancy F. Cott and Elizabeth H. Pleck. New York: Touchstone, 1979, pp. 311–342.

Spender, Dale. "Education: The Patriarchal Paradigm and the Response to Feminism." In *Men's Studies Modified: The Impact of Feminism on the Academic Disciplines,* ed. Dale Spender. Oxford: Pergamon, 1981.

——— . *Invisible Women: The Schooling Scandal*. London: Writers and Readers, 1982.

——— . *Learning to Lose: Sexism in Education*. London: Women's Press, 1980.

———. *Man-Made Language*. London: Routledge and Kegan Paul, 1980.

Squirrell, Gillian. "In Passing . . . Teachers and Sexual Orientation." In *Teachers, Gender and Careers*, ed. Sandra Acker. Barcombe, Lewes, East Sussex: Falmer Press, 1989, pp. 87–105.

———. "Teachers and Issues of Sexual Orientation." *Gender and Education* 1, No. 1 (1989): 17–34.

Stanfield, Rebecca. "Confessions of a Lesbian Teacher." *Off Our Backs* Vol. 17, No. 9 (October 1988): 14.

Stanley, Julia Penelope, and Susan J. Wolfe. *The Coming Out Stories*. Watertown, Mass.: Persephone Press, 1980.

Stanworth, Michelle. *Gender and Schooling: A Study of Sexual Division in the Classroom*. London: Hutchinson, 1983.

Steakley, James. "Gays Under Fascism." A Slide Presentation. Sex and the State Conference. Toronto: July 1985.

———. *The Homosexual Emancipation Movement in Germany*. New York: Arno, 1975.

Stearn, Jess. *The Grapevine*. London: Frederick Muller, 1965.

Stoddard, Thomas B. *The Rights of Gay People: An American Civil Liberties Handbook*. New York: Bantam, 1983.

Stone, Sharon D., ed. *Lesbians in Canada*. Toronto: Between the Lines, 1990.

Strober, Myra, and David Tyack. "Why Women Teach and Men Manage? A Report on Research on Schools." *Signs* 5, No. 3 (Spring 1980): 494–503.

Swallow, Jean, ed. *Out from Under: Sober Dykes and Our Friends*. San Francisco: Spinsters, Ink, 1983.

"The Threat of RC Funding." *Rites* 2 (October 1985): 4.

Torton-Beck, Evelyn. *Nice Jewish Girls: A Lesbian Anthology*. Watertown, Mass.: Persephone Press, 1982.

"Tory Opponents Criticize Miller for A Remark on Homosexuality." *The Toronto Star*, January 26, 1985, p. 47.

Valverde, Mariana. *Sex, Power, and Pleasure*. Toronto: The Women's Press, 1985.

Vicinus, Martha. "Distance and Desire: English Boarding School Friendships." *Signs* 9, No. 4 (Summer 1984): 600–622.

———. *Independent Women: Work and Community for Single Women, 1850–1920*. Chicago: University of Chicago Press, 1985.

Walker, Stephen, and Len Barton. *Gender, Class and Education.* Sussex: Falmer Press, 1983.

Waller, Willard. *The Sociology of Teaching.* New York: John Wiley and Sons, 1932; rpt. 1976.

*We the Teachers of Ontario.* OTF/FEO. Toronto: OTF, 1990.

Weeks, Jeffrey. "Discourse, Desire and Sexual Deviance: Some Problems in a History of Homosexuality." In *The Making of the Modern Homosexual,* ed. Kenneth Plummer. London: Hutchinson, 1981, pp. 76–111.

————. "Movements of Affirmation: Sexual Meanings and Homosexual Identities." *Radical History Review* 20 (Spring/Summer 1979), pp. 164–179.

————. *Sex, Politics and Society. The Regulation of Sexuality Since 1800.* London: Longman, 1981.

————. *Sexuality and Its Discontent.* London: Routledge and Kegan Paul, 1985.

Weiler, Kathleen. *Women Teaching for Change: Gender, Class and Power.* South Hadley, Mass.: Bergin and Garvey, 1988.

Weis, Lois, ed. *Class, Race and Gender in American Education.* Albany: State University of New York Press, 1988.

West, D. J. *Homosexuality.* Harmondsworth, England: Penguin, 1955; rpt, 1963.

Wheeler, Glenn. "Separate Schools of Sex Ed." *Now,* Oct. 31–Nov. 6, 1985.

Wheelwrite, Julie. *Amazons and Military Maids: Women Who Dressed as Men in the Pursuit of Life, Liberty and Happiness.* London: Pandora, 1989.

Widdowson, Frances. *Going up into the Next Class: Women and Elementary Teacher Training 1840–1914.* London: Hutchinson, 1983.

Willis, Paul. *Learning to Labor: How Workingclass Kids Get Workingclass Jobs.* New York: Columbia University Press, 1977; rpt, 1981.

Winsloe, Christa. *The Child Manuela.* Trans. Agnes Neil Scott. New York: Farrar and Rinehart, 1933.

Wolpe, AnnMarie. *Some Processes in Sexist Education.* London: Women's Research and Resources Centre Pub., 1977.

Woolf, Virginia. *Three Guineas.* London: Hogarth, 1938; rpt. Harmondsworth: Penguin, 1982.

Yogis, John A. QC. *Canadian Law Dictionary.* Toronto: Barron's Educational Series, 1983.

Zaremba, Eve. "Shades of Lavender: Lesbian Sex and Sexuality." In *Still Ain't Satisfied,* ed. Maureen Fitzgerald, Connie Guberman, and Margie Wolfe. Toronto: The Women's Press, 1982, pp. 85–92.

# Index

Abbot, Sidney, 123
AIDS, 5, 31, 83, 133, 177, 241
Althusser, Louis, 68; education and ISAs, 67; Ideological State Apparatuses, (ISAs), 66–67; Repressive State Apparatuses (RSAs), 67
American Psychiatric Association, 26, 79
Apple, Michael, 72, 145
Arbus, Judith, 44, 48
Ashenden, D. J., 74–75
L'Association des enseignants franco-ontariens (AEFO), 46
Atkinson, Ti-Grace, 114

Bailey, Derek Sherwin, 12
Barnes, Djuna, 21
Barney, Natalie, 21
Barrett, Michele, 63
Barton, Len, 58–59
Beard, George, 16
Beecher, Catharine, 35
Beechy, Veronica, 57
Berube, Alan, 17
*Body Politic*, 155, 189
Boggs, Carl, 78
Bowles, Samuel, 68
Brownmiller, Susan, 212, 214, 216
Buci-Gluckmann, Christine, 64
Bullough, 12, 16–17
Burstyn, Varda, 60

Canada: bilingualism, 97; capitalism and patriarchy in, 60–61; Charter of Rights and Freedoms, 32; decriminalization of homosexuality, 32; history of women and teaching in, 33–55; jurisprudence in, 14; lack of source material in, 7; patriarchy and, 69; political economy of, 60–61; setting for study, 6; schools in, 145, 203. *See also* Human Rights Code
*Canada Education Monthly*, 38–39
Caprio, Frank S., 85; definition of lesbian, 23
*Chatelaine*, 47
Chauncey, George, Jr., 15, 16, 18
Chessum, Rosemary, 74
Christian, Meg: "Ode to a Gym Teacher," 111
Clarke, Sir Fred, 36
Class: education and, 19, 55, 68, 69, 70, 72, 146; Foucault and, 29; hegemony and, 63–64, 76; ideology and, 63–64, 77, 79, 88–89, 90, 91; lesbians and, 9, 29, 30, 31, 32, 140, 215; lesbian teachers and, 103, 108–9, 121, 122, 125; patriarchy and, 58; Victorian women and, 34. *See also* Hegemony
Coming out: definition of, 114–15; feminism and, 124, 142; lesbian teachers and, 120–124
Coming out, pre-1969, 107, 113, 121; alcoholism and, 134; butch/femme roles and, 108, 123; deviance and, 121, 132; labeling and, 125, 131, 132; sexuality and, 111; social conditions of, 143
Companionate marriage, 19